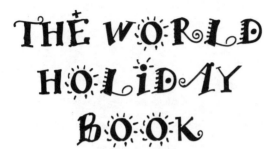

# THE WORLD HOLIDAY BOOK

CELEBRATIONS FOR EVERY DAY OF THE YEAR

## Anneli Rufus

HarperSanFrancisco
*A Division of* HarperCollins*Publishers*

Illustrations by Anneli Rufus © 1994

FIRST EDITION

Library of Congress Cataloging-in-Publication Data
Rufus, Anneli S.
    The world holiday book : celebrations for every day of the year / Anneli Rufus. — 1st ed.
        p.    cm.
    ISBN 0–06–250912–8 (pbk. : alk. paper)
    1. Holidays.   2. Festivals.   I. Title
GT3932.R84    1994
394.2'6—dc20
                                        94–557
                                        CIP

94  95  96  97  98  ❖  HAD  10  9  8  7  6  5  4  3  2  1

# introduction

*A* friend of mine has a favorite story about Passover.

There were going to be thirteen at the *seder* table that year, a fact which filled my friend with superstitious dread. It was asking for bad luck on a holiday already fraught with warnings, omens, outbursts, and plagues.

"Couldn't we just not invite the Provines?" my friend pleaded with her mother, brutally targeting the only four nonrelatives on the guest list. "Then we'd be nine."

"Are you *crazy*?" her mother shrieked indignantly. The three Provine children were fatherless, after all. "This is *Passover.*"

Which was funny because on all other nights my friend's mother seethed with a xenophobic fervor, her home a fortress, her table with its three lonely place settings a margarine-redolent sanctum sanctorum to which no magic word on earth could buy the wayfarer an introduction.

No magic word, that is, except *Passover.* At the onset of the holiday, my friend's mother waxed suddenly warm, even jolly, oozing the milk of human kindness the way wooden statues of the Madonna are sometimes said to cry or bleed.

That's what I love about holidays: how they transform us, how they remind us of the things we hold sacred. Holidays affirm our traditions and proclaim our loves as stalwartly as pushpins in a map. Like body-piercing and canapés, holidays set us apart from other species, turning every celebrant into a vessel for ritual, bonding us with every other celebrant throughout the world and throughout time. Holidays are collective dreams, wishes, fantasies, and myths made glorious flesh; and to share other people's holidays is to trade dreams. Holidays—holy days, festivals, feasts, *fiestas,* rites—bring out the best in us: their gongs and hymns and fires bring us back to our sacred selves, our social selves. Even the starkest and most ascetic of holidays, such as fasts and vigils, have an austere beauty that sharpens the senses and clears the mind the way horseradish clears the palate.

And that's why we should celebrate *more* holidays. Lots more. All kinds, from all over, enough to celebrate every day, if you have the energy. Read this book, find the rites that resonate, and *do* them. You can use this book to replace, with sly self-reliance, some of those holidays that you've been coaxed into observing all your life but never felt quite right about. Just being born in a country founded by Puritans doesn't automatically ensure that someone is going to 𝓵𝓸𝓿✲ Thanksgiving or sunrise services on Easter morning. In fact, some of the most "American" holiday traditions came from somewhere else. Christmas trees came from Germany, via England; Plymouth Plantation's Governor William Bradford, designing the first Thanksgiving feast, used *Sukkot,* the Jewish "feast of the tabernacles," as his model for an outdoor harvesttime repast.

By including holidays from all over the world, I run the risk of yanking them wholesale out of their natural contexts and delivering them naked and quivering, as a cat smugly proffers baby birds stolen from the nest. But I hope they do not look that way to you. I hope the holidays here vibrate with a deep universal humanness, leaping effortlessly across seas and centuries in their passionate reverence for season and sun and moon, endings and beginnings, animals and miracles and goddesses and gods. One problem in assembling this book was that in adhering to the Gregorian-calendar format, I had to omit a very rich body of holidays that are scheduled according to other timetables: consider the Muslim calendar, the Hindu, the Hebrew, the lunar calendar to which most of Asia adheres. Any holiday plotted according to one of these alternate calendars would fall on a different date every year in the Gregorian calendar. Space permits me to regretfully offer a mere handful of these "moveable feasts"; hundreds more exist, representing diverse cultures.

I for one can never bear it when a holiday ends, when the last candle gutters out and the last shout or toast or incantation dies trailingly away. For then there comes a sad hush, and too soon the clamor of ordinary dailiness closes in, as if to say, "Back to work. Party's over. Gods've gone home." For in a hard-working society, it is rare and even subversive to celebrate too much, to revel and keep on reveling: to stop whatever you're doing and rave, pray, throw things, go into trances, jump over bonfires, drape yourself in flowers, stay up all night, and scoop the froth from the sea.

# The World Holiday Book

# January 1

**S**atisfying (because it indicates having survived the previous year) yet scary (because who knows what the next year will bring), New Year's Day calls for safeguards, augurs, charms, and proclamations. All over the world, people kiss strangers, shoot guns into the air, toll bells, and exchange gifts. In Scotland and northern England, people keenly watch their thresholds to ensure that the "first footer"—the first visitor to come through the door in the new year—is of the propitious kind. Some regions swear by dark-haired men, others by blonde men; no one seems to want a woman. No first footer worth his salt arrives empty-handed: Preferred gifts are herring, bread, and fuel for the fire. In Japan, temple bells usher out the old year, and then comes the *joyano-kane*—the "night-watch bell," a series of exactly 108 peals. These, it is said, free the faithful from the 108 "earthly desires" lambasted in the Buddhist canon. Bulgarian, Serbian, Macedonian, and Rumanian bells also ring in the new year. Paraguayans rearrange the figurines in their Christmas crèches and address the baby Jesus as *Niño del Año Nuevo*. In Greece, January 1 is the feast day of the beloved Saint Basil, who is fêted with his own nut-and-lemon–laced cake, the *vasilopita*. Swedes, meanwhile, go to church, go to smorgasbords, and drink spicy *glögg*.

# January 2

## First Writing
### Kakizome

The Japanese New Year season begins on January 1 and lasts two weeks. Symbols of the season include pine branches for endurance, paper lobsters for longevity, and *daidai,* a bitter orange whose name is a homonym for "from generation to generation" and "forever." These two weeks are full of *hatsu,* portentous "firsts," all to be savored with acute awareness and a sense of the bittersweet, quicksilver nature of first-time–ness. *Hatsu-dori* is the year's first cockcrow, *hatsu-mode* the year's first shrine or temple visit; *goyo-hajime,* the year's first day of business, is traditionally January 4. Musicians embark mindfully on *hatsu-geike,* the year's first practice session, and carpenters on *chona-hajime,* the year's first use of an adze.

January 2 is set aside for *kakizome,* "first writing." Each member of the household takes a turn dipping a brush into freshly mixed ink and inscribing a favorite poem or proverb onto a long strip of paper. The goal is to write as beautifully as possible, every brush stroke an *ouevre,* the characters vivid against a sheet that started out as pure and open as the year ahead. Households, schools, and community organizations sponsor contests in which prizes are awarded for children's best kakizome. The poet Issa captured the spirit of one of these contests:

> *How he looks and looks at the prize*
> *For the year's first calligraphy—*
> *That orange!*

# January 3

## Saint Genevieve's Day

### Sainte-Geneviève

Genevieve took the veil at fifteen, but not before an unpleasant tiff with her mother involving the latter's refusal to take Genevieve to church one busy morning. In anger, the girl struck her mother blind. Later, she relented and gave the woman back her sight. As a handmaiden of the Church, Genevieve went to live in Paris, where, we are told, she fasted, prayed, wept for humanity's sins, and worked many miracles.

The most notable of these happened when barbarian hordes were besieging the city. Genevieve not only managed to feed the starving Parisians, but she also convinced the barbarian leader, Childeric, to release the prisoners he had captured. Later Genevieve exerted similar power over Attila the Hun. This plucky saint came to reign as the patron of Paris (as well as of secretaries, actors, and the Women's Army Corps, the WACs). She has been successfully invoked in times of plague, and a fair in her honor has been a longtime tradition in the city.

# January 4

## Pilgrimage to Chalma

### Nuestro Señor de Chalma

In 1533 two Augustinian friars were evangelizing the Oculteco people of Ocuilan, about a hundred miles from Mexico City. The natives were devoted to their own god: They prayed and sacrificed to his idol in a cave.

One day, it is said, the priests and some of their Indian converts marched up to the cave carrying a big wooden cross with which they planned to supplant the idol. When they got there, the idol already lay smashed to bits and in its place stood a crucifix. "A miracle!" they declared. The moribund fellow on the crucifix soon became known as Our Lord of Chalma, and he was credited with great powers. In 1683, he was moved to a nearby church, to which flock as many as twenty thousand worshipers every year from January 1 through January 7. The pilgrims, which include Zapotecs, Aztecs, and many other native groups, make the last part of the journey through the valley to the shrine on foot. They dance and sing for *el Señor*, perform mystery plays, and leave offerings. A popular good-bye song goes:

*Good-bye, blessed sanctuary, until next year. . . .*
*Good-bye, delight of the soul; give me your benediction.*
*Good-bye, Señor de Chalma,*
*divine benefactor . . . adiós, adiós, adiós.*

# January 5

The baby-stealing, chicken-riding, shape-shifting, snaggle-toothed, honey-voiced demons called *kalikandjari* come to earth, Cypriots say, at Christmas, and they depart with spiteful reluctance every January 5. Said to be wraiths of children who died unbaptized, *kalikandjari* spend their days on earth hovering around lakes and crossroads making evil plans. They sneak down chimneys and urinate all over freshly bought groceries and defecate into people's hope chests. They insinuate their way inside by tapping on front doors while uncannily mimicking the voices of loved ones. Often, they loiter maliciously on rooftops, berating their mothers for not having had them baptized in time.

One *Kalanda* custom has the housewife kneading pastry dough at midnight in total silence. This she fries along with some sausages and throws the whole panful onto the roof for the kalikandjari. She sings:

> *Little piece, piece of sausage,*
> *Knife with a black handle,*
> *Piece of pancake:*
> *Eat and let us go.*

# January 6

## Epiphany

Epiphany, commemorating Jesus' baptism and the Three Kings' visit to the manger, is one of Christianity's most widely celebrated holidays. In Greece on this twelfth day after Christmas, processions march to the sea, where the priest throws a cross into the water. Local youths dive for the cross and are heaped with gifts and blessings upon its retrieval. Similar rites—echoing ancient propitiations of river gods, sea gods, fishing gods, and storm gods—are *de rigueur* all along the Danube and in Albania, as well as in American and English fishing ports. The Greeks believe this is a day for wearing new clothes and for making wishes, a day on which seawater is sweet enough to drink and on which beasts in the stable may suddenly start to speak.

In France, the day's main event is a low-slung, butter-rich, shiny-with-egg-yolk cake called the *Galette des Rois*, the Kings' Cake; in England, it is called the Twelfth Cake and is taller, fluffier, and elaborately frosted. The cake has lucky charms baked inside that foretell the destinies of those who eat it: A coin portends wealth, a ring portends marriage. Whoever finds the cake's hidden

bean is crowned king- or queen-for-a-day and is urged to choose a consort and to order everyone around. A Mexican variant is the *Rosca de los Reyes,* a crown-shaped cake in which is hidden a tiny china baby. The one who finds the doll in his or her slice must throw a party three weeks hence, on Candlemas Day.

# January 7

## Ukrainian Christmas

### Rizdvo

*R*izdvo is steadfastly Christian
. . . which is only appropriate
in the birthplace of Eastern Orthodoxy.
It also bears the stamp of ancient earth
worship . . . appropriate in this land
long known as Europe's breadbasket.

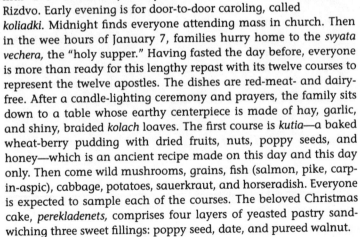

The twinkling of the first star in the
eastern sky on the Ukrainian Christmas Eve—which is January 6—ushers in
Rizdvo. Early evening is for door-to-door caroling, called
*koliadki.* Midnight finds everyone attending mass in church. Then
in the wee hours of January 7, families hurry home to the *svyata
vechera,* the "holy supper." Having fasted the day before, everyone
is more than ready for this lengthy repast with its twelve courses to
represent the twelve apostles. The dishes are red-meat- and dairy-
free. After a candle-lighting ceremony and prayers, the family sits
down to a table whose earthy centerpiece is made of hay, garlic,
and shiny, braided *kolach* loaves. The first course is *kutia*—a baked
wheat-berry pudding with dried fruits, nuts, poppy seeds, and
honey—which is an ancient recipe made on this day and this day
only. Then come wild mushrooms, grains, fish (salmon, pike, carp-
in-aspic), cabbage, potatoes, sauerkraut, and horseradish. Everyone
is expected to sample each of the courses. The beloved Christmas
cake, *perekladenets,* comprises four layers of yeasted pastry sand-
wiching three sweet fillings: poppy seed, date, and pureed walnut.

# January 8

A veritable bevy of ancient goddesses watched over mothers-to-be and women in childbirth. And midwives were these goddesses' earthly helpers. Thus, in the mountains of Greek Macedonia, this date was long ago set aside for the honoring—for the toasting, anointing, propitiating, and venerating—of village midwives.

Nominally dedicated to the obscure Saint Domenika, the day finds all women of childbearing age hastening to the midwife's home, bearing gifts. Most traditional are things she will need for her work: new towels, soap, scissors. Women also bring the midwife festive foods and bottles of wine. Each guest in turn solemnly washes the midwife's hands with warm water—in symbolic anticipation of the day when the midwife will come and assist in the supplicant's own childbirth. The midwife's assistants create a *schema,* a phallic figure made of a leek or a sausage. This the guests pass back and forth; they pat and kiss it; some weep. The guests crown the midwife with garlands, streamers, and necklaces made of figs and currants, and then all sit down to a meal during which they tell rude jokes and drink as much as they want, because this is the only day of the year on which women are granted the right to public displays of drunkenness. At days' end, the village women pull their midwife in a flower-decked carriage through the streets to the public fountain, where they sprinkle her most reverently with fresh water.

# January 9

## Feast of the Black Nazarene

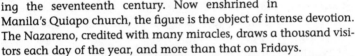

**E**ven the pickpockets, local legend has it, come clean on the day of the *Nazareno*. Over a hundred thousand pilgrims throng the Manila streets north of the Pasig River for the year's biggest festival. The Nazareno is a life-size statue of the crucified Jesus. Carved of dark wood by Indians in colonial Mexico, the statue was carried across the Pacific to the Philippines in a Spanish galleon during the seventeenth century. Now enshrined in Manila's Quiapo church, the figure is the object of intense devotion. The Nazareno, credited with many miracles, draws a thousand visitors each day of the year, and more than that on Fridays.

Every January 9, a local penitent takes it upon himself to haul the huge Nazareno on its wheeled *carroza* through the streets of town. He does this barefooted, straining and gasping, protected by a cluster of young male companions. The neighborhood all around them is a swirling, jostling mass of humanity. Everyone struggles to get close enough to touch the Nazareno with a towel or handkerchief. Thus imbued, it is believed, the cloth has both the power to heal illness and to dissolve sin, and is effective when rubbed on the body from head to toe. The procession winds slowly along and ends with a mass at the Quiapo church. Filipino tourism officials recommend watching the procession not from street level but from the top of some nearby building.

# January 10

## Ebisu Matsuri

*A*mong Japan's *shikifukujin,* "Seven Lucky Gods," that septet of Buddhist deities who sailed from China in their *takarabune,* or "treasure ship," Ebisu is the god who smiles the most brightly. He is the plump, bearded one with the fishing pole tucked under one arm and a huge sea bream tucked under the other, the one who knows all about credits, debits, algorithms, spreadsheets, loss leaders, and accounts receivable.

A god of commerce as well as of food and fishing, Ebisu is at home with both net profits and drift nets. Thus, he is the businessman's favorite, and many days in the businessman's calendar are dedicated specially to him. January 10's festival, which became a popular tradition during the Edo period, was the year's first, and its purpose was to ask the god for a profitable year. Merchants would gather for New Year's banquets on this day, while the god stood by with rice cakes stacked up like fat coins on his altar. Far fewer of these lavish feasts are held now than a hundred years ago, but businesspeople still buy inexpensive Ebisu posters at New Year's to place, along with rice cakes, on home altars. And many is the shop in modern Japan where a statue of the ebullient god overlooks the transactions, his grin such a part of him that the expression "Ebisu-face" means "happy face."

# January 11

Carmenta, a goddess of prophecy and childbirth, was important enough to have one of Rome's portals named for her. The Porta Carmentalis, at the foot of the southern end of the Capitol, stood near the temple where the goddess's special priest, the Flamen Carmentalis, presided. The sacrifices he prepared for the goddess's altar were strictly vegetarian, as Carmenta eschewed all animal hide and flesh from her precincts. Scholars presume that a goddess of birth would naturally abhor any kind of slaughter.

It is reported that, with the exception of the Flamen Carmentalis, no males were permitted to enter the goddess's temple. (One legend suggested that women had even built the temple by themselves.) Midwife as well as sibyl—her name with its root *carmen* implies a spell, a charm, a prophecy, a poem, a song—Carmenta was doubly important to pregnant women and new mothers, who took care to visit the shrine on her festival day. Carmenta's specialty was telling babies' fortunes, and it was said that she did not merely deliver her oracles but sang them. As April was the traditional marriage month among Romans, January found many young Roman women expectant for the first time and in need of an assignation with Carmenta.

# January 12

## Burning the Clavie

This annual event in Burghead, Scotland, was already considered ancient in the eighteenth century, at which time a local chronicler denounced the practice as "superstitious, Idolatrous and sinfule." While it is now enacted every January 11, the *Daily News* reported in 1878: "On the last day of the year, old style, which falls on the 12th January, the festival of 'the Clavie' takes place at Burghead, a fishing village."

The article goes on to tell how the fishermen set fire to a tar barrel, and one of them hoists it above his head and carries it "round the town, while the assembled folks shout and halloo. If the man who carries the barrel falls, it is an evil omen." The "clavie"—today a sawn-in-half whiskey barrel, donated by a local cooper—is a heavy and dangerous burden. Custom demands that the clavie bearer not merely walk but run down the street, with the clavie splattering tar and showering sparks in every direction. The *Daily News* continues: "On a headland in that village still stands an old Roman altar, locally called the 'Douro.'. . . The man with the lighted barrel having gone with it round the town carries it up to the top of the hill and places it on the Douro. More fuel is immediately added. The sparks as they fly are supposed to be . . . evil spirits leaving the town; the people therefore shout at and curse them."

# January 13

The precise moment at which good times must end is a sticky and unpleasant matter. Thus when Christmas carols begin to grow stale in the throat, Norwegians wisely assign the role of killjoy to one of those erstwhile gluttons for punishment, a medieval saint. "Knut drives Christmas out," they sing as January 13 approaches. In fact, this eleventh-century Danish king, famous for two vicious raids on Yorkshire and

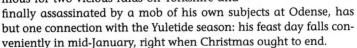

finally assassinated by a mob of his own subjects at Odense, has but one connection with the Yuletide season: his feast day falls conveniently in mid-January, right when Christmas ought to end.

The Norwegian Christmas—*Jul*—is a cozy time of eating buffet meals, visiting friends, exchanging gifts, and sitting by the fire. Many of these traditions date from the Viking era, when *Joulu* was the winter feast celebrating both fertility and death, the mystery of the world's emergence from and eternal return to the unknown, to darkness. Christmas buffets hark back to the old Joulu tradition of leaving tables heaped with food for the ancestral spirits.

On the twentieth day after Christmas—literally, *Tyvendedagen*—the Christmas trees are stripped of their ornaments, and the wood is chopped up and burned in the fireplace. Some rural Norwegians still stage Saint Knut's Day sleigh races. This is traditionally the last day on which the Christmas greeting, *Glaedelig Jul,* may be exchanged.

# January 14

**i**f you've always thought medieval Christianity, with its crusaders and indulgence salesmen, its sin eaters and black death, was a grim and harrowing institution, think again. Well into the sixteenth century, January 14 was an annual holiday that found the citizens of certain French towns crowding the streets, open sewers notwithstanding, for a procession that, with Christmas nearby, commemorated the Holy Family's search for lodgings. The pregnant Mary, it is said, rode on an ass. The ass is considered just as ludicrous a creature in France as elsewhere, so it was with jeers and hilarity that the people of Beauvais, north of Paris, led a teenage girl astride a gold-caparisoned donkey down the streets of town from the Gothic cathedral to the church of Saint Etienne. At the door of the church, the entire assembly including the priest brayed like donkeys. Then they all trooped inside and the beast was led to the altar. The mass that followed was a pray-and-bray affair, with the congregation hee-hawing at prearranged points during the *Kyrie* and the *Gloria in Excelsis*. The many verses of the service's Franco-Latin hymn praised the ass's strength, its skill at jumping, its velvety ears, and its "beauteous mouth," proclaiming:

> *Gold from Araby the blest,*
> *Sheba's myrrh, of myrrh the best,*
> *To the church this ass did bring;*
> *We his sturdy labors sing.*

# January 15

## Martin Luther King, Jr.'s Birthday

**B**orn on this day in 1929, the African-American clergyman Dr. Martin Luther King, Jr. worked hard for civil rights in his native South and elsewhere. Preaching peace and sensibility, he was in the vanguard of many demonstrations and rallies. In 1963, during the massive March on Washington, King gave the famous "I Have a Dream" speech at the foot of the Lincoln Memorial. In the speech, King prophesied a world in which his children "will not be judged by the color of their skin but by the content of their character." It was one of the most moving orations of the generation.

King's assassination in April 1968 in Memphis, Tennessee, sent shock waves around the world. In succeeding years, various cities and then states made King's birthday a legal holiday. Now a national holiday in the United States, it serves as the focus for discussions, national as well as international, about the issues King held dear, and about the progress—or lack of same—achieved since King had his dream.

# January 16

**i**n times of yore, many Japanese youths apprenticed themselves to skilled artisans, merchants, and tradesmen. It was a solid way of ensuring a career, but the experience—an ordeal of many years' duration—could also be a trying one. The young person would be living far from home and family, and usually the apprentice's tasks were the most menial, the hardest, the dullest, and the most exhausting. Two holidays every year were set aside so that apprentices could briefly go home to recharge their spiritual batteries and return, refreshed, to work. These *yabuiri* were occasions not to be wasted, as the poet Buson illustrated:

> *The apprentice at liberty*
> *steps over the fallen kite string*
> *and hurries on.*

Home at last, the apprentice rested, just as in childhood. Buson observed:

> *The apprentice on vacation*
> *is dreaming*
> *while the beans are cooking.*

For the apprentice whose parents had died, it was an opportunity for cemetery visits. The poet Issa mused:

> *The apprentices' holiday:*
> *The wind blows back there*
> *in the pine trees by the grave.*

# January 17

## Saint Anthony's Day
### San Antonio Abad

The Saint Anthony to whom this festival is dedicated was a hermit and an ascete, a keen observer of human psychology and a fount of good advice, when not holed up in his hermitage. In his solitude, Anthony was beset with many sensuous temptations and visions, which are represented by the pig with which Anthony is nearly always pictured. Thus he has acquired bestial associations.

On this day in Mexico, people bring their animals to church to be blessed by the priest. The animals—pets, beasts of burden, and future enchilada fillings alike—have been scrubbed and dressed for the occasion: cats wear satin capes, roosters wear tiny *sombreros*, amiable dogs wear dark glasses and leather belts. Pigs, goats, cows, mules, and horses have their flanks painted with polka dots or stripes in confetti colors. Old-timers in Oaxaca, Taxco, and Xochimilco tell tales of hoopskirted rabbits, pigs in feather boas, chickens in pinafores, and parrots with big bow ties. Farmers have been known to bring bags filled with writhing slugs or locusts (not dressed up)—in hopes that the priest's blessing will dissuade the vermin from devouring the farmer's crops. Poised atop the churchyard wall, the priest sprinkles the beasts with holy water from the vessel he holds in his arms. Altar boys scurry back and forth bringing fresh supplies of water.

Traditional dinner fare on this day is pork.

# January 18

## Assumption Day

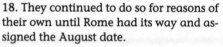 n modern times, the anniversary of the Virgin Mary's bodily levitation into heaven is celebrated around the world on August 15. The change to this date almost certainly represents an attempt to supplant an ancient festival in honor of the wildwoods goddess, Diana, which the Romans had long celebrated in mid-August. Other pre-Christian cultures, including the Celts, celebrated their harvest-home rites at that time: it is not surprising that in today's Assumption Day church rites, the Virgin is often saluted as Our Lady of the Harvest.

Be that as it may, as of the sixth century, Christians throughout Egypt and Arabia were celebrating Mary's assumption on January 18. They continued to do so for reasons of their own until Rome had its way and assigned the August date.

# January 19
## Robert E. Lee's Birthday

**N**either a slave owner nor a fan of slavery, Lee supported the Confederacy because he believed in his native South and all its traditions, for better or for worse. As a Marines commander in 1859, he led the attack on abolitionist John Brown at the federal arsenal in Harpers Ferry, West Virginia. As a Confederate general in the Civil War, he was hailed as the sharpest strategist on either side. His final surrender at Appomattox in 1865 was, they say, the result of insufficient manpower.

His birthday has been celebrated annually in many states, including Tennessee, Kentucky, Georgia, Arkansas, and South Carolina. In 1985 the date was officially dedicated to him in Florida, Louisiana, Mississippi, and North Carolina. In Alabama, he shares Martin Luther King, Jr.'s holiday. His home state of Virginia observes Lee-Jackson-King Day; and in Texas, Lee's exploits are the focus of January 19's Confederate Heroes Day.

At Stratford Hall, the Virginia mansion that was Lee's birthplace, the evening of January 19 finds some five hundred visitors enjoying an annual Lee birthday gala with cake and punch by candlelight. Docents in each of the mansion's eighteen rooms are on hand to tell stories about Lee and his distinguished family. Also on or near this day in Richmond, Virginia, the Confederate Museum holds a birthday reception, while the general's old haunt, Saint Paul's Episcopal Church, offers a memorial service.

# January 20

## Breadbasket Festival
### Festa das Fogaçeiras

Innocent youth as the symbol of hope, renewal, and abundance has been the theme of this festal day in the Portuguese coastal town of Santa Maria da Feira for over four hundred years. It started, as have many festivals worldwide, with a plague. The people of Santa Maria da Feira prayed to the long-suffering martyr Saint Sebastian, begging him to take away the plague. And so he did.

Now, people come from all over Portugal to commemorate the miracle. Hundreds of little girls, dressed all in white, wear beribboned baskets on their heads. Piled in each basket are flowers and loaves of bread—in such abundance that each child carries a towering burden that far outbalances her size. Then the girls proceed through the town, their backs straight and their heads erect, their baskets steady. Spectators cheer from the sidewalk. The sweet loaves used for this rite are called *fogaças*. The girls who carry them are called *fogaçeiras*.

# January 21

**P**atroness of chastity and of all Girl Scouts, Agnes was a Roman adolescent who during the reign of Emperor Diocletian took a vow of celibacy. She rejected all proposals of marriage, which got her into trouble when a certain angry suitor worked it so that Agnes was arrested, tortured, and finally stabbed in the throat.

Her feast day later became popular, especially in the rural north of England, for prophetic dreams in which women would see their future mates. Custom demanded an all-day fast. At bedtime the celebrant would eat a heavily salted hard-boiled egg, shell and all. (An alternate tradition held that a raw, salted red herring—with head, eyes, bones, tail, and all—worked just as well.) Thirsty, she would retire to bed. There she would dream, it was said, of a man who gallantly appeared offering a drink of water.

# January 22

## Saint Vincent's Day

**O**n this winemakers' holiday, the tradition in Burgundy villages, where grapes have flourished since the second century C.E., is to rustle up every single statue of Saint Vincent that can be found and to parade them all, en masse, through the streets. Villages in the Côte-des-Nuits region (famous for its red wines) and the Côte-de-Beaune region (famous for its whites) take turns hosting the festival. Accompanying the dozens of statues are vintners, vineyard workers, wine merchants, and richly robed members of the Confrèrie des Chevaliers du Tastevin, a distinguished sort of Knights Templars of the wine trade.

All over Europe, the feast day of this fourth-century Spanish martyr was crucial in determining the success or failure of the year's wine harvest. A jingle sung on the island of Guernsey in the sixteenth century advised:

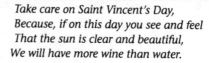

*Take care on Saint Vincent's Day,*
*Because, if on this day you see and feel*
*That the sun is clear and beautiful,*
*We will have more wine than water.*

# January 23

## Saint Ildefonso's Day

When the conquistadores came to the Rio Grande region, they strove to convert the natives. To this end they erected adobe churches in the Indian villages, cheek by jowl with the sacred subterranean halls called *kivas*. They renamed the pueblos and assigned patron saints. Today, ancient rites survive alongside the new, imported ones.

San Ildefonso Pueblo (twenty miles north of Santa Fe, New Mexico) marks its namesake's feast day with traditional dances. The most dramatic of these is the buffalo dance, recalling the people's ancestors' vernal treks north to the Great Plains to hunt bison for meat to help the community survive till spring. Several dancers impersonate hunters, while two long rows of "buffaloes" in heavy, horned masks shuffle back and forth into the kiva. Finally the buffaloes emerge to enact the dance's climax, which is an exuberant "slaughter." The buffaloes' bodies litter the plaza, and the hunters carry them away.

# January 24

This benefactor's mustache is genteelly trimmed to a pair of points like pigeons' wings. He wears the soft woolen cap of the Bolivian *altiplano*. He is Ekeko, the current edition of an ancient prosperity god. Hundreds of years before the Spaniards plumbed what is now Bolivia, the local Aymara Indians were already staging annual Ekeko fairs honoring the generous deity whose image held a prominent place in every household. After winning a battle against the Aymara at La Paz in 1781, the Spaniards tried to steal the Indians' thunder even further by attributing their victory to the Virgin of La Paz. They rededicated the Aymaras' Ekeko fair to her. The Indians, however, weren't buying it, because two hundred years later the Alasitas Fair still finds La Paz's main square full of booths selling handicrafts, holiday food, and innumerable statuettes of Ekeko. His painted lips curve in a benevolent grin; he carries the kinds of things the Aymaras want most: plump sacks of sugar, flour, beans, coffee. Over the figurines' clay shoulders are slung miniature aluminum coffeepots and frying pans, ropes, and crates of cigarettes.

# January 25

## Burns's Night

The eighteenth-century "common man's poet" who wrote of humble matters in his brash "Lallans" dialect, remains Scotland's favorite native son. Here his birthday is celebrated as Robert Burns himself would have liked it. Partyers assemble in the banqueting hall, where they tuck into such dishes as cabbie-claw (wind-dried cod with horseradish and egg sauce) and finnan toasties (smoked haddock). But these are merely the whets. The main event, of course, is the Scottish national dish: haggis, a sheep's stomach stuffed with chopped mutton, oatmeal, offal, and spices, sealed up tightly and boiled to a shiny brown. Flanked by bagpipers in full regalia, the cook enters the hall, holding the platter aloft. The master of ceremonies addresses the haggis in Burns's own words:

> *Fair fa' your honest sonsie face,*
> *Great chieftain o' the pudden race.*

With a sharp knife, he carves an X into the top—the "paunch." He turns back the flaps and all recite a Scottish grace as the haggis is served. At night's end, after many tearful toasts, the celebrants rise arm in arm to sing Burns's most famous work of all: "Auld Lang Syne."

# January 26

## Republic Day
### Basant Panchmi

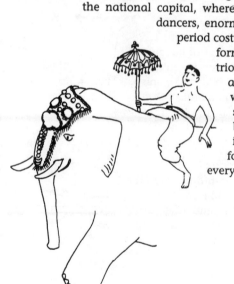

India—or, as it generally calls itself, *Bharat*—declared its independence from Britain and everybody else on January 26, 1950. The government adopted a new constitution, and now the anniversary is celebrated in all parts of the country. While many towns host fairs and parades, the biggest take place in the various state capitals. The most magnificent has always been in New Delhi, the national capital, where uniformed soldiers, military bands, dancers, enormous horse-drawn floats, marchers in period costume, and dozens of painted elephants form a procession that lasts for hours. Patriotic displays include flag dedications and political leaders' speeches; fireworks light up the night. Among the several days of pageantry surrounding Delhi's Republic Day ceremonies is an important dance festival that draws folk and tribal dance troupes from every region of India.

# January 27

**O**n this misty, frosty morning in Basel, Switzerland, a raft glides down the Rhine bearing a bizarre crew. Two drummers, two flag bearers, and two cannoneers in white stockings and three-cornered hats share the deck with a masked, ivy-covered savage, the *Wilde Mann*. He grips an uprooted pine tree, which he shakes in the direction of Kleinbasel, "Little Basel," the district on the river's right bank. At the bridge called Mittler Brucke, two more figures climb on board: a shaggy lion that stands erect on two legs, and a green-winged, cruel-beaked griffin. At noon and then into the evening the three figures dance together, as they have done at this festival for over four hundred years. They chase away winter with their dance, and they always take care never to face the left bank.

The three characters are emblems of three ancient Kleinbasel neighborhoods. The political significance they once enjoyed has long since mutated into a social function: that of inspiring community solidarity in Kleinbasel. Each of the three neighborhoods used to have its own separate festival day: January 13, 20, and 27. Now all three celebrate together, taking turns celebrating on one of those dates every year.

# January 28

## Saint Charlemagne's Day

**O**f all the charismatic figures who ever ruled France, Charlemagne—emperor, scholar, and sometime saint—was perhaps the most mythic of all. An energetic eighth-century Frankish king, he battled Teutons and Moors, and for this he was crowned emperor of the Holy Roman Empire.

This spawned an era known thereafter as the Carolingian renaissance, during which Charlemagne's court sparkled like an intellectual firebrand in the midst of a mostly illiterate and uneducated Europe. Gathering writers, teachers, and thinkers around him, Charlemagne established a system of monastic schools that taught music, grammar, classics, geometry, astronomy, rhetoric, dialectics, and arithmetic—namely, the liberal arts. Charlemagne is hailed as the founder of Paris's first university.

Because he was canonized not by a real pope but by an antipope who had broken away from the Vatican, Charlemagne is not an honest-to-God saint. Still, his feast day was for hundreds of years observed half in reverence, half in jest among French secondary school and college students. All those who had ranked at the top of their class at least once, as well as those who had ranked second at least twice, were invited to a festive champagne breakfast hosted by the principal or chancellor. The scholars were expected to recite poems that they had composed—in Latin, of course—for the occasion.

# January 29
## Dicing for the Maid's Money

**B**efore he died in 1674, John How of Guildford, Surrey, England, made a stipulation
in his will. The then-robust sum of four hundred pounds was to be invested, and the interest on this account should be awarded every
year to a local maidservant who had occupied her
position for at least two years. A different woman would win the
money every year. (This was one of many seventeenth-century
schemes for rewarding servants who performed long loyal service
and were of "good character.") The interest wasn't simply to be
handed over. According to How's will, the town magistrate should
choose two qualified candidates. On the anniversary of How's
death, the contestants would toss a pair of dice on a table in the
Guildhall; the high roller would get the money.

In 1702 another Guildford man, John Parsons, bequeathed six
hundred pounds. The interest on this was to be annually awarded
to some "poor young man who hath served an apprenticeship of
seven years." This ceremony took place on the same day as the
"dicing." The young manservant, per Parsons's instructions, must
swear before the magistrate: "I am worth less than twenty pounds."

But apprenticed manservants are a nearly extinct breed, so
Guildford's magistrates have recently altered the ceremony. While
the winner of the dice toss receives How's charity, as before, the
loser is awarded Parsons's charity. The "loser" gets more than the
"winner." The magistrate duly records the proceedings in the town
ledger; by the mid-1980s, Parsons's dole amounted to a few pence
more than twelve pounds.

# January 30
## Holiday of the Three Hierarchs

### Ton Treion Eirarkon

**O**bserved since the early Middle Ages, this battle of the archbishops commemorates three of Greek Orthodoxy's favorite saints. Each member of this fourth-century trio to this day enjoys an ardent fan club of his own. Saint John Chrysostom (c. 347–407), hailed as one of the great Greek "doctors of the church," was a renowned preacher, eventually exiled, whose compassionate sermons earned him the nickname John the Goldenmouthed. Saint Gregory of Nazianzus (329–389) was another Greek doctor of the church, shy but controversial. He was a bishop of Constantinople, eventually forced to resign, whose intelligent discourses earned him the moniker Gregory the Theologian. And Saint Basil (330–379), yet another doctor of the church and a confidant of Gregory's, railed against the Emperor Valens, who oppressed Orthodox Greeks. Called onto the carpet to defend his activism, Basil reportedly retorted, "Perhaps you have never before had to deal with a proper bishop." His nickname became Basil the Great.

In the centuries following the saints' deaths, Greeks argued much about which of the three had been the best. By the eleventh century, it is said, this dilemma was on everyone's lips. In 1081 Bishop John of Galatia is reported to have had a vision in which the trio appeared, explaining that they were all equal in the eyes of God and begging the bishop to tell the world. Thereafter, this holiday was established to honor the equality of John, Gregory, and Basil. Greek schoolchildren write special essays on the subject, and people attend assemblies and other programs throughout the day.

# January 31

## Nauru Independence Day

*A*t eight square miles one of the smallest countries on earth, the Independent Republic of Nauru, thirty-five miles south of the equator and twenty-four hundred miles northeast of Sydney, Australia, is not to be found on most maps. This comma-shaped speck of an island with its stands of coconut palm and inhospitable coral plateau has had more than its share of foster parents. Germany annexed Nauru in 1888 and administered it as part of the Marshall Islands group. In 1919 it was put under British mandate. It was jointly administered by Great Britain, Australia, and New Zealand until January 31, 1968, when Nauru—pronounced "na-OO-roo"—attained independence, hoisting its own flag, blue and gold with a twelve-pointed white star.

On that first Independence Day, Nauru natives (whose blood is a blend of Micronesian, Melanesian, and Polynesian) reveled, and the island's Chinese community sponsored a performance of Canton opera. Today in Nauru, Independence Day is remembered with beachfront barbecues—fried flying fish is traditional. By night, fireworks compete with stars in the vast Pacific sky.

# Moveable Feast

## Chinese New Year

**Chun Jie**

The lunar new year traditionally celebrates the earth's renewed fertility. The fifteen-day New
Year season finds celebrants sandbag-
ging themselves and each other with
the foods, colors, shapes, sounds, and
even syllables that bespeak health,
happiness, fertility, and fortune for
the coming twelve-month span.

In the spirit of setting things straight, all account books should
be balanced, debts paid off, and houses cleaned before New Year's
Day. Then houses, businesses, and streets are decked and draped
with banners, flowers, and scrolls of vivid red, a traditionally lucky
and demon-dispelling hue. People exchange red-wrapped gifts,
most commonly the *hong bao*—cash enclosed in a compact red
paper packet—and offer their friends propitious edibles such as red
dates (whose Chinese name, *hong zao,* sounds like the words for
"prosperity comes soon") and tangerines (whose Cantonese pro-
nunciation, *kat,* sounds like that of the word for "lucky").

While celebrants avoid using swearwords during this season,
and parents warn their children against inadvertently blurting out
such inauspicious words as *death* or *disaster,* this is by no means a
time for keeping silent. Street festivals are alive with the sound of
firecrackers. (When these were banned in Singapore, resourceful
celebrants played cassette tapes of exploding firecrackers.)

# February 1

**i**t's no coincidence that Ireland's patron saint, Brigid, has the same name as that country's once-favorite goddess, Brigid, aka Brigit, Brighid, Bride, and Brid. *The Penguin Dictionary of Saints* concedes that "ascertainable facts about [Saint Brigid's] life are few," and that existing accounts are "very far-fetched and not unmixed with folklore." The goddess ruled poetry, metalcraft, and healing; sick persons as well as poets seek out the saint. As abbess of the sanctuary at Kildare, she is said to have insisted that all her bishops be practicing goldsmiths.

Sir James Frazer in *The Golden Bough* recounts that "in the Highlands of Scotland the revival of vegetation in spring used to be graphically represented on Saint Bride's Day, the first of February. Thus in the Hebrides the mistress and servants of each family take a sheaf of oats, and dress it up in women's apparel, put it in a large basket and lay a wooden club by it, and this they call Bride's Bed, and then the mistress and servants cry three times, 'Bride is come, Bride is welcome.'" Elsewhere in the British Isles the women carried the sheaf all around town, and housewives prepared "Bride feasts" into which men were customarily allowed only if they stood outside the locked front door and begged to be let in.

# February 2

The anniversary of the day on which the Virgin Mary ritually cleansed herself and brought her forty-day-old child to the temple in Jerusalem was made an official holiday during the reign of Emperor Justinian. It was called, in full, the Feast of the Purification of Saint Mary and the Presentation at the Temple. Because Jesus was the "light of the world," the Church asserted that this February 2 event should be a feast of lights, a "candle mass." Pope Innocent XII, however, wrote in the seventeenth century: "Why do we in this feast carry candles? Because the gentiles dedicated the month of February to the[ir] infernal gods and as at the beginning of it, Pluto stole Porserpina, and her mother Ceres sought her in the dark with lighted candles; so they, at the beginning of the month, walked about the city with lighted candles. Because the holy fathers could not extirpate the custom, they ordained that Christians should carry about candles in honor of the Blessed Virgin, and thus what was done before in honor of Ceres is now done in honor of the Blessed Virgin."

In the wistful season between midwinter and spring, a candle represents the faint glimmer of faith, hope, and sunshine. The Celtic festival of *Imbolc,* dedicated to the goddess Brigid, was held at the beginning of February. It took two "new" holidays, Saint Brigid's Day and Candlemas, to replace the ancient rite.

# February 3

**O**n his way to being torn to shreds with iron combs in the year 316, an Armenian doctor who was later to be known as Saint Blaise encountered a boy who was choking to death on a fish bone. Blaise loosed the bone, saved the boy, and is now hailed as the patron saint of those suffering from throat ailments. All over the world on his feast day, churches hold throat-blessing ceremonies.

One of the best known of these takes place at London's Church of Saint Etheldreda. Hundreds come in hopes of a cure. After a service, the priest uses ribbons to fasten together two long white candles in the shape of an *X*. This he holds under each worshiper's chin in turn, intoning, "May the Lord deliver you from the evil of the throat."

In Spain, special cakes are named for the saint, and on his day the loaves, having been blessed in church, are distributed to friends and family as well as to domestic animals, in hopes of preserving their esophageal health in the coming year. Because he was torn to shreds with iron combs resembling those used to process wool, Blaise is also the patron of ironworking and woolworking districts. Until the mid-nineteenth century, such English towns as Norwich, Bradford, Bury Saint Edmunds, and Aberdeen celebrated "Bishop Blaise Day" with processions and bonfires.

# February 4

## Dividing the Seasons

### Setsubun

The name of this Japanese holiday literally means "dividing the seasons." And the thousand-year-old rite does precisely that, shutting down winter abruptly while opening up spring. It is, in fact, a noisy kind of spring cleaning. In private homes, the head of the household goes from room to room scattering roasted soybeans while the whole family chants: *Fuku wa uchi, oni wa soto!* "In with good luck, out with demons!" In public ceremonies, held between February 2 and February 4, celebrities are chosen to throw the beans off the balconies of shrines and other important buildings. While the ancient Romans threw beans to feed their ghosts in the ceremony called the *Lemuria,* the Japanese *mamemaki,* bean throwing, is an attempt to hit the demons and all the misfortunes they represent.

Why beans? It has been suggested that the reason is linguistic, as *mame* means both "bean" and "good health." The custom of eating one roasted soybean for every year of your age is an ancient Japanese health charm. Similarly, at *Setsubun,* the bean thrower flings as many roasted soybeans as he has years.

# February 5

## Mayoresses' Festival
### Fiesta de la Alcaldesa

**i**n memory of Saint Agatha, the stubborn third-century Sicilian virgin who was tortured and finally killed for refusing the attentions of a Roman consul, women in certain northern Spanish villages claim her feast day as their very own holiday. And beware the man who steps out of line on February 5.

In Zamarramala, a Segovia suburb, two matrons are elected co-mayoresses-for-a-day. Together they promenade regally around the town, dressed in lavish black-and-red vestments heavy with silver ornaments, laying down laws and making proclamations. Meanwhile, all men are confined to their homes, where they must perform domestic chores while their wives revel with the mayoresses in the streets. In nearby Sotosalbos, a single mayoress is aided by a phalanx of women counselors. At Miranda del Castañar, near Salamanca, it is the churchwardens' wives who rule as mayoresses. And

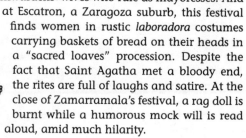

at Escatron, a Zaragoza suburb, this festival finds women in rustic *laboradora* costumes carrying baskets of bread on their heads in a "sacred loaves" procession. Despite the fact that Saint Agatha met a bloody end, the rites are full of laughs and satire. At the close of Zamarramala's festival, a rag doll is burnt while a humorous mock will is read aloud, amid much hilarity.

# February 6

## Bob Marley's Birthday

**i**n 1984, Jamaican reggae legend Bob Marley was selling more records than any of his compatriots, and more than most pop stars around the world. At the time, he had been dead for three years. Born February 6, 1945, to a white father and a black mother, Marley lived in poverty in Trenchtown, a slum district of Kingston. At fifteen, he formed his first singing group, the Wailin' Wailers, with his school chums Peter Tosh, Rita Anderson (later to become Rita Marley), and Bunny Livingston. Having dropped the "Wailin'," Marley's group went on to introduce reggae music to the world. Wildly successful, Marley was something of a peace activist and a shining role model for Jamaican youth. When he died of cancer in 1981, fans lined up for hours to pay respects beside his casket; the massive National Arena was not big enough to contain all the mourners at his funeral. Thousands lined the route from the arena to Marley's grave site in his native village of Rhoden Hall.

His grave is now a Jamaican national shrine. And his birthday is a national holiday, marked by concerts and memorials all over the island.

# February 7

lthough he is often referred to as Richard the King, this Saint Richard (not to be confused with his compatriot, Saint Richard of Chichester) was not a king but an ordinary native of eighth-century Hampshire. While on a pilgrimage with his family, the pious young Richard died at Lucca, Italy, circa 722. His relics were enshrined near the place of his death, and by the twelfth century a vivacious cult had arisen around this vague wisp of a saint. His feast day was widely celebrated, especially at Lucca.

It is perhaps not the popularity of Saint Richard but of sundry movie stars (Richard Powell, Ricardo Montalbán, Richard Burton) that has so popularized the name throughout the world. Nevertheless, Latin Americans named Ricardo are entitled on February 7 to host a "name day" party. Similar to a birthday party but less egocentric, this entails the gathering-together of friends for refreshments, gifts, and games on the feast day of the host's saintly namesake. In Mexico, a name day party is *piñata* time.

# February 8

**B**uddhism's relentless compassion for all beings sentient and otherwise finds perfect expression in this ceremony, which honors all the sewing needles that have been "killed" in action over the previous year. It is customary among Japanese dressmakers, home ec students, and others who sew to set aside needles as they break, not throwing them out but saving them for February 8. On this day the needles are brought to the local Buddhist shrine, where a triple-tiered altar is set up for the occasion. The bottom tier holds an array of sewing accessories: scissors, thimbles, thread. The top tier has offerings of seasonal fruit and white *mochi*, pounded-rice puffs. The center tier holds a vast slab of soy curd, *tofu*. Into this obliging, refreshing smooth coolness the participants plunge their broken needles. Meanwhile, priests sing sutras to comfort the needles, to heal their injured spirits, and to thank them for work done well and uncomplainingly.

It is customary to dress in *kimono* for the fifteen-hundred-year-old *Hari-kuyo* rite. All this day, Buddhists refrain from sewing: It is a funeral for broken needles, a well-deserved vacation for hale ones.

# February 9

**O**n her day, Apollonia is invoked against toothache. Attacked by a mob in Alexandria in the year 249 and exhorted to deny her Christian faith, the aged deaconess refused. Her assailants beat her about the head so enthusiastically that her teeth were knocked out. Soon thereafter, she leaped into a bonfire and died praying.

In religious art, Apollonia's emblem is a tooth clamped in a dentist's forceps.

She is especially well remembered in England, where in 1520 the author of the humorous play *Calisto and Meliboea* wrote:

> *It is for a prayer . . . my demandying,*
> *That is said . . . of seynt Appolyne*
> *For the toth ake wher of this man is in pyne.*

# February 10

## Saint Paul's Shipwreck

**B**y the time Saints Paul and Luke found themselves shipwrecked on the coast off Malta, circa 58 C.E., the island's civilization was already ancient. One of the Mediterranean's earliest cultures flourished here, predating even the Egyptians. As a Phoenician colony, Malta had enjoyed democracy. Then as a Roman province, Malta was renowned as a naval base and producer of sailcloth and fine honey, the best in all the empire. Temples to a prehistoric goddess, to Roman deities, and to the Phoenician god Moloch were scattered throughout the island.

What Paul and Luke had to offer the Maltese, then, was merely the latest in a five-thousand-year history of novelties. The two had been en route to Rome when their ship went down in a storm near what is now known as Saint Paul's Bay. The saints spent the rest of that winter in Malta, where Paul reportedly effected miracle cures and converted the island's governor.

This accomplished, as Paul tells in the Acts of the Apostles, "After three months in Malta we set sail in . . . an Alexandrian vessel with the Heavenly Twins on its figurehead." The apostles' brief visit is credited with Christianizing this now wholly Catholic island. The anniversary is celebrated with church services, dances, and fireworks.

# February 11

### Kenkoku Kinen no Hi

*K*igensetsu, Empire Day, was once Japan's most patriotic holiday. After World War II, at the American army's urging, it was officially stricken from the calendar. Extinguished by the winds of war, the holiday rose again twenty-one years later, with a softer, safer new name.

National Foundation Day honors the legendary founding of the imperial line. On February 11, 660 B.C.E. (according to a government ruling made in 1872), Japan's first emperor, Jimmu, is said to have ascended to the throne. This is how it happened:

When the sun goddess, Amaterasu, sent her grandson Ninigi down to earth, she entrusted him with her sacred sword, her mirror, and her "comma-shaped jewels." Headquartered on Kyushu, Ninigi soon learned that the locals didn't care who he was or that his grandma was divine. Several generations of Ninigi's progeny strove to subjugate the natives. Finally his great-grandson, Jimmu, led a successful campaign at what is now Osaka. Today Jimmu's feat is commemorated with speeches and patriotic school programs, as well as ceremonies in which the current emperor and empress and the prime minister take part.

# February 12

## Lincoln's Birthday

**D**uring his five years in office, the sixteenth president of the United States enjoyed an uncanny hold on the public imagination. He was hailed as the embodiment of American democracy; the Great Emancipator. His life story—that of steady upward progress from a log cabin to the White House— proclaimed that such things were pos-

FOUR SCORE AND SEVEN YEARS AGO—

sible in the "land of the free." Lincoln's assassination in a Washington theater threw the country into unsurpassed mourning and moved poet Walt Whitman to write:

*Coffin that passes through lanes and streets,*
*Through day and night with the great cloud darkening the land. . . .*
*I mourn'd, and yet shall mourn with ever-returning spring.*

Lincoln was a relative unknown until the age of forty. He had been a partner in a general store, a postmaster, a surveyor, and a lawyer by the time he entered the Illinois state legislature.

Lincoln's birthday became an official holiday the year after his death. At the first of these ceremonies, in Washington, D.C., the Marine Band played a selection from *Il Trovatore,* which seems in bad taste considering what happened when Lincoln last attended a theater. No longer celebrated on the president's actual birthday, "Lincoln's Birthday" is generally observed on the first Monday in the month, and in some states is lumped together with Washington's birthday.

# February 13

The Roman holiday dedicated to honoring (some say worshiping) dead kinfolk began precisely at the sixth hour on the thirteenth day of February and lasted a full nine days thereafter. These *dies parentales* (parental days) were not a spooky time for the average Roman citizen. Rather, these were days of obligation and feasting, quiet and respectful, introspective, like a wake. During the *Parentalia,* all temples were closed, weddings were forbidden, and governmental magistrates uncharacteristically appeared in public devoid of the insignia of their office. People visited their parents' and other relatives' graves, bringing offerings such as milk, wine, honey, oil, and spring water. Some brought sacrificial blood from the bodies of black animals. They decked the graves with roses and violets. "Dining with the dead" at the grave site, the celebrant would offer the traditional greeting and farewell of the holiday: *Salve, sancte parens,* "Hail, holy ancestor."

The Vestal Virgins, the priestesses who tended the goddess Vesta's shrine in the Forum, performed rites of their own at the *Parentalia.* The senior Vestal paid a ceremonial visit to the group's "parental" tomb—that of the early Vestal, Tarpeia.

# February 14

**O**ne thing is nearly certain: Valentine's Day has nothing to do with either of the two third-century martyrs who share the name Valentine and share this as their feast day.

The date is heavy with the scent of coupling. A medieval folk belief held that wild birds choose February 14 to begin their spring mating. The ancient Roman custom, enacted every year at February 15's *Lupercalia,* of "lovers' lots"—drawing partners' names at random from a box—enjoyed enduring popularity through the ages. In mid-sixteenth-century France, Saint Francis de Sales struggled to abolish the custom. As a contemporary described it, Francis tried to interest his flock instead in the practice of "giving boys billets with the names of certain [female] saints for them to honor." One can imagine how well that went over.

Another old tradition held that the first person seen on the morning of the fourteenth (excepting blood relatives) would be that day's "valentine." So Shakespeare has Ophelia chirruping to Hamlet:

> *Good morrow, 'tis Saint Valentine's Day,*
> *All in the morn betime,*
> *And I a maid at your window,*
> *To be your valentine.*

# February 15

*A* wolf (*lupa*) according to legend nursed a pair of abandoned human twins in her cave (the Lupercal) on the Palatine Hill. These twins, Romulus and Remus, went on to found Rome. The poet Ovid explains: "A she-wolf who had given birth to her whelps came, wondrous to tell, to the abandoned twins. . . . She halted and fawned on the tender babes . . . and licked into shape their two bodies . . . fearless, they sucked her dugs. . . . Great is the reward owed the nurse for the milk she gave." At the *Lupercalia,* a band of priests called *Luperci* gathered at the Lupercal on the southwestern slope of the Palatine. Here they sacrificed goats and a puppy, and made offerings of a sacred grain mixture, the *mola salsa.*

Two youths were smeared on the foreheads with the sacrificial blood. They duly wiped this off with swatches of milk-soaked wool. Then—this was mandatory—the boys had to laugh. Feasting, then stripping naked, then winding themselves in the still-warm, still-wet skins of the sacrificed goats, the pair fled down the hill. They ran around its circumference, slapping everyone they met with goatskin thongs, *februa,* also cut from the sacrificial beasts.

One of Rome's most important holidays, the Lupercalia began as an earthy fertility rite. Plutarch maintains that a slap from the *februa* granted the slappee many children and easy childbirth. The holiday lasted well into the Christian era, until Pope Gelasius I outlawed it in 494 C.E.

# February 16

**D**uring Japan's period of self-imposed isolation, it was important for people to demonstrate their nonattachment to Western imports
and influences, including Christianity. Literally
translated as "stepping on a picture," *Fumi-e* was
the ceremonial practice of stamping on pictures
of Jesus, Mary, the saints, or the cross, which had
been specially printed for this purpose. The
lunar-calendar date corresponding with February 16
marked the start of the annual three-month Fumi-e
season, a custom first established in 1626 by Mizuno Morinobu,
magistrate of Nagasaki. In 1716 the government enacted a law
whose purpose was "to make certain the extinction of Christianity."
Those who refused to perform the rite were often persecuted for dis-
loyalty to the then-state religion, Buddhism. Fumi-e, finally abol-
ished in 1857, inspired the haiku poet Shuchiku to write of:

> *An old woman*
> *trampling on a picture of Christ*
> *and chanting.*

# February 17

QVIRINVS

**E**very classicist worth his or her salt knows without a doubt that this day was an ancient Roman holiday, a festival dedicated in all reverence to the god Quirinus. This was the god after whom Rome's Quirinal Hill was named. The god's temple stood on that hill; in a house adjoining the temple lived the god's priest, the Flamen Quirinalis. Flanking the temple gates was a pair of myrtles, one called the Patrician and the other called the Plebeian. And February 17 was beyond the shadow of a doubt the *Quirinalia*.

It's just that no one today knows the slightest thing about Quirinus. For example, what was he the god of? Who were his consorts? Did he prefer lamb sacrifices or dog? Some scholars have suggested that Quirinus was merely another name for Romulus, one of the legendary twin brothers (the other being Remus) credited with the founding of Rome. In the *Aeneid*, Vergil wrote of *Remo cum fratre Quirinus,* "Remus with his brother Quirinus." Others think Quirinus was Mars under a different name. They base this theory on the fact that votive offerings addressed to both Mars and Quirinus have been unearthed on the Quirinal Hill. The same archeological evidence, however, has led still other scholars to exactly the opposite conclusion. So the activities of February 17, whether solemn or festive, remain a mystery.

# February 18
## Saint Bernadette's Second Vision

In 1858 an undernourished, asthmatic fourteen-year-old citizen of Lourdes named Bernadette encountered a radiant woman hovering around a rocky outcropping. The woman called herself the Immaculate Conception, and Bernadette called her *aquero*, "that one." The pair met eighteen times, during which the woman revealed to Bernadette a spring that from that time to this produces 27,000 gallons of water a week and is said to possess miraculous healing powers. The shrine of Our Lady of Lourdes is now the top pilgrimage site in France and one of the most popular in all the world.

During and after her visions, clergy and parishioners alike ridiculed Bernadette. They called her stupid and accused her of making the whole thing up. She stuck by her story, however. With Lourdes's increasing fame, Bernadette more fiercely sought privacy, finally entering a convent at Nevers where she suffered further ridicule. But enduring ridicule is one of the surest paths to sainthood, and she was canonized in 1933. The anniversary of her second vision on February 18 is the day Saint Bernadette is celebrated—in Lourdes and elsewhere in France.

# Fèbruary 19

n the town of Villanueva de la Vera in eastern Spain, this date has long been dedicated to a ritualized scapegoating ceremony in which the victim is an effigy called Pero (a diminutive of Pedro) Palo (meaning "stick" or "twig"). Allegedly a reenactment of a Jew's interrogation and torture during the Spanish Inquisition, this event was authorized by the Tribunal of the Inquisition, which long ago dedicated festival banners and drums to the townspeople for use in the "trial."

In the days preceding the event, a group of townsmen called *Pero-Paleros* labor to erect the wooden platform on which the effigy will be displayed. Another group creates the Pero itself. This work is done in secret, and those who do it are ensured, so it is said, of good luck in the coming year. Life-size and stuffed with straw, the effigy is clad in black, with a black hat and a black skirtlike garment around the waist. At dusk on the festival day, Pero rides on his platform. His body is impaled on a wooden pitchfork; a sign on his back reads "Condemned to death by the popular Tribunal for high treason." To the shuddery whisper of drums, the mock trial is enacted with its inevitable guilty verdict. Pero Palo is decapitated and then tossed to the howling revelers, who rip and tear the body until the street is strewn with straw. Afterwards, sausages are distributed to the local poor and a banquet is held in the home of the head Pero-Palero.

# February 20

**W**ho knows what that distinguished Londoner, Sir John Cass, would have written in his will? No one knows, because Cass died of a sudden hemorrhage just as he was picking up a  quill pen to write the blasted thing. That was in 1718, and every year since, an annual memorial marks the anniversary of Cass's death. The entire student body of Sir John Cass College attends the melancholy service at Saint Botolph's Church, Aldgate. In commemoration of the fact that their founder died with pen in hand, the scholars wear quills on their uniforms. In honor of his hemorrhage, the quills are blood red.

# February 21

T he last day of an extended ancestor-honoring festival, *Feralia* was the ancient Roman version of Day of the Dead. Its name comes from the verb *ferre*, "to carry," as in "to ferry."

As is the custom in similar holidays all over the world, the Roman family would hike to the ancestral graveyard, ferrying offerings. As Ovid explains: "That day they . . . carry to the dead their dues; it is the last day for propitiating the ghosts." The ghosts, it was believed, were hovering expectantly over their graves. "Honor is paid," Ovid goes on, "to the tombs. Appease the souls . . . and bring small gifts to the extinguished pyres. The ghosts ask but little: they value piety more than a costly gift; no greedy deities are they. . . . Votive garlands, a sprinkling of grain, a few grains of salt, bread soaked in wine, and some loose violets: these are enough: set these on a potsherd and leave it in the middle of the path. Now doth the ghost fatten upon his dole."

# February 22

## Caristia

**O**n the heels of the ghost-ridden *Parentalia* (see February 13) and its attendant *Feralia* (see February 21), when deceased ancestors were duly honored and fed, came the *Caristia*—from *cara,* meaning "dear." This was a life-affirming holiday, a day of affectionate family reunions, which offered Romans an opportunity to relish the company of those loved ones still living.

All squabbling was forbidden, old feuds were forgotten, and chronic sibling rivalries were set aside. Concordia, the peace goddess, ruled this day with an overflowing cornucopia in one hand and an olive branch in the other. Ovid notes Concordia's "gentle presence . . . on that day more than all others." Of the Caristia with its banquets and its gift exchanges, he explains: "A crowd of relations comes. . . . Sweet it is, no doubt, to recall our thoughts to the living after they have dwelt upon the grave and on the dear ones departed from us; sweet, too, after so many departed, to look upon those of our blood who are left, and to count kin with them."

# February 23

## Terminalia

This festival honoring Terminus, god of boundaries, encouraged neighbor to feast with neighbor—thus smoothing one of the most potentially awkward of human relationships.

The festival was observed in the countryside. A pair of neighbors would walk out to the boundary marker (usually a stone) dividing their properties. Each man garlanded his side of the stone, erected a makeshift altar on his side, and decked it with offerings to the god. Then from out of each house came the men's families, the wives bearing firebrands that had been ignited on their own kitchen hearths. The sons carried baskets of their fathers' produce, and the daughters bore sacrificial honey cakes. Using the firebrands, the wives kindled twin altar fires made of neatly interlaced sticks. A boy held his basket over the fire while his sister shook the basket three times to scatter its contents into the flames. Then the girls fed their cakes to the fires. Meanwhile, the men's employees gathered and stood by in silence, dressed all in white, wine in hand. Together, the two landlords slaughtered a lamb and a suckling pig on the spot, and the blood spattered the boundary stone. Afterwards, the families joined together for what amounted to a proto-block party.

# February 24

*Regifugium*

**L**iterally "running for office," ancient kings of Rome fled on foot, every year on this day, from the Forum. No mere parlor game, the *Regifugium* descended from an annual rite in which the king was pursued by an eager band of would-be usurpers. If overtaken, the sovereign faced certain dethronement and possible death. This flight (*fugium*) of the king (*regis*) was a rite of a kind practiced all over the world to test a ruler's mettle, physically as well as spiritually. Rome's ancient kings were high priests and monarchs rolled into one. Such a ruler underwent the Regifugium, Sir James Frazer notes in *The Golden Bough,* "with particular rigor to ensure that no personal defect should incapacitate him for the performance of those sacred rites and ceremonies on which, even more than on the despatch of his civil and military duties, the safety and prosperity of the community depended."

Every February 24, a sacrifice was offered in the Comitium after which the king took off running. While in later years the Regifugium was, in Frazer's words, "an empty form," it was in spirit, he tells us, "a relic of a time when the kingship was an annual office awarded, along with the hand of a princess, to the victorious athlete or gladiator who therefore figured along with his bride as a god and goddess in a sacred marriage to ensure the fertility of the earth by homeopathic magic."

# February 25

This Wessex-born Anglo-Saxon, a sister of both Saint Willibald and Saint Winebald, became a nun at Wimborne in Dorset. Then she moved on to Germany, where she was made abbess of a double monastery at Heidenheim. She was a skilled healer. But unlike many saints—that is, ones who really existed— she lacked a contemporary biographer. Thus nothing is known of her days in Germany. Walburga, aka Waldburg, died in 779; in 870 her remains were moved to a shrine in Eichstatt. Shortly thereafter a mysterious oil was discovered flowing from the rock surrounding her tomb. The oil was soon hailed as having miraculous healing powers. In 893 Walburga's body was disinterred, dismembered, and parts of it were distributed to churches in Germany, Belgium, and France.

The oil still flows from Walburga's tomb in Eichstatt, where the saint's feast day is a special event. She has become more closely associated with another holiday, however. *Walpurgisnacht* (see April 30), the anniversary of the date on which her remains were moved to Eichstatt, supplanted a pre-Christian German revel.

# February 26

## Zamboanga Festival
### Bale Zamboanga

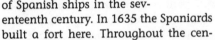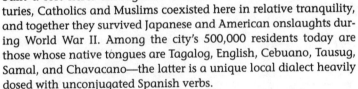

**i**f multiculturalism is the status quo in the Philippines, then Zamboanga on the island of Mindanao is as Filipino as the Philippines get. Early Malay settlers—tribal pagans who converted to Islam—witnessed the arrival of Spanish ships in the seventeenth century. In 1635 the Spaniards built a fort here. Throughout the centuries, Catholics and Muslims coexisted here in relative tranquility, and together they survived Japanese and American onslaughts during World War II. Among the city's 500,000 residents today are those whose native tongues are Tagalog, English, Cebuano, Tausug, Samal, and Chavacano—the latter is a unique local dialect heavily dosed with unconjugated Spanish verbs.

Zamboanga celebrates its diversity every February 25 and 26 with the *Bale Zamboanga.* During the festival, Catholic and Moslem groups present cultural programs, religious rites, regattas, and exhibitions, which are open to all.

# February 27

*A*n amazing number of English gentlepersons managed to singlehandedly create holidays in their own memory by means of cleverly wrought bequests in their wills. One of these was Provost Bost, administrator of the public school, Eton. Upon his death in 1504, it was revealed that Bost had willed a sum of money that, properly invested, was earmarked to provide tuppence a year in perpetuity for each of Eton's "collegers." (Collegers are boarding students whose families live far away; the remainder are town boys or "oppidans.") The money was to ensure that the boys would get enough to eat. At the time of Bost's death, tuppence bought nearly half a sheep, and it was an Eton tradition, dating back to the reign of Henry VI, that collegers were to be fed no meat except mutton.

Provost Lupton, Bost's successor, added his own posthumous bequest to the orginal charity so that the annual dole would amount to thruppence. Every February 27, the collegers gather—a diginified cadre of jackets, vests, and ties—in College Hall for the Threepenny Ceremony. Each boy in turn plucks his three-pence from the crown of a tall silk hat. As consideration for the gift, each boy must recite a prayer for Bost's soul.

# February 28

## Kalevala Day

The modern world owes virtually all it knows about Finnish folklore to one man, Dr. Elias Lönrott. For countless centuries, the wealth of Finnish myth and legend had existed solely within the oral tradition, locked in people's hearts but fading with every passing decade. In 1822, one Zacharias Topelius published a few scant bits of the lore. This inspired Dr. Lönrott to go further. With a team of assistants, Lönrott combed the countryside, interviewing his compatriots. He gathered thousands upon thousands of lines, writing them down exactly as the peasants had chanted them. Here were stories of Kalevala, the mythical land of heroes. Here were its denizens, such as the magician-scholar Lemminkainen, the blacksmith god Ilmarinen, the fire-bringer Vainamoinen. Here were tales about the point of a swan's feather, the milk of a sterile cow, spells and incantations, thirty-year gestations, evil bears, a golden plough, necromancers, a musical instrument made of fish bones. The result of Lönrott's research became the national epic, the 22,000-line *Kalevala*.

Dr. Lönrott, preparing the first edition of his manuscript for final publication, dated his preface February 28, 1835. On the anniversary of that day, Finns celebrate with parades and concerts—and, of course, readings from the *Kalevala*.

# February 29

Ladies' Day

**T**hree years out of every four, the Gregorian calendar and all the people who adhere to it neatly leapfrog over February 29 as if it didn't exist. The chronological conundrum called Leap Year was incorporated into the Gregorian system to accommodate the inconvenient fact that the earth takes five hours and forty-eight minutes longer than 365 days to circle the sun. Crowning this upheaval of the "natural" order of things is its social equivalent, the old English custom of Ladies' Day. As of the Middle Ages, women were entitled every Leap Day to reverse the natural order and propose marriage to men. A Scottish parliamentary law of 1288 stipulated that "for [each] yeare known as lepe yeare, any maiden ladye of both high and low estait shall hae liberte to bespeke ye man she like." She could ask, and he had his right to accept or refuse. But any refusal, according to the law, would cost the man a pound.

A booklet published in London in 1606 further detailed the practice: "It now become a part of the common lawe . . . as every leap yeare doth return, the ladyes have the sole privilege during the time it continueth of making love, either by wordes or lookes, as to them it seemeth proper. . . . No man will be entitled to . . . in any wise treat her proposal with slight or contumely."

# Moveable Feast

## Feast of Lots

### Purim

*W*ith its raucousness, relentless clowning, and borderline-bawdy theatrics and masquerades, Purim is the most unbuttoned of Jewish holidays, inadvertently echoing Mardi Gras and other pre-Lenten carnivals occurring at this same time of year. Some anthropologists hold that Purim is no less than a descendant of the orgiastic Babylonian New Year, on which Marduk and his fellow gods were said to gamble by casting lots (*purim* in the Babylonian language). The consensus, however, is that Purim commemorates one Queen Esther, who with her cousin Mordecai, thwarted a massacre that had been engineered by the anti-Semitic royal adviser, Haman. (Haman, it is said, ended up on the gallows.)

Purim is the only day of the Jewish year on which celebrants are canonically permitted—in fact encouraged—to drink themselves silly. After a formal reading from the Book of Esther to usher in the holiday, many temples sponsor Purim carnivals, complete with song, dance, and games of the knock-over-bottles-painted-with-Haman's-face variety. Carnival booths offer *hamentaschen,* triangular filled cookies that represent Haman's three-cornered hat. Throughout the day, revelers are encouraged to stomp the floor, blow horns, and whirl *graggers* (special low-pitched noisemakers) whenever Haman's name is mentioned.

# March 1

**i**n the holiday-obsessed world of ancient Rome, even the gods had birthdays. Garrulous Mars had his on March 1, the beginning (*kalends*) of the month that bore—and still bears—his name. However, Mars's day was celebrated not with mock battles or other predictably martial demonstrations, but with reverence to Mars's mother, Juno. The goddess became pregnant with him, the poet Ovid tells us, immediately upon finding a special wildflower: "She touched it, and by her touch conceived in her womb . . . and Mars was created."

Juno, as one of the Roman pantheon's biggest cheeses, was worshiped under many names and many aspects. As Juno Lucina she held the secrets of childbirth and was represented in artworks with a flower in her right hand, a swaddled infant cradled in her left, and a veil hiding her face. It was to Juno Lucina's temple on the Esquiline Hill that Roman women journeyed every March 1 to pay their respects, to pray, and to leave their offerings. At home, too, they offered up prayers for a good, happy marriage; on this day husbands gave presents to their wives. While the *Saturnalia* (see December 17) was the Roman men's chance to subvert the social order, with masters waiting hand and foot on their slaves, the *Matronalia* was the women's chance to do the same. On this day they doted on their female servants from morning till night.

# March 2

S aint Chad—the brother, oddly, of Saint Cedd—was every inch an Englishman. Born in Northumbria, he served as an abbot in Yorkshire, founded a monastery in Lincolnshire, and was bishop of Lichfield by the time of his death in 672. Many English cathedrals bear his name, as do a great number of wells and springs whose waters are said to boast miraculous healing properties. Chad was famous, in his time, for his love of walking. (Saint Theodore of Canterbury finally insisted that Chad ride on horseback; he said traveling on foot was beneath a churchman of Chad's stature.) It was Chad's reputation as a nature boy that makes his feast day such a favorite for weather prognostication and agricultural lore. One old folk rhyme alludes to the weather on the first three days of March, vis-à-vis three English saints:

> *First comes David,*
> *Then comes Chad,*
> *Then comes Winnold, roaring like mad.*

Another states:

> *Sow beans and peas on David and Chad,*
> *Be the weather good or bad.*

# March 3

This holiday's other name, *Momo no Sekku* or Peach Blossom Festival, is a double entendre, suggesting both the blossoms themselves in all their pastel tremulousness and the Japanese ideal of equally tender, equally tremulous girlhood. This is the day when little girls host their friends for tea-and-poetry parties with diamond-shaped pink and green *mochi* cakes. The guests politely amuse themselves in the shadow of the hostess's set of *hina,* dolls. These are not playthings at all but heirlooms, passed down from mother to daughter. Kept in storage all year, the hina are unwrapped only for this occasion and are arranged in a proscribed order along special shelves that display them to best advantage.

The hina represent members of an imperial court. The empress in her twelve-layered silk kimono (*jyu-ni-hito*) stands on the top shelf alongside her purple-robed emperor. On the second tier are three ladies-in-waiting and three young male musicians: one with a drum, one with a flute, and the third—the singer—with a fan. Also here are government ministers, footmen, scribes, tea ceremony experts, palanquin bearers, and caterers laden with tiny lacquer dishes. Not every child owns a whole set of hina; museums often stage exhibitions at this time of year featuring sets three hundred and four hundred years old.

# March 4

## Saint Casimir's Day

Thirteen-year-old Prince Casimir gloated over the failure of his father's plans to make him king of Hungary. Kingship wasn't young Casimir's bag; he had dedicated himself to Jesus. His irate father, King Casimir of Poland, banished the intractable boy—albeit to a castle on the outskirts of his hometown, Kraków. Serving reluctantly as a viceroy while his father was away in Lithuania, Casimir pursued the spiritual life diligently, going so far as to reject the hand of Emperor Frederick III's daughter in favor of his foresworn celibacy. On March 4, 1484, he died, not yet thirty years old.

At his tomb in Vilnius, Lithuania, miracles were soon reported. Now the youthful would-be monk is patron saint of Lithuania (where he is called *Sventas Kazimieras*) as well as of his native Poland. In both countries, special church services mark his feast day.

# March 5

The Romans' annual March 5 festival honored the goddess Isis as the sailors' patroness and inventor of the sail. In his second-century C.E. book *The Golden Ass,* Roman author Lucius Apuleius has the goddess Isis addressing the protagonist on the eve of her March 5 festival: "Devote to my worship the day born of this night . . . for at this season the storms of winter lose their force, the leaping waves subside and the sea becomes navigable once more."

Observed at a port city near Corinth, the celebrations included flower-garlanded women strewing petals; other women held mirrors in which the goddess might observe herself; other worshipers sprinkled the streets with perfume. Then came devotees who carried lamps, torches, and candles. Next came the pipers, flutists, and choirboys. Beadles called out, "Make way! Make way for the goddess!" as a horde of priests advanced toward the sea, dribbling milk onto the ground from a breast-shaped golden pitcher.

At the seashore, a boat was waiting. Built especially for this ritual, it sported "hieroglyphics painted over the entire hull," a sail of "shining white linen," and a "long fir mast with [a] shining head." The "gilded prow [was] shaped like the neck of Isis's holy goose, and the long brightly polished keel cut from a solid trunk of citrus wood." Its hold was loaded with spices and other offerings. The priests cut the moorings and launched the vessel. Unmanned, this was the people's annual gift to "the queen of the stars, the mother of the seasons, the mistress of the universe."

# March 6

lthough later a bloody battleground, the Alamo started life early in the eighteenth century as a mild Franciscan mission. With a convent, a hospital, an over-two-acre plaza, and—a detail that would prove crucial—a three-foot-thick surrounding wall, the mission ministered to the local Indians. By the end of the century the Indians were much diminished and the mission was abandoned. Locals took to calling the place the Alamo, either after a settlement in Mexico or because of a nearby grove of *alamos,* cottonwoods. The Alamo was a crumbling ruin by the time Texan colonists decided it was time to declare independence from Mexico.

The Mexican president, General Antonio López de Santa Anna, did not agree. So in late February of 1836, a band of Anglo-American Texan colonists held fast behind the thick walls of the Alamo, determined to bar Santa Anna's threatened incursion into the interior. Santa Anna's troops arrived as expected, red "no quarter" flag fluttering, and demanded unconditional surrender. The Texans refused, and the thirteen-day siege that ensued ended March 6, when the Mexicans charged the Alamo and killed nearly everyone inside. (Among the dead was Davy Crockett, king of the wild frontier.) The bloodbath infuriated many; the war intensified. Texas celebrates its victory with Alamo Day.

# March 7

**M**assachusetts-born Luther Burbank dabbled, as a child, in backyard gardening. At twenty-one he bought some land of his own, and by twenty-four he had developed a new variety of potato. Then he resettled in Santa Rosa, California, which had a longer growing season than his native East, and began work in earnest. Over the next fifty years, this self-described "partner of nature" produced over eight hundred new strains and varieties of flowers, fruits, vegetables, and other plants, including new kinds of tomatoes, corn, squash, beans, peas, artichokes, asparagus, chives, and rhubarb. He was particularly interested in plums (and the resultant prunes), roses, and lilies, and he is responsible for the cheery Shasta daisy and a spineless cactus. Burbank was a plant breeder who emphasized the hands-on approach and did not keep thorough records.

Nevertheless, many of his successes now form the base of entire fruit and vegetable industries, particularly in his adopted state of California. In gratitude, the state legislature passed a bill in 1909 declaring that every March 7, "being the anniversary of the birthday of Luther Burbank . . . [be] set apart and designated Bird and Arbor Day." The legislature urged teachers to include "in the school work of the day suitable exercises having for their object instruction as to the economic value of birds and trees, and the promotion of a spirit of protection toward them . . . and the desirability of their conservation."

# March 8
## International Women's Day

**M**ost of the world's holidays, it can be cynically stated, are in one way or another men's days. Patriotic, religious, historical—take your pick. International Women's Day was inspired by a pair of mid-nineteenth-century Ladies' Garment Workers' strikes, and now it is celebrated on this day all over the world in many different fashions. A longtime staple in the former U.S.S.R., this was an official day off for women workers. On this day, men stood on the bread and grocery lines, cooked the meals, cleaned house—and bought traditional bunches of mimosa flowers for the females in their lives.

In the United States, a congressional resolution designating March as Women's History Month laments that "American women of every race, class, and ethnic background have made historical contributions to the growth and strength of our nation in countless recorded and unrecorded ways . . . [and have been] early leaders in the forefront of every major progressive social change movement . . . whereas despite these contributions, the role of American women in history has been consistently overlooked and undervalued, in the literature, teaching and study of American history." Throughout the month, women's groups in American towns hold celebrations and events, exhibitions, concerts, and rituals, recalling heroic and gifted women of every stripe.

# March 9

In the Rumanian countryside before World War II, farm families implored the Forty Saints to provide good weather on their feast day. This in turn would ensure good weather for the next forty days thereafter. To curry favor with the Forty Saints, a pious Rumanian would execute forty genuflections before retiring to bed on the evening of March 8.

The saints who share this feast day were soldiers of the Twelfth (aka Thunderstruck) Roman Legion. In the year 320, Emperor Licinius abruptly threatened to execute all Christians then living in the East. Those who repudiated Christianity would be spared. The forty soldiers, stationed at Sebastea in what is now Turkey, held fast. They were rounded up, stripped, and marched out to the middle of a frozen pond, where they huddled naked on the ice as their tormentors teased them by kindling fires and preparing warm baths on the shore. But the forty stayed out on the ice all that day and night, and on the morning of March 9, those few who had not yet frozen to death were slaughtered.

Having felt so keenly the chill of this season, the Forty Saints might well be expected to have mercy on those who beg them for good weather. Their feast day is a time for cleaning barns and organizing farm tools.

# March 10

Tibet shimmers in many Westerners' minds as an enigmatic aerie, faintly holy, peopled with Buddhists and yaks. In fact, Tibet is truly remote, but only partly because of geography. The Chinese government invaded Tibet in 1950, commencing an occupation that imperiled virtually every aspect of Tibet's distinctive culture. On March 10, 1959, after nine years of Chinese occupation, Tibetans rioted in Lhasa, their capital. The People's Liberation Army marched in, and in the bloody aftermath some 80,000 Tibetan refugees fled to neighboring India and Nepal and beyond. Tibet's spiritual leader, the Dalai Lama or "ocean of wisdom," went into exile in India. In the wake of continued hostilities, the Chinese government closed Tibet's doors to individual foreign tourists and particularly to the foreign press.

Meanwhile, Chinese rule continued apace. To this day, Tibetans and their supporters mourn their homeland, dreaming of its restoration. Annually, on the anniversary of the Lhasa uprising, the exiled Dalai Lama issues his statement. Expatriate Tibetans and their supporters hold political and cultural fairs, bazaars, and gatherings to mark the day.

# March 11

**O**n the night of March 11, 1644, while the English Civil War was raging on all sides and Cromwell's Roundheads were clamoring on the outskirts of town, Hercules Clay, the mayor of Newark, Nottinghamshire, lay dreaming that his house was on fire. He awoke in alarm, but finding nothing amiss, he went back to bed. Soon he dreamed a second time of flames. Again he awoke, found nothing wrong, and went back to sleep. Almost immediately he dreamed yet again of fire. At this point, he sat bolt upright, vaulted from under the covers, and dragged his protesting family out of the house.

Moments later, a Roundhead bomb smashed into the mayor's home, which burst immediately into flames. The family watched from afar, horrified but—thanks to Clay's prophetic dream—safe.

Mayor Clay attributed his dreams to supernatural intervention, and so in his will he provided for the preaching of an annual "Bombshell Sermon" in the Newark parish church on the anniversary of his dream. The tradition continues to this day. Reading passages from a bible that once belonged to Hercules Clay himself, the vicar discusses the nature of danger, dreams, and deliverance.

# March 12

## Receiving the Water
### O-mizutori

This Buddhist ceremony attracts huge crowds to Todai-ji Shrine in Nara, Japan, reputedly the world's largest wooden building and home to a fifty-three-foot statue of the Buddha. After a two-week period of austerities, undergone so as to lessen the errors of mankind, the shrine's eleven priests are ready for the rite. *O-mizutori* is said to have been initiated in the year 752 following a mystical dream. On March 2, the priests of Kyoto's Jinu-ji shrine celebrate their own *Mizu-okuri* festival, during which they "send" sacred water to Todaiji's priests via a legendary underground stream. Close to midnight on March 12, Todaiji's white-robed priests "receive" the water, drawing it from Wakasa well, as monks blow into conch shells to create a powerful roar. The priests then light ten huge torches, whose glow flickers along the temple walls. The crowd waits, breathless. As midnight approaches, the priests carry the torches along the veranda, scattering a rhythmic shower of golden sparks in every direction.

The spectators lunge and jostle in an effort to "catch" sparks on their skin (the tingle is supposed to have healing properties). They bend to scoop up ashes and cinders from the floor, to be kept at home as potent relics.

# March 13

**B**eginning every year on this day, Valencia's Fallas Festival is a week-long extravaganza whose brilliant fireworks and towering bonfires "burn away" the last vestiges of winter and welcome the cheering, healing glow of the summer sun.

Las Fallas has parades, bullfights, music, and costumed revelers dashing down the streets at all hours, downing golden brown fritters (*churros*). But what gets people really excited are the *ninots,* hilarious, huge wood, plaster, and papier-mâché statues that now make their appearance all over the city. Neighborhood committees have been laboring for months, designing and building their *ninots* in secret. Now here the statues stand, hundreds of them, some as tall as houses. Lavishly detailed, the satirical *ninots* can employ up to twenty-five different characters—mermaids, naked politicians,

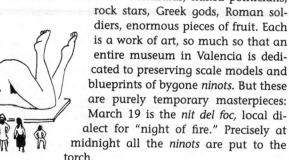

rock stars, Greek gods, Roman soldiers, enormous pieces of fruit. Each is a work of art, so much so that an entire museum in Valencia is dedicated to preserving scale models and blueprints of bygone *ninots.* But these are purely temporary masterpieces: March 19 is the *nit del foc,* local dialect for "night of fire." Precisely at midnight all the *ninots* are put to the torch.

# March 14

**S**capegoats suffer so that we don't have to. Every March 14, a man dressed in animal skins was led through the streets of ancient Rome. His companions prodded him with long rods—branches with the bark peeled off, then polished till the wood gleamed smooth and white. After much marching and prodding, the scapegoat's tormentors pummeled him with their sticks, shouted "Mamurius!" at him, and drove him from the city. No one is exactly sure of Mamurius's precise identity. One legend tells of Mamurius, a metalsmith, who was driven from Rome when some shields he had made for the army were deemed unlucky. Other sources identify Mamurius with the similarly named Mars, whose month this was. Some believe that the character's name, Mamurius Veturius, refers to the driving out of the "old Mars"—that is, the old, impotent year—to make way for the new fruitful one. (The Romans celebrated their New Year in spring.) Mars was associated with a holiday of earth renewal because, as Sir James Frazer notes in *The Golden Bough,* in earlier times, he ruled woods and vegetation:

"It was to Mars that the Roman husbandman prayed for the prosperity of his grain and vines, his fruit trees and his copses." During the Mamurius Veturius rite, he explains, "The representative of the god appears to have been treated, not only as a deity of vegetation, but also as a scapegoat. . . . It becomes necessary to drive him beyond the boundaries, that he may carry his sorrowful burden away to other lands."

# March 15

## Phallus Festival

### Tagata Honen-Sai

*i*zanami and Izanagi were Japan's parent gods. Having first created the Japanese islands out of bubbling oily chaos, they then set out to create everything else. While their mating produced a spate of deities, the incendiary birth of the fire god Ho-Masubi proved too much for poor Izanami. As she lay dying, her blood, vomit, and urine spawned more deities still. Then Izanagi mourned her, and his left eye secreted the sun goddess; his right eye secreted the moon god, and from his nose oozed Susanoo, guardian of the sea.

It should come as no surprise, then, that this supercouple is to this day the focus of annual Shinto fertility festivals. The temple precinct at Izanami's Oagata-jinja shrine near Inuyama in central Honshu features large cleft rocks, huge clamshells, and other sacred items that resemble female genitalia. (At the Hime-no-Miya festival on the first two Sundays in March, worshipers career out of the temple and through the streets shouldering a *mikoshi,* a portable altar, packed with vulva replicas.) *Tagata Honen-Sai,* held every March 15, takes place at Izanagi's shrine, Tagata-jinja, and stars a ten-foot-long wooden phallus. Carried sedately along the road on a litter,

 the gleaming member tours the local countryside. Throughout the afternoon, its bearers offer libations to the farmers whose fields they pass.

# March 16

**S**aint Urho, the grasshopper slayer, is Finland's answer to Saint Patrick. The legend tells how, faced with a plague of locusts bent on devouring Finland's entire wine-grape crop, Urho raised his staff and thundered the Finnish equivalent of "Grasshopper, grasshopper, go to hell!" And, legend has it, they did—forever, like Patrick's serpents. Miracle accomplished.

The first problem is that Saint Urho probably never existed. (But then, neither did a lot of perfectly respectable saints.) Secondly, *what* Finnish wine-grape crop? Thirdly, Finland still has grasshoppers.

We turn our attention, then, to the American Midwest, long a stronghold of transplanted Finns. Rumor has it that a Finnish-American department store owner in Minnesota grew weary of his Irish-American employees always asking for March 17 off in honor of Saint Patrick. The store owner wanted his compatriots to have a day off, too—and (perhaps and perhaps not) so Saint Urho was born.

Finnish Americans all over the U.S. embrace this day as a focus for solidarity. The town of Hood River, Oregon, for example, celebrates with a Saint Urho's Day parade in which locals dress up as locusts. The Urhomobile, a VW bug painted lime green (for the locusts) and purple (for the grapes) rumbles down the street as its occupants shout in unison, "Grasshopper, grasshopper, go to hell!"—in Finnish, of course.

# March 17

The very names of the Roman god Liber and his female counterpart Libera are exhilarating—smacking of liberality, liberation, freedom. In fact their festival, the *Liberalia,* promised freedom: liberation from the powerlessness of childhood. On this day every year, boys aged about seventeen took off for the last time their purple-bordered childhood togas (the *toga praetexta*) and proudly donned a manly unbleached woolen *toga virilis,* aka *toga libera.* The *bullae,* penis-shaped charms that had protected them throughout their youth, were removed from around the boys' necks and offered to the household gods. Then their fathers led them to the Forum and presented them at the shrines as citizens and responsible adults.

But little is known about the actual nature of Liber and Libera. They weren't exactly freedom gods. They were worshiped in Italy long before the time of the Empire, and originally they had something to do with germination and creation, although later the Romans merged Liber and Libera with aspects of their loose-living wine god, Bacchus. At this point, according to one scholar, "Liber [had] become the object of obscene ceremonies which need not be detailed here."

As the fathers and their teenage sons strode to and fro on this day, old women called Sacerdotes Liberi—Liber and Libera's priestesses—sat along the sidewalks tending *foculi,* portable altars. On these, for a small fee, they would sacrifice oily honey cakes called *liba.*

# March 18

**C**lose on the heels of the better-known Saint Patrick's Day, March 18 was for many years known in rural Ireland as Sheelah's Day. The holiday's adherents, wrote one sarcastic observer at the turn of this century, "are not so anxious to determine who 'Sheelah' was as they are earnest in her celebration." They toasted the mysterious Sheelah in whiskey, he tells us, while still wearing the previous day's shamrock pinned to their clothing. Then at day's end, he writes, the "very devoted" celebrant would unpin the shamrock, plop it into his or her drink, and "drown it in the last glass." Some have suggested that since this enigmatic holiday falls right after Saint Patrick's, Sheelah must be some female relative of Patrick's: his mother, some have said, or (such things having been possible) even his wife.

Still others point to a Celtic curiosity known as the sheela-na-gig. A grimacing female figure with hugely spread vulva, carved of stone and tucked amid the masonry of many old Irish and English churches, the sheela-na-gig is perhaps a fertility figure, the image of some goddess, or a device for warding off evil. Nobody is sure what the name means, although some folklorists define it as "hag."

# March 19

## Saint Joseph's Day
### San Giuseppe

**F**ood, faith, and folk art merge as Sicilians prepare their *tavole di San Giuseppe*, their "Saint Joseph's tables." Anticipated months in advance, the *tavola* both embodies a family's gratitude for Joseph's continued protection and displays the earth's bounty. Traditionally the tavola is meant to be shared with the poor. Three disadvantaged children are invited to every home, where (often dressed in bed sheets to represent the Holy Family) they are treated as guests of honor. These so-called *virgineddi* are urged to sample at least a taste of every one of the table's hundred-plus pastas, soups, salads, fruits, fish dishes, and breads, not to mention cookies, fritters, doughnuts, cream puffs, and frosted cakes. (Joseph is the patron saint of pastry chefs and fry cooks.) The mandatory *maccu di San Giuseppe* stew includes five kinds of legumes, along with chestnuts, tomatoes, onions, celery, olive oil, wild fennel, and borage shoots—herbs of the season.

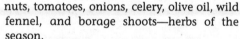

What really distinguishes this holiday, however, is its bread. Sicilians craft thousands upon thousands of *grano duro* loaves, some weighing twenty pounds, in the shapes of flowers, fruits, baskets, suns, moons, cats, fish, angels, butterflies, beards, shoes, trees, rats, roosters, mating birds, leering stars. Certain towns (including Calatfini and Salemi) stage annual bread processions on this day.

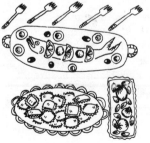

# March 20

Wulfran, born to wealth, gave all his lands and money to the Abbey of Fontenelle in Normandy, and in 682 he was made archbishop. Becoming increasingly obsessed with converting the pagans of Friesland, he relinquished the bishopric and hastened to the domain of the idolaters among whom he baptized great multitudes. Those whom Wulfran failed to convert went about their merry way, and one day the priest happened upon a crowd preparing to sacrifice a young man named Ovon. Wulfran strove to prevent this. There ensued heated negotiations with the local king, who had not yet made up his mind about Wulfran's strange new religion. At last it was determined that the throng could string Ovon up on a gibbet, but that Wulfran's prayers might save him from death. After hanging for two hours, the would-be victim was still alive.

Taking Ovon with him, Wulfran returned to Fontenelle, where eventually he died. His feast day is still honored among his French compatriots. The town of Abbeville marks the occasion with a solemn procession.

# March 21

After a methodical spring cleaning (whose name literally translates to "house-shaking"), Muslims and non-Muslims alike settle down on the eve of *No-Ruz* to a traditional omelet heavy with finely chopped spinach, dill, and parsley. Arranged for the enjoyment of visitors are bowls of *ajeel-e moshgel goshah*, "unraveller of difficulties," a snack mixture with pistachios, walnuts, hazelnuts, pumpkin seeds, dried figs, peaches, and raisins.

A shimmering table is laid with all the symbols of the holiday. Gnarled branches represent the twisting path of human life. An orange floating in a bowl of water represents, according to ancient Zoroastrian tradition, the world floating in space-time. Also here are tinted eggs, milk, rose water, a goldfish swimming in a bowl, candles, fruit, incense, narcissi, pastries, coins, and mirrors—one for every member of the household. Also here are the *haft-sin*, the Zoroastrian "seven *S's*": apples (*sib*), hyacinth (*sonbol*), garlic (*seer*), sumac (*somagh*), jujube fruit (*senjed*), sprouted seeds (*sabzeh*), and a wheat-germ dish called *samanon*. Glowing candles cast the table in a perpetual pearly glaze. At the stroke of midnight, the family sits absolutely still. According to legend, the earth trembles ever so slightly every time it rolls into a new year.

# March 22

*C*ybele was a blockbuster of a goddess. Mother of earth, mother of mountains, mother of wild beasts, she rode with lions. Her lover was her grandson, Attis (see March 24). When he betrayed her, she hunted him down (not difficult, as she was omniscient) and drove him insane. Frenzied, he tore off the genitals that had caused him to betray her. And so he perished—but not forever.

Originally Phrygian, Cybele was duly imported to Rome by a populace hungry for her power. They called her Magna Mater, great mother. Cybele's spring rites, the *Hilaria*, celebrated the mysteries of Attis's death and eventual rebirth. (Shades, definitely, of Easter.) In Rome, Emperor Claudius popularized the Phrygian tradition of bringing into the city a young pine tree, felled in the forest. The tree, representing Attis, was swathed like a corpse in linen and woolen sashes, then decked with wreaths of violets—the flowers said to have sprung from Attis's spilled blood. Members of the Tree-Bearers' Guild, *dendrophori*, carried the tree through the city gate and into Cybele's sanctuary, which stood on Vatican Hill, near where Saint Peter's now looms.

And thus, with a funereal hush and symbols of death, the *Hilaria* began. It would last amidst tears and rejoicing for the next several days.

# March 23

**R**everently known as the Lourdes of the Greek Orthodox church, the Cycladic island of Tinos, near Mikonos, is beloved for an icon of the Virgin Mary that was mysteriously "discovered" there in 1822. This item was soon credited with amazing healing powers. Built directly over the spot where the icon was discovered, the Panagia Evangelistria church now hosts a constant stream of the faithful—generally the *ill* and faithful. They have decked the shrine with so many gold and silver offerings that museums have been constructed in the church's courtyard to display the overflow.

During the last week in March, the island is full to the rafters with pilgrims (again, mostly ailing pilgrims and their companions). On March 23, the church's priests take the icon from its altar, carry it outside, and proceed with it along a quarter-mile route through the streets of Tinos Town. What is unusual is that the streets—not the sidewalk but the streets—are littered with the prostrate bodies of infirm pilgrims, who have strewn themselves across the asphalt in hopes of a miraculous cure. The priests, icon in hand, tread directly on the worshipers, using their limp forms as soft, willing stepping-stones. It is traditional that the priests wear special thin-soled slippers for the occasion.

# March 24

The god Attis castrated himself in a fit of crazed guilt and subsequently bled to death. And then, said the Romans who allied themselves with Attis's cult and that of his lover/grandmother, Cybele (see March 22), the young god was resurrected. March 24 was an annual day of agonized mourning. Worshipers moaned, shrieked, wailed, and keened, clashed cymbals, played whining flutes, and generally worked themselves into such a froth that they slashed themselves with knives so that they might bleed as the god had done.

Through the night they fasted. They held a vigil over a mock tomb as if it were that of the dead Attis. At one point the head priest opened the tomb, revealing that it was actually empty. This proved that Attis wasn't dead after all, and the worshipers erupted into happy yells as the priest enjoined them: "Be of good cheer, neophytes, seeing that the god is saved; for we also, after our toils, shall find salvation."

Sound familiar? The Attis rite, folklorists assert, was nothing more or less than a reenactment of the life cycle of vegetation: cut down, only to rise again in spring.

# March 25

As Lady Mabella de Tichborne lay dying, she begged her husband, Sir Roger de Tichborne, to organize an annual charity in her memory. Roger responded with a challenge. He agreed to donate the yield from a portion of his lands—but only as large a portion as the moribund Lady Mabella was able to circumambulate in the time it took a firebrand to burn itself out. As Roger held the flaming brand aloft, she heaved herself out of bed and crept on all fours out the door. Gasping, she headed for the cropland. By the time Roger's flame burned out, Lady Mabella had managed to crawl around a twenty-three-acre parcel. To hold her husband to his side of the bargain, she laid a curse on his descendants should the charity ever be discontinued. Then she fell dead.

Every March 25, from 1150 onward, poor people lined up at Tichborne Park in Tichborne Village, Hampshire, for a portion of loaves made from the grain harvested on the acreage that had come to be known as the Crawls. Sir Roger's descendant, Henry Tichborne, discontinued the dole in 1794, as it had become a magnet for vagrants from all over the country. Disasters immediately began befalling Henry and therefore his heir, Edward, reinstated the dole in full force.

Today the dole continues. Not loaves but a ton and a half of flour are now distributed from the steps of Tichborne House—one gallon for every adult parishioner of Tichborne and neighboring Cheriton, and one half-gallon for every child.

# March 26

In 1920, in the wake of the sadly lamented Hawai'ian monarchy, Prince Jonah Kuhio Kalanianaole had the foresight to design the Hawai'ian Homes Commission Act, by which 200,000 acres of the islands were set aside to be homesteaded exclusively by native Hawai'ians. Ninety-nine-year leases at the rate of one dollar a year were available to applicants of at least 50 percent Hawaiian ancestry. (Granted: Nearly two million better acres remained firmly in the hands of the U.S. government, as per its 1898 annexation of Hawai'i.)

Kuhio didn't achieve this through his status as an *ali'i*, a Hawai'ian royal—not directly, at least. The adopted son of Queen Kapiolani, Kuhio staged several attempts to overthrow the U.S. government and to restore the Hawai'ian monarchy. For these activities, the highly educated prince was arrested and jailed. Upon his release, he served as the Territory of Hawai'i's first delegate to the U.S. Congress. During his tenure he initiated the Homes Commission Act. Engraved on his casket are the Hawai'ian words *Ke Ali'i Maka'aina'aina*, "Prince of the Citizens."

Kuhio's birthday spearheads a week of festivities on his native island of Kauai. Floats decked with local flowers form a fragrant parade, and a formal-dress ball recalls the grandeur of the monarchy. Hula performances and outrigger canoe races round out the celebrations.

# March 27

**F**ollowing the joyous resurrection of Attis (see March 24), Rome turned its attention to the god's grandmother/lover/tormentor: their Magna Mater, great mother, the awesome earth goddess, Cybele.

On the final day of the vernal equinox festival of death and renewal, the goddess was given a bath. Her image, with its forebodingly shapeless, dark, and jagged visage, was placed in an oxcart and led out of town in a grand procession through the Porta Capena. On the banks of the Almo—a brook that flows into the Tiber just below the city walls—the procession halted. In the waters of the brook, the purple-robed high priest washed the wagon, the goddess's image, and other holy objects. "All was mirth and gaiety" on this day, writes Sir James Frazer in *The Golden Bough.* "Even the eunuchs forgot their wounds." All thoughts of death and blood, so much a part of the preceding days' rites, were far away now as the party, strewn with fresh spring flowers, reentered the city and marched in triumph to the Palatine Hill, where the freshly washed image of Cybele was reinstalled in its shrine.

# March 28

## "Oranges and Lemons" Service

**G**enerations of London children have prattled the nursery rhyme that begins,

*"Oranges and lemons," say the bells of Saint Clement's;*
*"You owe me five farthings," say the bells of Saint Martin's.*

This Church of Saint Clement Danes in the Strand long served the spiritual needs of London's Danish merchant community, hence the "Danes" in its title. Historians have noted that at one time fruits, imported from Spain, used to be unloaded at a wharf on the Thames that once adjoined the old churchyard. Other researchers suggest that there was once a custom in the neighborhood of employers distributing fruit to their servants on certain occasions. Still others, however, are satisfied with the explanation that precious few words besides "lemons" rhyme with "Clement's." In March 1920 the first "Oranges and Lemons" service was held. Fruit donated by the local Danes was distributed to all children in attendance. Today's service is performed by youngsters dressed in the red and white of the Danish flag. They recite the nursery rhyme in its entirety while playing the tune on handbells. Afterwards the children line up under the ivy-wreathed stone doorway. Each child receives one orange and one lemon.

# March 29

These two fourth-century Persian-born brothers heard one day that in the city of Hubaham, a number of their fellow Christians had been imprisoned. These Christians had been sentenced to death by the Sassanian king, Shapur II. The brothers hastened to Hubaham, where they urged the prisoners to gladly die for their faith. Sure enough, nine were executed. Then officials arrested Jonah and Berikjesu, who were still hanging around making trouble. Asked politely to worship the moon, the sun, fire, and water, the brothers refused, leaving the king no choice but to have them tortured to death. Jonah was beaten with rods and knotty clubs,

then a cord was tied around his ankle, and he was dunked through a hole in the icy surface of a frozen pond. Berikjesu had two red-hot iron plates and two red-hot hammers jammed under his arms; then melted lead was dripped into his nostrils and his eyes. The brothers gamely survived these adventures, at which point Shapur had them locked up in prison, where Berikjesu suffered the further indignity of being hung upside-down by his foot.

Finally Jonah was dismembered and his parts were flattened in a press. Berikjesu had burning pitch poured down his throat. Today the martyrs' feast day is observed in the Eastern church as well as in the West, where the brothers are known as Jonas and Barachisius.

# March 30

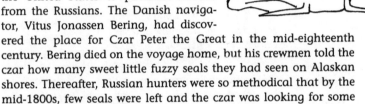

They all laughed when on March 30, 1867, Secretary of State William Henry Seward signed a treaty enabling the United States to purchase Alaska from the Russians. The Danish navigator, Vitus Jonassen Bering, had discovered the place for Czar Peter the Great in the mid-eighteenth century. Bering died on the voyage home, but his crewmen told the czar how many sweet little fuzzy seals they had seen on Alaskan shores. Thereafter, Russian hunters were so methodical that by the mid-1800s, few seals were left and the czar was looking for some way to dump the colony.

The Russians laughed: Having planned to charge $5 million for the territory, the czar's agent, Baron Edoard de Stoeckl, managed to squeeze $7 million out of Seward, plus an extra $200,000 in processing fees.

The Americans laughed: They called the seemingly worthless new acquisition "Seward's folly," "Seward's icebox," and "[President] Johnson's polar bear garden." A little while later, gold was discovered in Alaska. Since then, even more valuable resources have been found there, including coal, oil, and natural gas—not to mention tungsten and molybdenum. Now Seward's Day is an Alaskan state holiday.

# March 31

*A*ccording to a European folk belief, the last three days of March are not rightfully March's at all. An old Scottish ballad tells how capricious March begged generous April for a loan and then gleefully rendered the three days awful:

> *The first o' them was wind and wet,*
> *The second o' them was snow and sleet,*
> *The third o' them was such a freeze*
> *It froze the birds' claws to the trees.*

Originally Roman, superstitions surrounding the "borrowed days" endured well into the nineteenth century. They were dangerous days, fraught with taboos and the specter of bad weather. After King James I died at the tail end of March during a storm that battered the Scottish coast, a contemporary writer mourned that this would be "long after remembered as the storm of the Borrowing Days." An earlier document, titled *Compleynt of Scotland,* laments that "the borial blasts of the three borouing days of Marche had chaissit the fragrant floureise of evyrie frut-tree far athourt the fieldis."

# Moveable Feast

**P**assover takes events like plagues and slaughter and turns them into a message of hope and reunion. The seven-day festival is based on a series of events which took place during the Hebrews' captivity in Egypt. An irate Jehovah, deeming the Egyptians cruel, visited a number of plagues upon them and then killed all their firstborn sons, meanwhile safeguarding the Hebrews' escape. It is said that in their haste, the Hebrews snatched the yet-unrisen loaves from their ovens, accounting for today's Passover tradition of abstaining from all breads (and, among many Jews, all grain products) except matzoh, the flat wheaten crackers produced for the occasion.

The adventure is recounted in the *Haggadah* (Hebrew for "a telling"), the little book forming the liturgy for the ritual meal, or *seder,* that begins the holiday. The home has been swept completely clean of all *chametz*—bread—by the time the family gathers around the seder table. Taking turns reading aloud, they work their way through the Haggadah, with its refrain of "Why is this night different from all other nights?" and its ruminations on slavery and freedom. Symbolic seder foods are many, including *maror,* or bitter herbs, to recall the bitterness of bondage; an egg, with its implications of hope and rebirth; and *charoset,* a finely chopped fruit-nut mixture recalling the mortar with which the Hebrews labored.

# *April* 1

## *April Fools' Day*

The Romans celebrated their New Year's Day in spring, the unmistakable season of rebirth and renewal, with an eight-day revel from March 25 to April 1. This tradition persisted for centuries, until the French King Charles IX altered the calendar, officially adopting January 1 as the new New Year's Day. Some people took much longer than others to find out about the change. And once the news spread, still it was hard for many to fully absorb and adopt the shift. From this confusion sprang the now-worldwide custom of marking the old New Year's Day, April 1, with mean-spirited pranks.

In France, the prankee has come to be known as a *poisson d'Avril,* an April fish: that is, young and naive, easily caught. *Poor Robin's Almanack* of 1728 detailed the day's trademark "sleeveless errands":

*No sooner doth All-Fools' morn approach*
*But waggs, ere Phoebus mount his gilded coach,*
*In sholes assemble to employ their sense,*
*In sending fools to buy intelligence:*
*One seeks hen's teeth, in farthest part o' th' town;*
*Another, pigeon's milk.*

# April 2

pril Fools' Day reigns as one of the world's most popular and enduring secular festivals. For hundreds of years it has been a European favorite. It flourishes, too, in the United States, Australia, New Zealand, and—a British legacy—India. In Mexico they celebrate it, too, but on December 28.

April Fools' Day is also one of the year's shortest holidays. Custom demands that all fooling cease precisely at noon on April 1; after which the joke rebounds upon the joker, as one English saying scolds:

> *April Fools' Day's past and gone,*
> *And you're the fool for making one.*

And there it ends—everywhere, that is, except in Fife, the seagirt peninsula north of Edinburgh, Scotland. There, April 2 is a continuation of April Fools' Day. Highly specialized, Taily Day is entirely dedicated to pranks involving buttocks and other parts of the hindquarters. "Kick me" placards enjoy immense popularity on this day.

# April 3

## Sizdar Bedah

**T**raffic jams clog Iranian highways on the morning of this, the thirteenth day of the New Year's festival, *No-Ruz* (see March 21).

Even if *Sizdar Bedah* were not considered the year's unluckiest day on which to stay indoors—which it is—people would still be tempted outside, where the fragrant pines and sparkling breezes of Iran's brief springtime beckon and tease. Preparations are made, picnic foods assembled before leaving the house—ripe melon, marinated salads, strips of meat to be grilled alfresco. But the most essential item, one which absolutely cannot be forgotten, is the *sabzeh*. This little cushion of sprouted seeds was started in a pan of water several weeks back and has been steadily growing in a place of honor on the New Year's table.

Now everyone heads for the hills, where picnic sites await and where folksingers wander and New Year's clowns caper in blackface

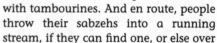

with tambourines. And en route, people throw their sabzehs into a running stream, if they can find one, or else over a garden wall—scattering the feathery sprouts like so many springtime wishes, or like fertility itself.

# April 4

**F**earful of losing a war against Carthage, Roman leaders consulted the Sibylline oracles, only to be told that the only way Rome could save itself was by importing a certain black meteorite that was currently enshrined in Phrygia. No mere doorstop, this rock was revered by the Phrygians as the Great Mother, the goddess Cybele.

Negotiations ensued. Finally in 204 B.C.E. the meteorite was brought to Rome, where on April 4 it was installed in the Temple of Victory on the Palatine Hill. That summer, a bumper harvest thrilled the populace, who applauded Cybele's generosity. The next year, the Punic War finally ended. The annual *Megalesia* lauded the goddess. A wild parade was followed by a sacred banquet, then *ludi* (games), and sacred skits. Lucretius described the parade, headed by the goddess's ecstatic *castrati* priests: "Taut timbrels thunder in [the priests'] hands and hollow cymbals all around, and horns menace with harsh-sounding bray, and the hollow pipe goads their minds. . . . And they carry weapons before them, the symbols of their dangerous frenzy, that they may be able to fill with fear through the goddess's power. . . ." The meteorite, borne in the procession, Lucretius wrote, "blesses mortals with unspoken salutation; with bronze and silver they strew all the path of her journey . . . and snow roseblossoms over her."

# April 5

*L*ong ago, before Taiwan's current population boom, corpses were buried all over the countryside, wherever the *feng shui* (geomancy) was favorable—on hills and in lonely groves, not necessarily in graveyards. Now the government requires that everyone be buried in official cemeteries.

Nevertheless, a Taiwanese grave is not something simply to be paid for and forgotten. Continued upkeep of loved ones' tombs is the purpose of a Chinese holiday called *Qing Ming Jie,* which means "clear and bright." Traditionally falling on the 105th day after the lunar winter solstice, this is the time for inspecting and cleaning graves. In this balmy, crystalline time of year, the very sky looks fresh-swept and flawless, refreshingly "clear and bright." Taiwan's version of *Qing Ming Jie* is celebrated every April 5, to coincide with the anniversary of the death of Chiang Kai-shek, Taiwan's first president. On this national holiday, families pack up brooms, incense, candles, flowers, drinks, and food—pastries are mandatory—and head for loved ones' graves. After thoroughly scrubbing the stone, clipping the grass, pulling up weeds, and sweeping away debris (some forward-thinking people bring seeds or seedlings to plant at the site), everyone sits down and relaxes for a tombside picnic. The departed spirit is considered the guest of honor, and pastries are left behind afterward for its continued enjoyment.

# April 6

Chakri Day commemorates King Chao Phaya Chakri, aka Rama I, whose coronation in 1782 established Thailand's Chakri Dynasty, which has continued unbroken to this day. Its current figurehead is H.M. King Bhumibol Aduljadej, a jazz composer and avid saxophonist.

Although a constantly changing modern government actually runs the country, Thai kings are still important symbols, revered almost as deities. To be overheard in Thailand criticizing any Thai king of any dynasty is punishable by a jail sentence.

To celebrate Chakri Day, the royal temple—the Wat Pra Keo—is opened to the public. On the grounds of Bangkok's Grand Palace, this most sacred of chapels boasts an array of frescoes, pagodas, and statues depicting the denizens of ancient Thai legendry. In the temple are life-size gold statues of the Chakri monarchs. Today's Bhumibol Aduljadej is Rama IX; a prophecy has declared that this dynasty will have nine kings only.

# April 7

**i**n the Lincolnshire village of Burgh-le-Marsh there was once a chunk of land called Bell String Acre. It got its name, the local legend tells, because of a near escape. On a dark winter's night early in the seventeenth century, they say, a ship's captain was threading his craft along this difficult stretch of coast when he suddenly heard church bells. "If I can hear those," the captain reasoned, "then I must be far too close to shore for comfort." Swiftly he adjusted his position, thus saving himself and his ship. In gratitude, he soon afterwards bought a piece of property at Burgh-le-Marsh. Rent on this Bell String Acre, he specified, should go toward the upkeep of the church bell's pull-rope, so that it might ring out its helpful warnings, he stipulated, "for ever."

Another less charming story tells how the townspeople refused to ring the bell, for they all relished the idea of plundering shipwrecks, but that a clergyman ran to the tower and clanged the bell. His heroic act saved the ship, but then the cleric died of exhaustion. (And then, it is said, the grateful captain married the clergyman's daughter.)

In any case, the sailor's request is honored all winter long in Burgh-le-Marsh. Beginning every October 10, the "curfew bell" rings nightly at 8 P.M. April 7 is the last night of the bells—that is, till the next October.

# April 8

## Buddha's Birthday
### Hana Matsuri

Unlike other big spiritual honchos, the Buddha was not a god. He was just a man, albeit a royal one, the princely son of an admittedly corrupt Brahman monarch. Some 2,500 years ago, in India, a white elephant intimated to the monarch's wife that she had conceived a child. She strode into the palace garden, where according to legend she painlessly birthed a son. As a young man, this Siddhartha Gautama bade farewell to all princely delights and sallied forth seeking—and eventually finding—enlightenment.

While most Asian Buddhists celebrate the Buddha's birthday according to the lunar calendar, Japanese Buddhists observe it every April 8. The Japanese name for it, *Hana Matsuri,* means "flower festival," an allusion to the season and to the garden in which he was born. On this day, every Japanese Buddhist temple sports a flower-festooned, peaked-roofed, portable shrine, a *hanamido.* Under the peaked roof stands a bronze statue of the infant Buddha, pointing up at the sky with his right hand and down to earth with his left. He stands in a basin filled with a dark, naturally sweet tea, *ama-cha,* brewed from hydrangea leaves. A ladle lies poised in the basin. After the temple service, the congregants line up at the hanamido, taking turns using the ladle to pour tea over the statue's head.

In Hawai'i, where it is an official state holiday, Hana Matsuri is known as Buddha Day.

# April 9

The Allies' calamitous battle against the Japanese Imperial Army on this Philippine peninsula—the battle that ended in the famous "Bataan death march"—was one of the sorest, saddest spots in American military history. The anniversary of the battle is a national holiday in the Philippines. Veterans and locals alike gather at the *Dambana ng Kagitingan,* the Altar of Valor, atop Mount Samat, Bataan. The shrine's signal feature is a 311-foot steel-and-concrete cross, visible for miles in every direction and illuminated by night. Nearby stands a "Fall of Bataan" marker and another marker indicating the exact spot where U.S. General Edward King officially surrendered to the Japanese commander. After the *araw ng kagitingan,* the wreath-laying ceremony, the crowd descends to the waterfront for a commemorative boat race.

# April 10
## Salvation Army Founder's Day

**P**erusing the aisles with all their pantsuits, vests, and neckties, it's easy to forget that the Salvation Army store is, after all, an army camp, and its general is in London.

Born April 10, 1829, William Booth was a Methodist minister who longed to evangelize among London's street poor. With his wife, Catherine Booth, he established in 1865 a movement complete with tents, soup kitchens, and outdoor revival meetings. At first, the movement's name was East End Mission. As it spread to other locations, the name broadened to the Christian Mission. Then an evangelist at one of Booth's seaport missions got the idea that if he added the title "Captain" to his name, it might attract sailors. This he did, and when Booth himself visited the port and saw the "captain's" success, he promptly declared himself a general and announced that after all, "The Christian Mission *is* a 'salvation army.'"

Officially adopting the catchy new name, Booth reorganized the mission along military lines, with officers, higher and lower corps, commanders, an initiatory pledge called the "Articles of War," and a plan of assault against all the world's "fortresses of sin." Today Booth's brainchild flourishes in cities all over the world, each of which has its own chain of command.

# April 11

The Roman goddess Fortuna, whose name bears a not entirely coincidental resemblance to our word *fortune,* was a deity well worth placating. The holder of destiny and luck, it was she who decided the outcome of every human venture. Fortuna's emblem, the ship's wheel, marked her as a "divine captain."

Fortuna's temple at Praeneste, east of Rome, was the biggest shrine in all of Italy, so big that an entire modern city, Palestrina, thrives today inside the old sanctuary walls. In its prime, a sanctum sanctorum enshrining the goddess's statue crowned the hilltop, and downhill from there cascaded a dizzying complex of niched terraces, altars, domes, and chapels. Along the second terrace was a series of stone-built chambers. It was to these that the faithful traveled from far and wide every April 11. It was here that the goddess answered the supplicants' knotty questions by means of advice printed on slips of oakwood drawn at random from a jar. The temple at Praeneste was renowned as Italy's most powerful oracle, and Fortuna's messages were no mere fortune cookies. They meant a great deal to the Romans, a pragmatic people determined to hedge their bets and minimize their risks.

# April 12

## Cerealia (First Day)

**I**f the name of the Roman goddess Ceres evokes visions of Cheerios, that's because it's the source of the English word *cereal,* as in grain crops. Like the Greek Demeter, Ceres was a grain goddess. She gave her rewards to the clever hands of the farmer, the cultivator, the deliberate sower.

Especially popular with the plebeians—that is, the hoi polloi—Ceres's temple was one of Rome's oldest, flourishing in the historic Boarian Forum as early as 490 B.C.E. Upon the founding of the temple, an annual week of games was established in Ceres's honor. This *Cerealia* began every April 12. The poet Ovid wrote of "the games of Ceres. There is no need to declare the reason; the bounty and services of the goddess are manifest. The bread of the first mortals consisted of the green herbs which the earth yielded without solicitation. . . . Ceres was the first who invited man to better sustenance . . . more useful food. She forced bulls to yield their necks to the yoke; then for the first time the upturned soil beheld the sun. . . . You may give the goddess spelt, and the compliment of salt, and grains of incense. . . . Good Ceres is content with little, if that little be but pure. White is Ceres's proper color; put on white robes at Ceres's festival."

# April 13

## Thai New Year
### Songkran

The Thai people celebrate *Songkran* by chasing each other down the street with buckets of water. An aqueous theme runs all through this waiting-for-the-rainy-season holiday. In the morning, young people demonstrate filial piety by washing their

parents' hands in scented water. Then all proceed to the local *wat,* the Buddhist temple, with offerings for the altar. They also bring rice and fruit for the resident monks. The big Buddha statue in the *wat* gets a flower-water bath; after the service, when the people go home, they similarly lustrate the statues in their own household shrines.

This is a day for good deeds, for karma-polishing acts. In a gesture of mercy for, as they say, "all sentient beings," young girls purchase small live fish for the purpose of bringing them down to the river on *Songkran* and setting them free. Similarly, this is a prime day for liberating songbirds from their cages. Along riverbanks, revelers gather to build pyramids of sand, called *chedis,* into which they stick tiny colored flags. While this is an ancient holiday derived from India's *Holi* (in which the water thrown at passersby has dye in it), it has modern trimmings in Thailand. Numerous Miss Songkran beauty pageants take place on this day, as well as gift exchanges between friends, family members, and coworkers. The gifts are nearly always towels.

# April 14

*i*f you ask the thousands of *Sanno Matsuri* revelers whom it is that they've come to see, they might not mention the mountain god Sanno at all, even though the festival is in his honor. The gorgeously carved *yatai* wagons are the real stars of the show. Shortly after the town of Takayama's miraculous deliverance from a plague over three hundred years ago, skilled craftsmen made the floats, to be used in an annual festival commemorating the god's beneficence.

Peopling the floats are *karakuri,* mechanical wooden puppets that bow, wave, and perform stunts. Acrobat puppets swing from trapezes and walk balance beams; a geisha puppet in kimono twirls while scattering flower petals. About twelve of Takayama's twenty-three floats are selected for each year's festival on a rotating basis, but the city prints a booklet for festival goers that describes each of the twenty-three in detail, even the ones not appearing in that year's *matsuri.* The wagons and their bearers, who dress in elaborate Edo-period costume for the occasion, gather at Hie-Jinja shrine on the morning of the 14th; several processions take place over the next two days, accompanied by musicians who play rare antique instruments.

# April 15

## Metal Phallus Festival

### Jibeta Matsuri

*A* hungry demon lodged itself, legend tells us, inside the vagina of a certain maiden of Kawasaki, southwest of Tokyo. The demon bit off the penises of two successive bridegrooms, which left the maiden distraught; in fact, the entire town was in a frenzy. But then a local blacksmith had the idea—some called it a divine inspiration—of making a lifelike iron phallus. Legend fails to record the emotions of the young woman on the night city officials brought the phallus into her bedchamber and thrust it deep inside her. The demon, just as they had hoped, chomped down eagerly on the iron morsel. Its teeth shattered, the monster slithered out, doomed to die of starvation. The townsfolk rejoiced: No more virile youths would be unmanned on their wedding nights, and the maiden could go on to fulfill her destiny as wife and mother.

Kawasaki's annual festival honors the *kanamara-sama,* literally the honorable metal phallus. The festival had lapsed for many years and was almost entirely forgotten when a group of local businessmen decided to reinstate it. After folk music performances comes a procession in which masked and costumed women and men advance down the street carrying diverse phallic effigies of all sizes. Toward evening, local smiths ritually reenact the forging of the *kanamara-sama,* amid much jollity. An outdoor banquet follows.

# April 16

## Saint Fructuosus's Day

**B**orn in Spain, Fructuosus was no mere workaday Visigoth but the son of Visigothic royals. His father was a military officer, but the iconoclastic Fructuosus became a monk, giving away nearly all his riches to churches and to recently freed slaves and other poor people. He saved one small portion with which he founded the Benedictine monastery of Compulta, not far from León. He aspired to hermithood, but wherever he went he was followed by crowds of disciples, including entire families. Despite his longing for the solitude of desert places, Fructuosus was made a bishop in 656—forced to accept the bishopric, as his biographers put it—and was then promoted to Archbishop of Braga.

*He went thataway!*

As Saint Fructueux, this reluctant leader is fêted in many European towns, including Champfremont and Semur in France.

# April 17

## Yayoi Matsuri

The temple complex of Nikko is Japan's most prized tourist attraction, boasting a spiritual heritage dating back to the mid-eighth century as well as possession of the indisputably original carving of the hear-no-evil, see-no-evil, speak-no-evil monkeys.

A team of 15,000 artists and craftsmen worked for over two years to put the finishing touches on Nikko's main shrine, the burial site of a seventeenth-century shogun. The annual *Yayoi Matsuri* is celebrated at that temple's more modest neighbor, the Futara-san-jinja, built in honor of a mountain god, his wife, and their child. The festival culminates on the 17th. During the preceding few days, *mikoshi* or portable, hand-carried mini-shrines are brought to Futara-san-jinja from several other nearby temples. As each mikoshi makes its way down the road to Futara-san-jinja, it is accompanied by a procession of dancers, singers, long-robed priests, and musicians, men and women alike. On the 17th, Futara-san-jinja hosts over fifteen festively decorated mikoshi, all of which are joined together in a striking Shinto ceremony, the year's biggest at this shrine.

# April 18

## Flower Festival

### Hana Matsuri

Cherry blossoms, which last only a few days on the branch before falling away to the spring wind and rain, have inspired countless Japanese, warriors and poets alike. Along with peach and plum blossoms, cherry blossoms embody the tender fullness of spring just as surely as they assert life's ephemerality. It's easy to sympathize with the haiku poet, Raizan:

> *I'm very sorry*
> *to have to die at this time*
> *with plum trees in bloom.*

and the exultation of his colleague, Sodo:

> *Who cares to notice carrot flowers*
> *when the plum trees*
> *explode into bloom!*

Many towns, temples, and villages in Japan hold flower festivals at this time of year. At Kameoka-shi, near Kyoto, where the annual festival is held on April 18, lines of men and women offer prayers for a beautiful spring as they dance, beating small drums and wearing broad, flat-topped hats decked with blossom-tipped branches of cherry, plum, and peach.

# April 19

**D**evastated by famine in 496 B.C.E., Rome lay in despair. Her leaders did the most logical thing: They took their problem to a Sibylline oracle and begged for a message from the gods. They got what they had come for. Obeying the oracle to the letter, they set to work constructing a temple to Ceres, the cultivator goddess, the bread bringer. A few years later, the sanctuary was firmly established. Rowdy games and amusements thrilled the mostly plebeian crowd at the Circus Maximus during the week of Ceres's annual festival, beginning every April 12. On the 19th—the anniversary of the date on which Ceres's temple had been officially dedicated—the games climaxed with the odd spectacle of red foxes careening around the Circus Maximus with their tails on fire.

While no one knows for certain the meaning, origin, or relevance of such a ritual (sticks were tied to the animals' tails and then set alight), Ovid relates an ancient Italian folktale in which a farm youth captured a vixen that has been plundering his father's crops. The boy, according to the story, bundled the fox into a pile of straw and hay, which he then set on fire. But the fox squirmed free, and as it ran across the fields, the flaming straws entangled in its fur sent off sparks that burned down the entire farm.

# April 20

## Drum Festival
### Furukawa Matsuri

Wild boars, evil spirits—who needs 'em? Certainly not the people of Furukawa, central Honshu, Japan. For over 1,500 years, they have been celebrating this annual festival whose function is to scare away both kinds of marauders, the bristly ones that raid farmers' crops and the metaphysical ones that haunt people's houses. Chief among the revelers' artillery is a pair of enormous drums—so huge that two men straddle them as if riding horseback, beating with all their might. It takes a whole team of youths to carry drums and riders on a bamboo palanquin, and the going is strenuous as the procession careens through the streets of town. The sweating, saké-bedazzled men in their scanty breechclouts lend the event its nickname: *Hakada Matsuri,* "Naked Festival."

The town is always packed with tourists for this two-day affair, which begins on the evening of the 19th and rollicks all through the night and into the 20th with bonfires at every street corner and saké distributed free to passersby. A key feature of the festival is the *shishi-mai,* "lion dance"; then comes a parade with complex floats depicting mythical animals and characters from folklore. Then come the drums, lantern-lit and thunderous.

# April 21

**N**ow hailed as Indonesia's first feminist, Princess Raden Ajeng Kartini fought an uphill battle throughout most of her brief life.

Born in eastern Java on April 21, 1879, Kartini was the daughter of the Javanese Regent of Jepara. Determined to loosen the bonds that traditional Javanese and Islamic life imposed on women, she established a school for regents' daughters in a time and place where the very idea of educating girls had long been deemed ridiculous. Emphasizing a Western-style and thus (as she saw it) a freer educational system, the princess nourished her pupils' intellects while at the same time offering them the chance, previously unheard of, to venture outside their homes before marriage. In letters to her many Dutch friends, later published, Kartini lamented of her frustrations with rigid, restrictive mores that had held her countrywomen under lock and key for so long.

After the princess died at twenty-five, other "Kartini schools" opened up throughout the country, known for their lofty educational standards mixed with alfresco diversions such as dress-up picnics. Today, the princess's birthday is a national holiday, celebrated with especial fervor—not surprisingly—in schools, where students and teachers share buffet lunches in memory of brave Kartini.

# April 22

**B**orn in America as an outgrowth of the 1960s' ecology movement—remember those green-and-white "e" flags?—Earth Day is a very young holiday: flexible, ripe with potential, and very, very green. The ecologists who dreamed up Earth Day hoped that it would serve as a focus for discussions about environmental dangers and possible solutions. First observed in 1970, Earth Day enjoyed a brief flurry of media attention. Ecology was hip. Soon enough, however, attention dwindled, and so did Earth Day. For years it went "underground," almost universally forgotten. By the time the holiday's twentieth anniversary approached, ecology—by this time it was called environmentalism—was hip again. Earth Day, phase two, blossomed with a vengeance.

Contemporary environmental dangers were greater, more numerous, and more widely known than in 1970. In its latter incarnation, Earth Day has become a focus for activism: broad-based and diffuse, but all with the same impassioned sense of save-the-planet urgency. Now Earth Day is the framework on which communities worldwide hang their annual environmental fairs, highway cleanups, fund-raisers, tree plantings, auto-free days, earth-healing rituals, and bike-a-thons.

# April 23

*A*llegedly a third- or fourth-century martyr, George enjoys vast dominions. He is patron of both boy scouting and the entire kingdom of England. Many an army has marched into battle praying for the protection of this soldier-saint. Yet "earnest endeavors have been made," writes hagiographer Donald Attwater, "to prove that he never existed, or that he was somebody else." Generations of British rulers and subjects alike have venerated George, the dragon slayer, yet the legendry linking him with dragons is of purely medieval vintage, and the dragon served as a handy metaphor for heathen hordes requiring extermination—such as those whom the Crusaders had battled in the East.

In 1415, Saint George's Day was declared a national holiday of the loftiest rank in England. It was celebrated with processions, horse races, and pageants in which the dragon slaughter was acted out. Some 250 years later, the revelers' piety had diminished, as evinced by the 1680 jingle that proclaimed, "Most say there are no dragons; and tis sayd there was no George."

In Catalonia, where *Sant Jordi* is also revered as patron and soldier, parades feature smoke-belching "dragons" and mock battles between the Moors and Christians. Traditionally on this day men give women roses; women return the favor by giving books to men. Bakeries display oblong pastries with the saint's name scrolled along one side and red and yellow stripes down the other.

# April 24

S aint Mark's Eve was, in the rural Britain of recent centuries, the year's best night for dreaming of one's future mate. Not just imagining, but really dreaming, while asleep. Unmarried girls and women would gather after dinner in groups of three or fewer. Together they would mix and bake a "dumb cake"—prepared, as its name suggests, in total silence. At the stroke of midnight, the celebrants would sit together eating the cake, also in silence. Then each would hurry home to climb backwards into

bed (it had to be backwards), where dreams would reveal the future mate's face. The 1770 edition of *Poor Robin's Almanack* tells of the sleeper who shuts her eyes, longing "to find her husband in the dark, by praying unto good St. Mark." A grimmer aspect of this festival was the belief that those females destined to die unmarried would dream of newly dug graves, shrouds riffling in the wind, or wedding rings crumbling to dust.

History does not record what all this has to do with Saint Mark, a devoted evangelist who, according to *The Penguin Dictionary of Saints,* was "the young man who ran away naked when Christ was arrested in Gethsemane."

# April 25

**E**ver comprehensive in the forms and objects of their worship, the ancient Romans celebrated their *Robigalia* in honor of Robigus, the mildew god. (Such deities, apparently, were well represented in ancient pantheons. The Greeks at Rhodes, for example, worshiped an "Apollo of the Blight.") By thus appeasing Robigus, it was hoped, farmers might keep their grain crops free of *robigo*, the rusty mildew that was always a danger to young plants in this season. Pliny explains that the disease is an unfortunate effect of warm weather combined with excessive dampness.

At the grove of Robigus, five miles from Rome on the Via Claudia, the *flamen*, priest, would light an altar fire and offer the god incense and a bowlful of wine. The poet Ovid recorded the priest's prayer: "Thou scaly mildew, spare the sprouting grain. . . . O let the crops . . . grow till they are ripe for the sickle. No feeble power is thine. . . . Grip not the tender crops. . . . Forstall the destroyer."

A dog and a sheep were sacrificed, after which, as Ovid reported, the priest threw "into the altar fire . . . the flesh of the sheep and the hideous entrails—I saw him do it—of the dog."

# April 26

## Confederate Memorial Day

**O**n April 26, 1865, at a cemetery in Vicksburg, Mississippi, a group of women went sedately down the path with armloads of flowers, decorating the graves of Civil War soldiers—their own friends, lovers, and relatives, and total strangers as well. Inspired by newspaper accounts of that unofficial "Decoration Day," other groups of women throughout the South turned their attention to the tending and adorning of Confederate graves. Contemporary reports tell of processions headed by young girls in white dresses, followed by widows and mothers in black. A *New York Tribune* reporter was on hand one day in Columbus, Mississippi, when members of one of these processions spontaneously whirled around and started laying magnolia blossoms on Union graves. The reporter was touched: "The women of Columbus . . . have shown themselves impartial in their offerings to the memory of the dead. They have strewed flowers alike on the graves of the Confederates and of the National soldiers."

While an official U.S. Decoration Day—later to be called Memorial Day—eventually came to be observed on a Monday in May, Southern states still observe various memorial days of their own. On April 26, for example, a legal holiday in Florida and Georgia, special graveyard services are followed with wreath-laying ceremonies, conducted while fifes and drums play "Dixie."

# April 27

## Humabon's Conversion
### Bahug-Bahugan Sa Mactan

**W**hen Ferdinand Magellan and his depleted crew reached the Philippines on March 16, 1521, they had just endured a terrible voyage from Patagonia, during which one of the Portuguese explorer's three vessels was wrecked and a third one was deserted. Establishing a camp on the coral isle of Mactan, just east of Cebu, he found the islanders to be enthusiastic Muslims, thanks to a much earlier wave of missionizing seamen. The headmen called themselves rajahs. All the headmen save one took a liking to Magellan and his men. (The sole rajah who disliked Magellan was called Lapu-Lapu. But more on him later.) One of them engaged the explorer in a friendship-sealing rite in which the pair mixed their blood with wine and shared a cup of it.

On April 14, Magellan looked on with pride as his ship's priest, Father Pedro de Valderrama, celebrated mass. Rajah Humabon, his wife, and eight hundred islanders were having themselves baptized, thus becoming the Philippines' first Christians. Magellan erected a large cross in honor of the occasion. Thirteen days later, on April 27, Lapu-Lapu killed him. An annual festival commemorates Magellan's landing, his adventures, and his murder, all of which are acted out on the beach at Mactan.

# April 28

Flora was a goddess most unabashedly erotic, sensual, and lush: the goddess whom the prostitutes of Rome chose as their own personal guardian. Of more ancient vintage than most of her fellow Roman deities, Flora may originally have been the Sabine people's goddess of spring, or possibly of the metaphorical "spring" that is human adolescence. By the year 238 B.C.E. she was Rome's goddess of flowers and thus of the sexual aspect of plants. As such, she merited an annual festival. By 173 B.C.E. the Senate made the *Floralia* official, decreeing that it begin every April 28 and last in all its licentious extremism until May 3.

Romans wore their most colorful clothes and draped themselves as well as their domestic animals with blossoms in honor of the spring goddess whom Ovid describes as "decked with a garland of a thousand varied flowers." From the outset a drunken revel, the Floralia later featured *ludi* (games), pantomimes, and playlets, all of a salty nature as befitted a fertility deity. Prostitutes often took the stage and performed stripteases in the goddess's honor. Chroniclers allude to orgies and the exchanging of erotic medallions. While the festival declined in the third century C.E., a northern version of it persisted as May Day. The goddess Flora, too luscious to be quite forgotten, lingered in the public imagination—often in the form of the village "May Queen."

# April 29

A lot of things about the Japanese empire changed during Hirohito's tenure, much of which he effected himself. In a country whose rulers had always been hailed as at least partly divine, this 124th emperor, born in 1901, defied tradition by attending public theaters, handling money, dabbling in marine biology, and otherwise acting almost like an ordinary human being. Nevertheless, people made devoted pilgrimages to his palace from all over the country—just for the purpose of picking litter off the imperial lawn. During the reign of this shy, mustachioed figure, his birthday prompted special services at the imperial shrine, military revues, a state banquet, and ceremonies invoking Hirohito's ancestors, the deified emperors of eras past. Every school in Japan performed its own semireligious, semipatriotic imperial birthday program. Shortly after World War II, Hirohito broadcast (at the behest of the victorious Allies) a message over public radio—another "first"—announcing that he was not, definitely *not,* divine. For more reasons than one, the nation wept.

Upon his death in 1989, Hirohito's birthday remained a national holiday, albeit with a new name and a generic seasonal connotation. *Midori no Hi* has become a popular time to depart for spring vacations.

# April 30

In Germany, May Eve is called *Walpurgisnacht,* after Walburga, the eighth-century Anglo-Saxon nun credited with converting the locals (see February 25). Long associated with witches' sabbats, the holiday is here observed, as Goethe recounted in *Faust,* with ecstatic paranoia, mountain revels, and uproarious mock witch burnings.

Modern Swedes, recalling their Viking ancestors, celebrate May Eve with mountaintop bonfires that "frighten" away the stubborn winter darkness while gladly beckoning the summer sun. At Stockholm's outdoor folk museum, Skansen, logs and tar barrels are piled up into an impressive heap atop Reindeer Mountain and set ablaze just after dusk, to the cheers of hundreds of urbanites. In Sweden the holiday is called *Valborgsmassoafton*—there's that pesky saint again.

Valborgsmassoafton is a special time for college students, who don their white velvet school caps, pin flowers to their lapels, and lollop about singing spring songs at the tops of their lungs. Similar student rites are also popular in Finland, where the holiday is called *Vapun Aatto.*

# May 1

*W*hile the Romans, the Celts, and others all welcomed the first of May with festivities, it was probably the Anglo-Saxons who popularized the maypole, that most potent and evocative of emblems. Like other May Day customs, this freshly cut and stripped tree trunk, planted in the village square, is unsubtly erotic. The Elizabethan Puritan, Philip Stubbes, was moved in his *Anatomie of Abuses* to rail against "this May-pole (this stinking Idol, rather) which is covered all over with floures and herbs . . . and sometimes painted with variable colours. . . . And thus being reared up, with handkerchiefs and flags hovering about the top . . . then fall they to dance about it like as the heathen people." He lamented the practice of sleeping outdoors on May Eve: "Of fortie, three score or a hundred maides going to the wood overnight," he wrote in 1583, "there have scarcely the third part of them returned home again undefiled."

Banned in England during the Reformation, maypoles rose again and are popular all over Europe to this day. The season's potency persists. In his poem "Corinna's Going A-Maying," the seventeenth-century poet Robert Herrick urged his love:

> *Come, we'll abroad; and let's obey*
> *The proclamation made for May.*

# May 2

## Big Kite Flying
### Odakaoge

The master of Hamamatsu Castle, living in the mid-sixteenth century and thus in the dark days before the invention of "It's a Boy" cigars, longed for a proper way to announce the birth of his first son. According to legend, the master's faithful retainer hit upon the idea of inscribing the baby's name on a huge kite, which would fly from the castle's battlements and could be seen from far and near.

Hamamatsu retains its reputation as Japan's "kite town." *Odakaoge* is an annual kite fight, a tradition now over four hundred years old. The kites measure up to four square yards, and many are too big to be handled by a single person. For the festival, several dozen teams, representing various districts, assemble with their kites on Hamamatsu's parade ground. The kitesters dress in striking period costume to accent the kites' bold calligraphic and animal designs. Two by two, from May 1 to May 5, the teams send their kites into the air to do "battle." Airborne, the mammoth kites soar and dip, striving to sever each other's moorings by means of glass shards glued to their tails. Meanwhile on the ground thousands of spectators cheer their favorites with whistles, horns, and rhythmic chants. Thousands of revelers bring their own normal-sized kites—not to fight with but to fly peacefully along the seashore.

# May 3

**D**epending on which fourth-century clarions you choose to credit, Saint Helen may or may not have discovered the True Cross (that is, of Crucifixion fame) while engaging in a bit of amateur archaeology on Calvary Hill in the year 326. To commemorate this event, people in El Salvador set up crosses in gardens, backyards, and patios and adorn them with fresh fruit, which guests are free to pluck as they come and go. *Día de la Cruz* is a continuous all-day party, complete with folk music, dancing, feasting, fireworks, and intermittent rosaries. The evening's final rosary concludes with a thousand murmured repetitions of Jesus' name.

In Chile, people carry household crosses made of fresh green branches from door to door all through the evening. The Quechua people in the Peruvian Andes decorate living trees and dance around them.

In Mexico, virtually every village plaza cross, mountaintop cross, and roadside cross gets a brilliant ribbon garland. This is the emblematic holiday of all Mexican masons and builders. At construction sites all over the country, workers erect wooden crosses for the occasion and decorate them with paper flowers. Scaffoldings likewise are hung with paper streamers, and workers gather precisely at noon for on-site fiestas, toasting *Santa Elena* with shots of tequila and saluting the cross with firecrackers.

# May 4

**H**er name cloaks her in mystery now and for always. The goddess Bona Dea was mysterious even during her heyday, when her rites were performed strictly in secret. The rites were known to women only—and an elite klatsch of patrician Roman matrons and sacrosanct Vestal Virgins, at that.

In the wee hours that bridged May 3 and May 4, the worshipers gathered at the home of the consul's wife, the Roman equivalent of a First Lady. All the doorways of the ritual room were carefully sealed against prying eyes; all male statues in the vicinity were veiled for the occasion. Branches and flowers adorned the room. A fancy jug was brought forth, full of wine, but one of the strict rules of conduct was that this wine must throughout the ritual be consistently referred to as "milk." We know there was dancing, accompanied by pipes and stringed instruments. We know the purpose of the ritual was to ask Bona Dea to work for the common good.

Plutarch writes longingly of "far off . . . the laughter of cloistered maids . . . the secret place of the goddess of women . . . the sweet fire of incense."

# May 5

## Boys' Day
### Tango no Sekku

The holiday's original name, *Shobu no Sekku,* referred to a type of Japanese iris whose name, *shobu,* is a homonym for the ultimatum "win or lose." The plant's slender leaves harbor not only medicinal powers but also a resemblance to swords. A shobu-leaf bath, a traditional element of this festival, is said to protect boys' physical health while magically rendering them fearless. Another symbol of the day is the *koi no bori,* a cloth or paper wind sock in the shape of the sturdy, deter-mined carp. Parents hang these outside their houses, one for every son in the family. The biggest wind socks, representing eldest or only sons, can measure up to fifteen feet long. An indispensable Boys' Day dish is *chimaki*—glutinous rice soaked and then steamed in a three-cornered bamboo-leaf-wrapped bundle. For the occasion, box-lunch vendors make these to sell at railway stations.

The end of World War II put a damper on many of Japan's more vehemently warrior-spirited festivals and customs. At that time, May 5 was made a national holiday and was given a non-committal new name: *Kodomo no Hi,* Children's Day. People still cel-ebrate in the old ways, however. Boys are encouraged to display fierce-eyed samurai dolls, complete with miniature armor and pe-tite battle banners.

# May 6

## Saint George's Day

**W**hile the feast day of Saint George, dragon slayer and patron of soldiers, is generally celebrated on April 23, many Eastern Christians prefer the alternate date, May 6. Among Serbs the holiday is called *Dyurdyev Dan,* and it is a day for rising early, before the dawn, then riding into the woods, collecting flowers and greenery, and bringing these back to festoon homes, schools, and meeting halls. Considered a seasonal "hinge" day, *Dyurdyev Dan* is the official beginning of the swimming season.

On *Georgiovden,* meanwhile, rural Bulgarians used to smear their doorjambs with fresh lamb's blood as a charm against sickness and evil. They prayed to the saint to send them an even bigger lamb with which to perform the ceremony next year.

In prerevolutionary Russia, *Den' Georgiya Pobedonostza* was celebrated with especial relish by *Kavalier,* soldiers who had been decorated with Saint George's Cross. Following church services, military organizations staged reunions and banquets.

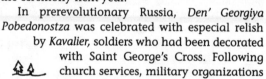

# May 7

## Pilgrimage of Saint Nicholas

### San Nicola

Nicholas was a fourth-century ecclesiastical Baron von Munchhausen. His legends are legion: He rescued shipwrecked sailors and liberated condemned prisoners. He resurrected murdered babies; he saved girls from prostitution.

Nicholas's bones are enshrined in the basilica at Bari, on Italy's southeast coast. Every year on the morning of May 7, the anniversary of the relics' arrival here in 1087, pilgrims converge on the basilica. (One historian reports how, until recently, the custom among pilgrims was, upon arrival, to lick the basilica's floor so vigorously as to draw blood.) Saint Nicholas's golden-haloed, carnation-wreathed statue heads a procession that leads to the wharf, where the bishop blesses the sea. Then the statue is put on board a boat, which sits all day at anchor in the middle of the harbor. All day, the vessels of Bari—fishing boats, rowboats, sailboats—go out to pay their respects. After dark, Nicholas's boat is towed back to shore, the statue is removed, and a torchlight procession accompanies it back to the church.

# May 8

## The Furry Dance

**N**othing whatsoever to do with fur, the name of the Furry Dance—as practiced every May 8 in Helston, Cornwall—is likely derived from the old Cornish word *fer*, meaning "rejoicing." Just as plausible is the theory that "furry" is a slurring of "Flora," for this annual gala has always borne the alternate name of Flora Day.

To do "the Furry," hundreds of local couples line up on the sidewalk, one behind the other in orderly fashion. As the town band plays a traditional tune, the dancers form a graceful human stream that winds up and down the streets and flows around corners—even through the front doors of shops and out the back; the dancers' footsteps are said to bring good luck. This spectacle transpires four times during the day, with well over a thousand Helstonians participating and several thousand out-of-towners gathered in the gaily decorated streets to watch. The first dance, beginning at 7 A.M., is for young couples only. The midmorning dance is for schoolchildren. The formal noon processional is the main event, with the men in top hats and frock coats, the women in gowns. Out-of-towners can at last join in the final dance just before dusk.

In 1790 *Gentleman's Magazine* reported on the rite: "They assemble and dance hand in hand round the streets . . . and thus continue. . . . In the afternoon, the local gentry go to some farm house and have tea, sillabub and other refreshments and then return in a . . . dance to the town and dance throughout the streets till dark."

# May 9

The *Parentalia* (see February 13) was ancient Rome's mellower day of the dead, dedicated to the feeding of mild-mannered ancestral spirits, the grateful *manes*. The *Lemuria*, on the other hand, concerns ghosts of an entirely different stripe: the hostile, hungry *lemures*. The chronicler Porphyrio shiveringly called them "wandering spirits of men who have died before this day, and are therefore fearsome." Nonius called them "nocturnal ghosts as terrifying as wild beasts." In homes and hallways, the lemures lurked.

The Lemuria was a homeowner's chance to palliate his own resident lemures. The celebrant walked barefoot at midnight through his rooms with one hand upheld in the potently protective "fig" gesture, thumb thrust between the fisted first and second fingers. His mouth was full of dried black beans, which he spat out one by one as he walked. The beans were ghost bait. As he walked and spat, the householder chanted nine times: "With these I redeem myself and mine." The lemures, he hoped, were trailing along behind him, eating the beans. It was forbidden to look back during the ritual. Having circled the entire house, the celebrant washed his hands thoroughly. Then he beat brass pans together, noisily bidding the lemures good-bye.

# May 10

## Bird Week (First Day)

### Tori no Mawari

Among Japan's many postwar environmental efforts was the establishment of Bird Week, a time for encouraging people to learn about and otherwise aid the native wild bird population. So much forest was cut down during the war to fuel munitions factories that a great quantity of bird habitat, not to mention the birds themselves, vanished. In the absence of natural predators, then, parasitic insects flourished and became a threat to agriculture. Seeing this, the Education Ministry organized Bird Week, which became very popular very quickly.

During Bird Week, ornithologists, bird-watchers, and other experts lecture to clubs and schools, and students work on such bird-related projects as the planting of pine trees. The Education Ministry awards prizes for the most creative projects.

# May 11
## Cormorant-Fishing Season (First Night)

**Ukai**

**O**n the Nagara River, in Gifu prefecture, west of Tokyo, May 11 marks the traditional opening of *ukai* season. Now and for the next five months, small boats ply the waters by night, bearing torches that attract shoals of river trout. The fishermen send their trained cormorants over the side. The sleek black birds obediently dive, and dive again, swallowing fish aplenty. Metal rings clamped around the bases of the birds' long necks prevent the fish from sliding all the way down. The fishermen periodically jerk the birds back into the boats by means of rope leashes, and they force them to ignominiously regurgitate their catch. Then they send the birds back over the side to fetch more.

This spectacle—resplendent with flickering torches, the soft splash of river water, and forced vomiting—is such a popular one that many tourists book space on an opening-night observation boat a whole year in advance. The fishermen, well over a hundred of them, dress in medieval-style grass aprons for the occasion. The poet Basho assessed his *ukai*-viewing experience in a haiku:

> *How exciting, the cormorant-fishing boat!*
> *But, after a time,*
> *I felt like weeping.*

# May 12
## Florence Nightingale's Birthday

**I**n 1837, at the age of seventeen, Florence Nightingale heard heavenly voices ordering her to serve humankind. She decided to become a nurse, which horrified her whimsical mother. In those days, nurses were little more than janitors, and hospitals were pits of squalor and neglect. Nightingale pressed on, and in 1853 she became superintendent of a small London hospital. She went on to the Crimea when war broke out there between Britain and Russia. She established the first of what we now know as war hospitals: sanitary, safe, and stocked with supplies. Her tireless ministrations to the wounded soldiers made her famous all over the world. Poet Henry Wadsworth Longfellow wrote of her in 1857:

> *A Lady with a Lamp shall stand,*
> *In the great history of the land,*
> *A noble type of good,*
> *Heroic womanhood.*

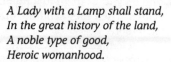

Following the war, Nightingale avoided fame and continued to train nurses, ever battling against what she herself declared "a commonly received idea . . . that it requires nothing but a disappointment in love, or incapacity in other things, to turn a woman into a good nurse." Since 1921, her birthday has been the centerpiece of National Hospital Week, observed in British and American hospitals with special exhibitions, workshops, and publicity drives.

# May 13

## Pilgrimage to Fatima

On May 13, 1917, three Portuguese children were tending their sheep when they suddenly encountered a woman sitting in an oak tree. Haloed and intense, the stranger implored the tots to pray for peace. Quickly realizing that this was the Virgin Mary, the children were breathless. The Virgin told them to meet her there again on the thirteenth day of the next month, and the next, and the next. This they did, each time accompanied by an ever-burgeoning crowd of spectators. No one except the children, however, could see or hear the Virgin, and of the three, only little Lucia could converse with her. The Virgin vouchsafed secrets, prophecies regarding the outcome of World War I, and imprecations for all of Christendom to pray for the collective soul of Russia. On the 13th of October, which proved to be the day of the Virgin's final visit, some 70,000 people were gathered at Cova da Iria, near the town of Fatima. They stood in the rain, waiting. Suddenly—too suddenly for any logical explanation—the rain stopped. Not only did the sun immediately start shining, it hopped—some say danced—across the sky all asparkle. This has since come to be known as Fatima's Miracle of the Sun.

Today, Fatima is home to innumerable Virgin Mary keychains, a wax museum, hotels, and a neoclassical basilica that crouches directly over the site of the apparitions. A vast esplanade fronting the church accommodates over 300,000 people. Every May 13, well over that many pilgrims arrive, many on hands and knees, for the vigil, rosary, procession, and mass.

# May 14

**N**o wonder San Isidro—Saint Isidore—is the patron saint of modern field-workers. Born in 1070, the sober Spaniard spent his entire hard-working (and, some say, miracle-working) life tilling the fields of the same farmer, in the countryside near his native Madrid. As the "ploughman saint," Isidro watches over plough-pulling animals as well.

In the Philippines, the broad-shouldered water buffalo, the carabao, is every farmer's sine qua non. Throughout the islands, especially in towns of whom Isidro is patron, people prepare their homes, themselves, and their carabaos to greet the saint on his feast day. With their hooves carefully scrubbed for the occasion and their horns wound with garlands, the beasts are hitched to flower-decked carts and then led in a solemn procession to church. Upon meeting the priest, the carabaos humbly kneel to receive their blessing.

Henceforth, solemnity gives way to hilarity, as the farmers race their beasts across the harvested fields. Then they gather for a lingering banquet, dropping in on friends and neighbors. For the occasion, homes are resplendent with *pahiyas*—lush arrangements of coconut, sugar cane, pineapple, banana, cookies, and translucent leaf-shaped *kiping*—candies made of steamed, tinted, then molded and hardened rice. As the festival winds down, householders give away their pahiyas as a gesture of goodwill.

# May 15

## Festival of Saint Dympna

### Dympna-Feest

To Belgians, the town of Gheel, just east of Antwerp, means one thing and one thing only: mental illness. Saint Dympna, patron of the insane, has her shrine here, and people have been bringing their afflicted loved ones here for centuries, each hoping that the saint will work yet another of her miracle cures.

Dympna was a seventh-century Irish princess savagely murdered after having fled to Gheel while trying to elude her incest-bent, lunatic father. It is said that, as a healing saint, she pleases more often than she disappoints. Nobody knows exactly how or why, but a lot of people *do* get better here. The town is a sort of mental hospital without walls: Its general population is almost entirely composed of nurses, priests, health-care workers, worried families—and, of course, the *non compos mentis*. A longstanding Gheel tradition is that the latter are boarded with local families to help them reintegrate into society.

On Dympna's feast day, a procession converges on the saint's tomb. Irreverent Belgian jokesters have made much of this "crazy pilgrimage," during which all sorts of things, obviously, have been known to happen.

# May 16

## Saint Honoré

*N*ot to be confused with the other French Saint Honoratus, a fifth-century bishop of Arles, the Saint Honoratus whose feast day is May 16 was a *sixth*-century bishop of Amiens. The Amiens Honoratus is the patron saint of French bakers, an enviable role (or roll, as the case may be). On the ancient banner of the Paris Bakers' Guild his image appears, dressed in bishop's miter and robe, with a hooked crozier firmly in his left hand and three loaves of bread just as firmly in his right. In the city where two thoroughfares, including the rue Saint-Honoré, are named for him, Parisian bakers and their apprentices used to honor Honoratus every year on the alleged anniversary of his death with a procession, which was headed by bakeshop girls in white dresses. After high mass in the Church of the Trinity, the bakers and their friends retired to a banquet and then a dance.

Bakers in many French towns, including Bordeaux, Poitiers, and Bourges, still hold processions and fairs on Saint Honoratus's Day.

# May 17

## Norwegian Independence Day

### Syttende Mai

Upon Napoleon's defeat in 1814, Norway gained its independence, and on May 17 Norwegian leaders signed the country's constitution. The anniversary is the occasion for great festivity not just among native Norwegians but among all people of Norwegian descent, especially in the American Midwest.

In Norway, the day begins with cannon fire—ceremonial blasts are shot from the castle in Oslo and from other fortresses throughout the country. Schools, offices, and factories are closed so that people might participate in the patriotic rallies, military demonstrations, and festive, flag-waving parades that fill the afternoon. The high point of Independence Day parades are the ranks of schoolchildren in national costume, who sing as they march.

Evening finds people celebrating at home with open houses and parties. These usually end with coffee, liqueur, and *bløtkake,* a favorite creamy layer cake. Also, no *Syttende Mai* fête is complete without *eggedosis,* the brandy-spiked Norwegian nog whose beaten egg whites make it so stiff that it must be served and eaten with a spoon.

# May 18

## Dunting the Freeholder

In the ancient British custom of "beating the bounds," already well established by the eighth century C.E., a landowner affirms his or her rights to a property by ritualistically marching around ("beating") its boundaries. A satisfying quantity of bounds-beating continues in Britain to this day.

A tract of land in Newbiggin-by-the-Sea, Northumberland, has been cooperatively owned for over seven hundred years by a constantly shifting group of (mostly absentee) landlords called the Freeholders. The land is divided into small shares called stints. Many of the sixty-odd Freeholders acquired their stints through inheritance; a stint can also be purchased. Dividing the income between themselves, the Freeholders cooperatively lease the land to homeowners, a campground, and the Newbiggin Golf Club.

Every May 18, or the Wednesday closest, the Freeholders meet in Newbiggin for their annual luncheon, after which they beat the bounds, inspect the property, collect outstanding rents, and distribute peanuts to whomever they meet.

On the golf course's eighth fairway there once stood a distinctive stone. After it was stolen, a concrete replica was erected in its place. Here the party of Freeholders pauses, and here the newest member of the group is bodily lifted up by his or her fellows. The new Freeholder is then bumped, buttocks first, three times upon the concrete. This is "dunting," and they say the rite dates back to the Freeholders' medieval beginnings.

# May 19

## Pilgrimage to Treguier

### Pardon de Saint-Yves

**B**rittany, in northwestern France, has its share of favorite saints, but native son Saint Yves is the overwhelming champion. Other saints are specialists: Saint Cado aids the deaf; Saint Herve quells fear; Saints Alar and Noyale protect horses; Saints Livertine and Tujanne relieve headaches. Only the Virgin Mary and Saint Yves are general practitioners, good for all purposes.

Born Yvo Heloury in the town of Minihy in 1253, Yves attended universities in Paris and Lyon. A judge, a priest, then a bishop, he was known for his love of the poor. In the Breton tongue, Yves is called *Sant Ervoan ar wirionez,* Saint Yves the truth giver.

The day of his annual *pardon* or pilgrimage is the anniversary of his death. An avenue of candles shimmers in the hands of the faithful as they traipse the pilgrimage route from Yves's childhood home, Kervarzin Manor, to his church at Treguier. This is a *pardon mut,* a silent pardon, and the thousands of pilgrims do not speak. Many complete the last part of the journey on their hands and knees.

Sometimes called the pardon of the poor, this is a special festival for the district's beggars and homeless, who have always called themselves "the clients of Saint Yves." A local legend tells how the saint has been known to miraculously fill poor families' stewpots on the eve of the pilgrimage.

# May 20

*A* band of patriots convened in Mecklenburg County, North Carolina, one night in the spring of 1775. They were through with British rule, they hotly agreed, and penned a declaration that "annull[ed] and vacate[d] all civil and military commissions granted by the Crown." This self-described Provincial Congress asserted its intention to govern the colony of North Carolina "until Parliament should resign its arbitary pretentions."

HEAR, HEAR!

What's wrong with this picture? You've got your patriots, you've got your Declaration of Independence. But you've got them in Mecklenburg, not Philadelphia, and you've got it in 1775, not 1776. That Mecklenburg was a year ahead of its time has not been forgotten in North Carolina, where May 20 is a legal holiday commemorating the adoption of the "Resolves of May."

# May 21

## Fire-Walking Festivals

### Anastenaria

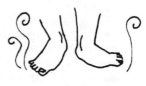

To the beat of the sacred drum and the whine of a one-stringed fiddle, members of the honored brotherhood called *Anastenarides* ("the groaners") sigh and stare as they stamp, barefooted, across the dance floor for frenzied hours at a time. Their fellow villagers watch in awe—because the Anastenarides' dance floor is made of live embers. The *Anastenaria*, celebrated in several villages of northern Greece, marks the feast day of Saint Constantine. The Anastenarides carry icons depicting Constantine, and it is said that the saint possesses the dancers, protecting their soles. They say the brotherhood comprises only those men whom the saint "summons," only those who are "clean enough." The event supposedly commemorates the miraculous rescue of the icons from a long-ago fire, but is more likely descended from pre-Christian fire rites.

After the dance, the celebrants go to the church, where the head dancer takes up the sacred axe and sacrifices an uncastrated black bull. The gore spills across the pillars of the church. Portions of raw, still-steaming meat are distributed to one and all, as are strips of hide, to be made into sandals. All year, the sacrificial tools, the icons, and the festival's requisite flute, bagpipe, drum, and fiddle are stored in the chief dancer's home. The icons are politely addressed as "Your Grace" and "Sire."

# May 22

**M**arried against her will, Rita lived for nearly twenty years with an abusive and ne'er-do-well husband. When he died violently, Rita did what she had wanted to do in the first place: She joined an Augustinian convent at Umbria in her native Italy. There she lived out the rest of her natural life, a span that was marked by a passel of supernatural occurrences.

All of this has virtually nothing to do with the fiesta held in Rita's name and on her feast day in the village of Apastepeque, El Salvador. The festival takes the

form of a dance-drama called *Tunco de Monte*, which follows the travails of a wild mountain-dwelling pig. A dancer dressed in a pigskin is chased back and forth by other dancers, and after several hours is finally "killed" by a dancer dressed as a sixteenth-century Spaniard. The "hunter" play-acts hacking his prey into pieces and distributing them to the assembled villagers, who at this point offer prayers to the saint for good weather and a fruitful harvest.

# May 23

**T**wice a year the ancient Romans held a *Tubilustrium,* which is just what it sounds like: a festival for the purpose of lustrating—that is, ritually purifying—trumpets. A devotedly militaristic people, the Romans put great stock in their battle gear. They had a festival for the dedication of shields, another for cavalry horses. On March 23 the year's first Tubilustrium marked the beginning of the fighting season and ostensibly made the army fit for war. Military as well as priestly trumpets were, as one ancient chronicler tells us, "purified in the Hall of the Shoemakers." But the location of that hall, where a ewe lamb was sacrificed for the rites, is lost in the veils of time.

The reason for May 23's Tubilustrium is more cryptic. It was too early to be welcoming home a returning army, and so it may have had more ancient connections, possibly even agricultural ones. It was nevertheless a repeat of the March 23 event, and the poet Ovid regarded it as a festival in honor of Vulcan, the divine smith and fire god who, the poet maintained, had forged the Roman army's original trumpets.

# May 24

## Saints Cyril and Methodius

### Sveti Kiril i Metodi

Cyril and Methodius were a pair of ninth-century brothers now known as the apostles of the Slavs. Cyril, the elder, was a noted university professor at Constantinople; Methodius was a provincial governor. The pious pair became priests, and circa 863 they went on a mission to Moravia, a backwater. The native Slavonic language was strictly a spoken, not a written, tongue. There was no Slavonic alphabet.

The brothers aimed to remedy this. Soon fluent in Slavonic, Cyril set about devising an alphabet. Now known as the Glagolitic, Cyril's invention later developed into the eponymous Cyrillic alphabet, which is used in the transcription of Russian, Bulgarian, and other Eastern languages.

Cyril died in 869. Soon after, Methodius was entangled in a religious dispute and landed in jail. Upon his release he regained his dignity and standing and was made archbishop of Moravia, where he continued the work he and Cyril had begun. When Methodius died in 885, one of his old enemies persecuted the archbishop's followers. They fled to Bulgaria, and there the brothers are honored as patrons of the national literature, culture, and educational system. The brothers' feast day is a national holiday, observed in every town with student parades, Bulgarian music concerts, and Bulgarian cultural programs.

# May 25

**O**n foot they come. In cars, trucks, and *campeurs* they come. Tens of thousands of Gypsies flock to the Provençal town of Les-Saintes-Maries-de-la-Mer to keep their annual appointment with a black-faced wooden lady who wears rhinestones and candy-pink satin. Hardly a bigwig on the biblical social register, the woman now known as Saint Sara was the Egyptian servant (so they say) of the Three Maries—Mary Magdalene, Mary Jacob, and Mary Salome (Jesus' aunt). According to legend, they all arrived here in a small boat (along with Saint Lazarus and the Magdalene's sister, Saint Martha) soon after the Crucifixion. While her fellow passengers went on to slay dragons and such, Sara was never noted for any feats at all. And yet . . . .

For some reason, her statue, enshrined here in a pale stone church, is the object of passionate year-round devotion. Rows of votive candles pulsate in the darkness of Sara's crypt. Once in May and again in October, the Gypsies come. They park their vehicles along the seawall. Then, in the crypt, they convene with the statue, commencing a ritual that was long scorned by Catholic officials and finally approved in 1933. The Gypsies fasten layer upon layer of satin raiments around Sara's neck, and then with riotous veneration they carry her down to the beach.

# May 26

*A*lthough Samuel Pepys is one of the most frequently quoted writers in the English language, Pepys himself would no doubt be horrified to see swatches of his private diaries so blithely bruited about in dictionaries and schoolrooms. In fact, the only thing he ever intentionally published was a 1690 missive titled *Memoirs Relating to the State of the Royal Navy.* A Cambridge graduate (class of 1655), employee of the Earl of Sandwich, secretary of naval affairs, short-lived Member of Parliament (1679), short-term prisoner in the Tower of London (also in 1679), and later an explorer in Tangier, Pepys was not so much a literary light as a well-rounded, industrious man of his era.

And that's exactly what makes him so useful. He kept a daily diary from January 1, 1660, until May 31, 1669, when failing eyesight forced him to stop writing. Four years later, Pepys died, and his library went through several inheritors before the diary was discovered. It was deciphered from the original shorthand and hailed as an incomparable record—frank, breezy, and gossipy—of daily life in seventeenth-century London.

Every year on the anniversary of his death, London honors its unwitting chronicler with a ceremony at Pepys's parish church, Saint Olave's on Hart Street. After the sermon, London's Lord Mayor places a laurel wreath on Pepys's grave, and the parishioners are treated to a concert of the music that Pepys himself most enjoyed.

# May 27

Consecrated archbishop of England in 597, Augustine, aka Austin, was charged with the task of converting the English. His boss, Pope Gregory, gave him very specific instructions: Pagan temples were not to be destroyed but were instead to be reconsecrated and renamed. Local customs and holidays were to be maintained, but Augustine was to rededicate them to saints whose feast days fell appropriately nearby.

Using these methods, Augustine is said to have converted thousands, starting with the king of Kent. He went on to evangelize at Rochester, Canterbury, and London, and is now known as the apostle of England. His feast day is celebrated on May 26 in Britain, on May 27 everywhere else.

# May 28

While pregnant with the future saint, Germain's mother endeavored to abort him. Unsuccessful, she bore him near the town of Autun, in France. She left baby Germain in the care of his grandmother, who tried to poison him. To save his life, Germain's religious uncle placed him in Autun's abbey of Saint Symphorien, where he developed a knack for prophecy, worked his way up through the ranks, and eventually was made an abbot. One night he dreamed that a kindly old man was offering him the keys to the city of Paris and urging him to take care of the Parisians.

In 554 he was made bishop of Paris, where he befriended, cured, and converted the Frankish King Childebert I. The king built Germain an abbey on the left bank of the Seine, which is now known as Saint-Germain-des-Près. Germain went about caring for Paris's poor. His *bonhomie* with the royals lost its shine when he excommunicated King Charibert, who had abandoned his wife so that he might marry another, meanwhile carrying on a relationship with his second wife's sister.

Germain is lauded for his fervent convictions. His feast day is honored, not just at his own eponymous shrine in Paris but also in other small French towns.

# May 29

*A*fter England's Civil War, Oliver Cromwell's victorious antiroyalist Republicans enjoyed a stint at the country's helm. The Republic came to an end, however, on May 29, 1660—when King Charles II emerged from a long exile to jubilantly reenter London and reclaim the throne.

Parliament rushed to establish a holiday commemorating this event. Church services and bonfires were mandatory; so was profuse oak imagery: branches, acorns, leaves, and the parasite-generated lumps that are prettily called oak apples. Ostensibly, the oak paraphernalia was to honor a lucky escape early in the war, during which King Charles, fleeing Cromwellian troops, hid himself among the boughs of a gnarled oak at Boscobel, Staffordshire. (Upon Charles's return to the throne, souvenir-hungry royalists mobbed the noble tree, clippers in hand.)

The holiday was almost absurdly popular, absorbing many May Day customs. Well into the Victorian period, enthusiastic Britons greeted every May 29 with oak leaves on their lapels and with oak-draped homes, churches, farm animals, and even locomotive engines. Those who neglected to properly decorate themselves were taunted and called Roundheads. It was the general practice to kick such people, sting them with nettles, and (in Sussex) tweak their buttocks.

Folklorists are quick to point out that oak worship was one of northern Europe's hoarier traditions, what with Thor's thunder-acorn and the druids' sacred oak groves.

# May 30

**O**pinions are divided concerning the origins of the United States' Memorial Day, a day set aside for honoring the graves of American war dead. While most historians credit Southern women with beginning the custom, an intriguing rumor concerns an anonymous German who fought in the American Civil War. (No record remains of which side he was on.) At the end of the war, this German allegedly was overheard commenting that in his native land, people scattered flowers on the graves of dead soldiers.

Be that as it may, in May 1868, Adjutant-General N. P. Chipman of the Union Army came to his associate, Commander John A. Logan, suggesting that the army make official an annual day for what was then called "decorating" Union graves. Logan was game, and he issued an order setting aside May 30 "for the purpose of strewing with flowers, or otherwise decorating the graves of comrades who died in defense of their country during the late rebellion, and whose bodies now lie in almost every city, village or hamlet churchyard in the land." His proclamation concluded "with the

hope that it will be kept up from year to year while a survivor of the war remains to honor the memory of the departed."

The patriotic holiday was later amended to include *all* the dead from *all* the wars, and its date was shifted to a convenient Monday in late May.

# May 31

## Flowers of May (Last Day)

**Flores de Mayo**

In the Catholic world, the month of May is dedicated to the Virgin Mary and is celebrated at the very least by the garlanding of Mary statues in churches, convents, and Catholic schools. In the Philippines, May is a time of intense festivity. All month, schoolchildren assemble bouquets and floral offerings and take them to church. Meanwhile, girls elected to serve as festival queens parade through the streets dressed in the national costume, the butterfly-sleeved *terna* dress, surrounded by page boys, flower girls who scatter petals, and their relatives and neighbors who sing and chant Hail Marys.

On the last night of May, this extended festival culminates with torchlight parades, open houses, games, and richly elaborate banquets. A feature of these is the Filipino variation on the Mexican *piñata:* a bamboo frame from which dangle packages of sweets, fruit, and toys on strings. Children leap at the packages while adults control the strings by means of a pulley system. In Manila, this is one of the biggest nights of the year, and many people attend formal balls.

# Moveable Feast

## Gay Freedom Day

There was a time in America when same-sex couples could be arrested for dancing together in public, when women could be arrested for wearing suits that had been manufactured for men. Throughout the paranoid fifties and well into the sixties, gay bars were both refuges and targets, and they were regularly—seldom justifiably—raided by jeering police. On June 27, 1969, police burst into the Stonewall in New York's Greenwich Village. Five gay bars nearby had been raided over the previous week, and now the Stonewall's clientele rose up in defiant anger, shouting, hurling furniture at the police, and refusing to leave. The standoff lasted all weekend, at the end of which the bar was a charred ruin. But the gay pride movement was born. In the wake of what is now known as the Stonewall Rebellion, myriad solidarity, support, and activist organizations sprang into being. Gay historians now cite two distinct eras: Before Stonewall and After Stonewall.

Gay Freedom Day, usually observed on the weekend nearest June 27, is a time for reflection, reunion, and renewed dedication—not to mention dazzling parades.

# June 1

## Clothes Changing
### Koromo-Gaye

**i**n Japan, this is the day when people pack away their winter clothes and don their pastel summer cottons, short sleeves, and sandals. Because it means so much, this is done no matter the actual condition of the weather. So what if one year winter decides to last until July? Many Japanese schools instruct pupils to start wearing their pale summer uniforms starting today, switching lighter cottons for navy blue flannel and wool. Similarly, employees of many companies start wearing their summer uniforms as of today.

The streets look completely transformed.

The holiday has its deeper spiritual side, too. With so much more of their flesh suddenly exposed, many people pay a special visit to their neighborhood shrines to ask for increased bodily protection.

An old legend of central Hoshu tells how June 1 is the day when snakes—like humans shedding their heavy clothes—shed their skins. The legend advises the prudent person to stay out of fields today, for to spy a snake shedding its skin can cause sudden irreversible blindness.

# June 2

## Rice Harvest Festival

### Gawai Dayak

At harvest time, whole Malaysian communities work together in the rice fields, gathering the stalks by hand. Traditional Malays harvest rice with a special knife whose carved handle is said to appease the *semangat* or rice spirit. (Rice spirits, rice mothers, rice souls, rice gods, rice babies, rice brides, and rice bridegrooms are known and venerated throughout Southeast Asia.)

On Sarawak, adjacent to Borneo in the South China Sea, the rice harvest is celebrated every year on the second day of June, sometimes the first. When the last of the grain has been collected, villagers gather at midnight in slant-roofed longhouses perched on tall stilts, deep in the jungle. First offering a thanksgiving for the current harvest and invoking blessings for the next one, the people tuck into a protracted banquet. An essential part of the meal is the local rice wine, also offered to the gods in the *miring* ceremony. A village poet recites appropriate prayers for the occasion asking for protection, guidance, and good luck. Then he swings a white rooster around in the air and sacrifices it. Dances follow, and often a particularly attractive couple is chosen from among the group, like a homecoming queen and king, to represent the harvest's fruitfulness.

# June 3

## Jefferson Davis's Birthday

The woman he loved died a mere three months after he married her. Thereafter, the West Point graduate and veteran of America's little-known Black Hawk War was, by turns, a Mississippi planter, a member of the U.S. House of Representatives, a senator, and the secretary of war. Come 1861, he was the general of the Mississippi militia. Then he was made provisional president of the provisional Southern government and, finally, president of the Confederacy. As the Civil War raged on, Davis, disliking bloodshed, counseled moderation, to the mounting disapproval of his opponents within the Confederate government. He found himself faced with so many enemies that an "anti-Davis" political party was clamoring for his dismissal: moot, anyway, because Robert E. Lee surrendered (without President Davis's approval) and the Confederate government collapsed. Davis himself was captured at Irwinville, Georgia. He spent two years in prison—in irons, in fact. Out on bail, he wrote the two-volume *Rise and Fall of the Confederacy.* Upon his death, Davis was buried twice, both times in the South: once in New Orleans and then four years later in Richmond, Virginia.

Davis's birthday is a public holiday in Florida, Georgia, South Carolina, and several other Southern states, where it is celebrated with banquets and graveside ceremonies in Civil War cemeteries.

# June 4

## Saint Francis Caracciolo's Day

*A*s a small child, this princely Neapolitan devoted himself entirely to repeating the rosary and distributing food to the poor. He was struck with leprosy, or something closely resembling it, and was horribly disfigured. When the disease lessened, Francis was so grateful that he became a priest and, at the age of twenty-five in 1588, founded a monastic order whose members took vows of poverty and chastity as well as a special "vow of indignity." Francis's barefoot monks specialized in missionizing prisoners and hospital patients. The rule of the order was that each day one monk fasted on bread and water, another monk flagellated himself, and a third wore a hair shirt. They took turns. Francis was renowned for praying while lying facedown before the altar, murmuring, "The zeal of your house has eaten me up."

Francis's feast day is the focus of veneration in his native Naples.

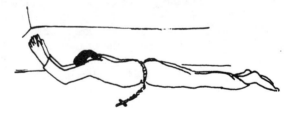

# June 5

*A*t the height of World War II, the Allies launched ambitious Operation Overlord along the Norman coast, targeting French beaches that were code-named Omaha, Utah, Juno, Sword, and Gold. The big day would be called D-Day. In its aftermath, bodies littered the shore, entire towns had been blown to bits, and the Allies' ascendance seemed assured.

The towns of Sainte-Mere-Eglise and Sainte-Marie-du-Mont commemorate the event with annual ceremonies beginning on June 5, D-Day Eve. Veterans and locals gather to hear speeches, participate in rites honoring the dead, and offer thanksgiving prayers.

Five miles inland from "Utah Beach," whose real name is Ravenoville-plage, Sainte-Mere-Eglise soared to instant fame when on D-Day American paratroopers landed here and fought a daring battle against German snipers inside the church tower. (The tower still displays its bullet wounds, and a stained-glass window down below illustrates the paratroopers' landing.) Sainte-Mere-Eglise was the first French town the Allies took that day, the first town to be "liberated." The road southward, marked with commemorative obelisks and more *musées des troupes aeroportées* than you'd care to imagine, is called the Way of Liberation.

# June 6

## Svenska Flaggans Dag

The Swedish flag with its yellow cross against a blue background was officially adopted upon the death of King Gustav Vasa in 1560, although Swedish armies had long been displaying those colors and that design in battle. In 1873, King Oscar II popularized the displaying of the flag, and to this day the old blue-and-yellow flaps atop a tall pole in the backyard of nearly every Swedish home.

In 1916, the government established *Flaggans Dag.* June 6 was the anniversary of several historical high points; most notably it was the date on which the beloved King Vasa ascended to the throne in 1523. Today crowds come to Stockholm's stadium every June 6 to watch the reigning monarch award flags to scout troops, housewives' organizations, military outfits, schools, and other groups. A military band plays Sweden's two-hundred-year-old national anthem, which contains the line: "Above the flower-crowned mound waves the blue and yellow Nordic flag." As evening falls, the crowd moves on to Skansen, Stockholm's open-air folk museum, for continued festivities including folk dance performances.

# June 7

## Saint Robert of Newminster's Day

This twelfth-century Northumbrian abbot amazed his brethren with his visions of angels and devils and with his powers of self-starvation. One Easter Day, it is said, he had been fasting so fiercely that his fellows feared for his health. At last he consented to try a slice of bread drizzled with honey. But before it was even brought to him, Robert decided that such a lapse of his principles would be a disappointment, even a danger, to his monks. Thus he sent the bread away untouched.

In 1147 Robert was accused of excessive familiarity with a certain pious woman, but he cleared his name with the

support of Saint Bernard, who as a gesture of goodwill sent him a cloth that boasted miraculous healing powers. Upon Robert's death on June 7, 1159, his friend Saint Godric of Finchale is said to have seen the abbot's soul departing his body in the form of a fireball. The anniversary of Robert's death is a special event among monks of the Cistercian order, especially in his native England.

# June 8

## Saint Medard's Day
### Sint Medardus/Saint-Medard

**B**elgium has its own "rain saint." Saint Medard (*Sint Medardus* in Flemish and *Saint-Medard* in French) is said to have startled everyone with his ability to walk through rainstorms without an umbrella or any special covering and stay completely dry while everyone else got soaked. This ability was attributed to Medard's faith, which protected him, it was said, better than any earthly cloak. Belgian farmers long maintained that the weather on Medard's feast day foretells whether the forthcoming weeks will be wet or dry. As an old Belgian saying puts it:

> *If it rains on Saint Medard's Day,*
> *It will keep raining for forty more days.*

# June 9

## Vestalia

The faceless goddess Vesta was fire itself: She was the spark, the heat, the generative fire that stoked the Roman Empire. The eternal flame in Vesta's temple in the Forum was Rome's great hearth, and Romans believed that it would burn as long as their empire lasted.

On only one day every year was Vesta's temple, a distinctively circular sanctum sanctorum, open to the public. That day was June 9, the *Vestalia*. And even then, only women—matrons, and barefoot at that—were permitted to enter. There they asked the goddess's blessing on their families and offered her food that they had baked in their own ovens. These dignified suppliants arrived in an orderly processional and were welcomed by the goddess's priestesses, the Vestal Virgins. For the *Vestalia*, the Vestals very carefully prepared the *mola salsa*, a kind of briny pastry that was said to be the goddess's favorite.

The festival-hungry poet Ovid, because of his gender, was naturally barred from the shrine. Still he mused longingly: "O Vesta, grant me thy favor! In thy service now I open my lips. . . . I was wrapt in prayer; I felt the heavenly deity and the glad ground gleamed with a purple light."

# June 10

*N*ihongi, the seventh- and eighth-century Japanese historical chronicle, tells how Crown Prince Tenchi was fascinated with a type of Chinese water clock that marked the hours by means of water dripping out of a vessel. Tenchi—who would serve as emperor from 663 to 671—created a Japanese version of the clock and installed it in the Imperial Palace. His passion for timekeeping didn't stop there. According to *Nihongi,* Emperor Tenchi officially proclaimed that while the average Japanese householder did not own a clock of his or her own, the passing hours should still be announced throughout the country by the ringing of temple bells and/or the beating of drums. Western-style clocks didn't make an appearance in Japan until 1551, when Portuguese ships brought them.

In 1920, the Japanese Federation for the Improvement of Living Conditions moved to institute a national timekeeping holiday whose date corresponded with that of Tenchi's proclamation. Today lectures focus on the importance of punctuality, and awards ceremonies honor the country's most punctual citizens. In former years, the Federation for the Improvement of Living Conditions set up booths at Tokyo's central railway station where watchmakers offered free repairs to all passersby.

# June 11

## Kamehameha Day

*A*s a young warrior in the service of his uncle, the Big Island's high chief Kalaiopuu, the ambitious Kamehameha is said to always have carried a wooden statuette of a war god. As Kamehameha launched into battle, they say, the statue's war cries terrified the enemy.

By 1782, Kamehameha had become, at the age of twenty-four, a Big Island chief. By 1790, he had conquered Maui. He went on to conquer all the other islands (except Kauai, which he came to govern anyway). He called his holdings Hawai'i, after his beloved home island, and he declared himself king. Forever after, his subjects, their descendants, and American history textbooks would call him Kamehameha the Great, as he had united the islands. It is also said that Hawai'i's old gods died with Kamehameha: One year after his death, Christian missionaries arrived.

In 1872, the late king's birthday was declared a national holiday. Today it is a state holiday, observed throughout the islands with boat races, hula shows, luaus, and formal balls. Parades on this day feature floats on which locals impersonate Hawai'ian royalty. A youth is chosen to impersonate Kamehameha, and in the parade he wears the sacred yellow *mamo*-feather cape and round Grecian-style helmet.

# June 12
## Philippines Independence Day

After the Philippines had been invaded, occupied, governed, fought upon, and fought over by seemingly every foreign nation and its brother, Filipino rebel leader Emilio Aguinaldo declared the islands independent on June 12, 1898. American generals had freed Aguinaldo from exile, urging him to declare his country's independence from Spain, with whom the United States was at war. A month and a half after Aguinaldo's declaration, American military reinforcements sailed into Manila and wrestled the islands out of Spain's grip. The following year's Treaty of Paris officially ended the Spanish-American War and permitted the United States to "acquire" the Philippines. Emilio Aguinaldo was somewhat disappointed.

In 1902 the United States promised to grant the Philippines full and unconditional autonomy—someday. In 1916 the United States granted the islands a bill of rights and all (male) citizens the right to vote. After World War II, the United States honored its promise at last, granting the Philippines its independence. Filipinos celebrated their Independence Day on July 4 until 1962, when then-President Diosdada Macapagal changed the date to June 12, in honor of Aguinaldo's 1898 declaration. People mark the holiday with patriotic outdoor ceremonies, after which church bells ring and fiestas ensue.

The state of Hawai'i honors its large Filipino-American community on this day with a cultural pageant.

# June 13

## Saint Anthony of Padua

Of the half-dozen or so Saint Anthonies, Anthony of Padua is the one whose statue, housed in myriad churches, holds a lily in one hand and the infant Jesus in the other. The bitter truth is that in real life the Portuguese-born Anthony never cradled Jesus at all, and never even knew him. Nonetheless, he was an eloquent biblical scholar whose preaching was said to have moved peasants and intellectuals alike. It is said that one day in Rimini, on Italy's east coast, Anthony went down to the seashore and preached to the fish, who lifted their heads above the surface of the water and listened, rapt. Another legend tells how a year after his death in 1232, the saint's tongue was found incorrupt, red, and meaty-fresh inside Anthony's dessicated head. The cleric who was to become Saint Bonaventure gathered up the member, it is said, and kissed it, weeping. The tongue, now enshrined in a silver case at Padua, where Anthony died, is the object of pilgrimage, especially on Anthony's feast day.

Also on his day it is customary to give alms to the poor, as Anthony was known for his fierce defense of the underprivileged.

# June 14

## Rice-Planting Festival

### Otaue Shinji

**S**own in "nursery" plots and then transplanted to the paddy as tender green seedlings—inserted by hand, one by one, into the deeply submerged soil—rice hardly seems a cost-effective crop. Yet it goes on record as yielding more calories per acre than any other known grain. Many Japanese eat rice with all three daily meals.

Rice sowing, rice harvest, and the emperor's first annual taste of a season's new rice are all causes celebres in Japan. Rice-transplanting festivals are the most widespread and the most popular of all, capturing the tremulous moment when the life-sustaining grain is at its most vulnerable. At this time of year, such festivals take place all over rural Japan. Traditionally, drums and flutes play as corps of kimono-clad female planters, knee-deep in the paddy, bend and plant, bend and plant the seedlings. They pause now and then amidst their rhythmic labors to exhort the Shinto rice deity.

Osaka's Sumiyoshi Jinja is one of Japan's most historically significant shrines, with longtime agricultural connections and its own sacred rice paddies on the temple grounds. Every year on June 14 the shrine holds its *Otaue Shinji*. In the early afternoon, thousands of spectators come to watch the young women working in the sunshine and to hear the special songs and prayers. It is said that the resident deity of the fields provides a good harvest as a reward to the faithful.

# June 15

## Saint Vitus's Day Fires

*A*ncient Teutons called their midsummer conflagrations need-fires. Not merely bonfires, these need-fires had a kinetic quality. They often took the form of cartwheels, set ablaze and rolled downhill. These were meant to duplicate the sun's swooping course across the sky; some folklorists suggest the fires were meant to "accompany" the sun on its journey. Strict regulations governed the lighting of the fires: In some places, only a pair of brothers could light the need-fire; some places, two male virgins did the job, or two youths with the same first name, or twins. In *The Golden Bough,* Sir James Frazer relates that "in the western islands of Scotland the fire was kindled by 81 married men, who rubbed great planks against each other. . . . Among the Serbians the need-fire is . . . kindled by a boy and girl between eleven and fourteen years of age, who work stark naked in a dark room. . . . In Bulgaria, too, the makers of the need-fire strip themselves of their clothes; in Caithness they divest themselves of all kinds of metal."

The feast day of Saint Vitus, one of Germany's favorite martyrs, became with that country's Christianization a handy focus for need-fire rites. Frazer tells how every June 15 "at Obermedlingen, in Swabia, the 'fire of heaven,' as it was called, was made . . . by igniting a cartwheel, which, smeared with pitch and plaited with straw, was fastened on a pole twelve feet high, the top of the pole being inserted in the nave of the wheel. The fire was made on the summit of a mountain, and as the flame ascended, the people uttered a set form of words, with eyes and arms directed heavenward."

# June 16

Bloomsday

*A*ll the events in James Joyce's cryptoexuberant novel *Ulysses* took place on a single day, and that day—Bloomsday—was the 16th of June. So every year on the anniversary of protagonist Leopold Bloom's sojourn through Dublin, Joyce fans from all over the world come to pay their respects. Festivities begin at the James Joyce Tower, which is on the seashore at Sandycove, a half mile south of Dun Laoghaire on Ireland's east coast. Joyce himself once lived in the tower.

After a special "Joyce Breakfast," followed by readings and festivities in the tower, the party moves on to Dublin, where afternoon walking tours start from in front of Dublin's Central Post Office. The tours retrace Leopold Bloom's route through the capital.

# June 17

## Bunker Hill Day

All fired up from their victories at Lexington and Concord, the Massachusetts patriots elected in April 1775 to gather an army of 30,000 with which to fight the British at Boston. By June they had amassed only half that number. Undaunted, they sallied forth. After numerous tussles with the redcoats, they found themselves at the battle of Bunker Hill. The Americans, short on ammunition, were reportedly reduced to picking up stones from the ground and hurling them desperately at the bayonet-wielding Britons. Nevertheless, when the battle was over, the number of redcoat casualties was about twice that of the Americans, a result that further inspired the patriots and led to still more daring and decisive battles.

The Bunker Hill anniversary is an annual holiday in Boston, where after morning ceremonies, a parade winds down Bunker Hill Street to the Bunker Hill Monument and beyond. Hundreds of thousands of sightseers gather along the four-mile route to watch over five thousand marchers—fife-and-drum corps, military bands, and buglers, among others.

# June 18
## Saints Mark and Marcellian's Day

These twin brothers were of a noble third-century Roman family. Although their parents, wives, and children all worshiped the Roman gods, Mark and Marcellian were Christians. Thus they were arrested and condemned to be beheaded. Their influential parents convinced local government officials to delay the execution for thirty days, during which time the brothers' friends and all their family members daily visited their cell, begging them to save their lives by giving up Christianity. Mark and Marcellian refused, egged on in their refusal by the future Saint Sebastian, an army officer who would later be martyred himself. At one point the brothers managed to escape and were hidden in the home of a friend. They were recaptured and tied to a wooden pillar. Their feet were nailed down to keep them from running away again. Finally they were stabbed to death with lances.

Their feast day is especially important in the churches in Rome, Bologna, and Volterra, which claim to possess parts of the brothers' bodies.

# June 19

The American Civil War was over; it was the summer of 1865 and Union General Gordon Granger had landed at Galveston Bay with federal troops. Their mission was to order recalcitrant slave owners—force them, if necessary—to free their slaves. Messengers rode out into the countryside to spread the news. It is said that the slaves of Texas, Oklahoma, Louisiana, and Arkansas finally got the word on June 19. Their counterparts in Mississippi had known since May 8; those in Florida had been savoring freedom since May 20. It is said that Texan slave owners held off from telling, and thus liberating, their slaves in a desperate effort to squeeze one last crop out of them. It is also said that army messengers were murdered en route to keep them from delivering the news.

June 19th—Juneteenth—has come to be identified with the official end of slavery in the United States. Also called National Freedom Day, its celebrations were originally confined to all-black farm towns in a few southern states. But the holiday has come to be observed in African-American communities throughout the country with rallies, picnics, concerts, and fairs.

# June 20

## San Antonio de la Florida

**O**ne of Saint Anthony of Padua's attributes is that he helps people find things—usually, this means lost keys or eyeglasses. But in Madrid's La Florida district, where Anthony was known as "the marrying saint," he helped with another kind of hunting entirely. In Goya's day and well into the twentieth century, chaste-as-a-lily Anthony was the guest of honor at a weeklong neighborhood ritual whose participants implored him to help them find mates.

On Anthony's June 13 feast day, the dancing began at dusk. The streets of the neighborhood filled with people; the whispers of the river—the Río Manzanares—formed a soft undertone to the music of the *tunas,* wandering bands of young musicians. Goya painted this scene, captivated by the sight of the chapel, where—in the midst of a whirl of costumed hilarity, music, and dance—a long line of silent young women snaked out the door, candles in hand. Each waited her turn to address the statue of the saint, to offer him a candle and a prayer. Into the church's holy water fonts, the supplicants tossed handfuls of special pins called *novios,* "sweethearts."

Climaxing on the 20th, the streets rang with music and the cries of vendors selling fritters, cider, and little rolls called Saint Anthony's loaves, made not to be eaten but to be kept as love charms.

# June 21

## Midsummer

**W**hile Celtic Britain was partial to May Day fires, midsummer was the festival of choice throughout Norse and Anglo-Saxon Britain (most of England, most of Scotland, Shetland, and the Orkneys). Fires, poles, dancing, games, and various shenanigans involving fertility were the general rule on this "longest day of the year." The passing centuries took their toll on this once-majestic occasion. By the 1680s, British folklorist John Aubrey was moved to report that "still in many places . . . they make Fires on the Hills: but the Civill Warres comeing on have putt all these Rites or customes quite out of fashion."

Millennia ago, Stonehenge's anonymous and long-vanished builders no doubt celebrated their own midsummer rites among the stones. More recently a British group called the Ancient Order of Druids, founded in 1781 by a carpenter named Hurle, instituted an annual June 21 ceremony at the site. The latter-day Druid rite, which attracted huge crowds, entailed a bread-and-wine sacrament, candles, bells, incense, and white-and-purple-surpliced priests who shared wine from a silver cup as the midsummer sun-

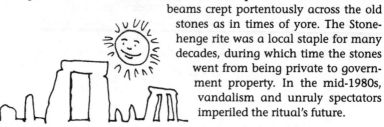

beams crept portentously across the old stones as in times of yore. The Stonehenge rite was a local staple for many decades, during which time the stones went from being private to government property. In the mid-1980s, vandalism and unruly spectators imperiled the ritual's future.

# June 22

**O**ne night early in the third century, a British Christian named Alban was whiling away the hours in his villa at Verulanium, in what is now Hertfordshire, when there came a knock at the door. Alban was startled to see his old friend Amphiabel, a fellow Christian who was fleeing persecutors sent after him by the emperor, Diocletian. Alban sheltered his friend, only to be arrested himself. Following a brief imprisonment that was peppered with minor miracles and angels' visits, Alban was hauled off to the chopping block. On the way he was dragged through rosebushes. The blood streaming from his wounds left a crimson trail all along the route. On June 22, Alban became England's first Christian martyr.

Near the old city of Verulanium, which is now called Saint Albans, stands his shrine. It is here that an annual rose festival commemorates Alban's martyrdom. Local schoolchildren form a solemn procession to the church, carrying roses that are then dedicated in a special church service. The flowers are spread out to form a fragrant "carpet," which stays in the church for a week.

# June 23

**B**onfires were and are a midsummer staple from one end of Europe to the other. The Celts of England and Ireland gleefully ignited them, as did the Norsemen, whose *Balders balar* flared up in honor of their god Balder every Midsummer Eve, June 23. The French, Austrians, Germans, Portuguese, and others all held fire rites to mirror the resplendent sun. Early Christian missionaries, knowing that they couldn't hope to extinguish these fires, had no choice but to announce that June 24 was Saint John's feast day and June 23 was Saint John's Eve and to pretend that the bonfires were lit in John's honor. Grudgingly the priests left the populace to its own incendiary devices.

To this day the midsummer fires blaze away. In Norway, *Sankthansbal* made of logs and tar barrels can be seen from miles away. To the whine of fiddles, Swedes caper around lofty midsummer poles. Revelers at San Pedro Manrique, in northern Spain, feast while a huge bonfire roars nearby. When the flames die down, pious penitents stomp barefoot over the glowing embers. Often they carry passengers on their backs to increase the intensity of the penance.

# June 24

## Saint John's Day
### Día de San Juan

I n Latin America, Saint John is a water bringer, *San Juan Bautista*, "the baptist." So in the midst of sultry summer, his day is a water festival, an exuberant respite from the heat. A longtime favorite tradition in Mexico City was to pack up guitars, picnic baskets, and summer flowers and gather at public swimming pools late on the night of the 23rd. Precisely at midnight, everyone would dive into the water, scattering petals as they leaped. The pool parties would last all through the night and into the next day. Similar customs are still popular all over Mexico, where people feast at poolsides and riversides. (Also popular are divinations involving raw eggs broken into tumblers of water.) When it rains on the 24th, they say that *San Juan llora*, "Saint John cries."

While today only its capital city is named after San Juan, the whole island now called Puerto Rico used to bear the saint's name. There the faithful believe that on his day, John renders all waters safe for swimming. As in Mexico, the festivities start on the night of the 23rd, when people flock to the beach for an all-night fiesta. At the stroke of midnight, custom demands that everyone line up at the water's edge and walk backwards into the moonlit waves. It is said that San Juan, gazing down from heaven, rebaptizes all who do this.

Saint John's Day is celebrated all over the Catholic world, usually with festivities of a fiery or watery nature.

# June 25

## After Saint John
### Après Saint-Jean

In the French countryside, the week preceding Saint John's Day (June 24) is a time for junketing around from village to village, gorging on bonfire viewing. French *feux de Saint-Jean* have been a tradition in Alsace, Brittany, Burgundy, and other regions since the Middle Ages. In westernmost Brittany, parishioners contribute the firewood, which is stacked up within sight of a church and then kindled by a priest. Afterwards, the embers are collected as talismans against fire and lightning. In other areas, the bonfires are made from haystacks, and couples jump over the guttering flames, hand in hand. In wooded Alsace, along the German border, huge logs are used to erect pyramids high on hillsides, which are set ablaze at night while crowds of people watch from the villages below.

The climactic day is Saint John's. In its aftermath, slack and blackened pyramid skeletons languish, crumbling against the green, and a postparty hush cloaks everything. But—at least for many rural people named Jean or Jeanne, after the saint—the pleasure is not entirely over yet. Often enough, the namesakes awaken on the morning of the 25th to find that friends have come by during the night and festooned their houses with fresh flowers, streamers, and greenery.

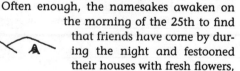

**O**ne summer day in the Middle Ages, a strange man in multicolored (that is, piéd) clothing strode into the German town of Hamelin. Learning that the town was infested with rats, the stranger offered to dispose of the rodents—for a fee. When the burghers gratefully agreed, the stranger whipped out a flute and played a mysterious tune that proved an irresistible rat lure. Rats swarmed out of every house in Hamelin and followed the Pied Piper to the banks of the Weser River. Then they followed him into the swirling waters and were drowned.

When the burghers refused to pay the piper, he devised a plan of revenge. Once again putting his pipe to his lips, he played yet another air—one that seduced not rodents but children. Parents watched helplessly as the Pied Piper, playing merrily, led all of Hamelin's youngsters out of town, after which they were never seen again.

Although opinions vary on the exact date of the piper's revenge (sixteenth-century chronicler Richard Verstegen claimed it was July 22, 1376), the German government holds with June 26, 1284. The town of Hamelin stages Pied Piper plays every Sunday from June to September. Children form the bulk of the cast, but as 130 was the alleged number who went with the piper on that fateful day in 1284 or 1376, the cast of today's productions is ritually limited to 130.

# June 27

## Saint Cyril of Alexandria's Day

*C*yril boasts the nicknames Doctor of Divine Grace, Seal of the Fathers, Tower of Truth, and Doctor of the Incarnation. He read and wrote much and, as a young priest, drove the Jews out of his native Alexandria. He also attacked other groups whose beliefs were not in accordance with his own. In 417 Alexandria's most influential philosopher was a pagan woman called Hypatia. Among the disciples who flocked to her from near and far were bishops and governors, who consulted her on matters of civil administration and asked her to critique their writings. A band of Cyril's followers attacked Hypatia in the streets, dragged her from her chariot, and tore her to pieces. Cyril himself was never directly linked to the murder.

He is most famous for his discourses on the divinity of Jesus and Mary. Hailed as one of the Church's foremost theologians, Cyril's feast day is a focus for much veneration, especially among the Copts.

# June 28

## Battle of the Bridge
### Gioco del Ponte

**E**ven before it had a leaning tower, Pisa had fangs. Founded circa 180 B.C.E., the city had by the early Middle Ages become a powerful republic, following its own code of laws, conquering its enemies, and blithely plucking prizes—Sardinia, Corsica, the Balearic islands, and even Jerusalem, via the second crusade—for its own enrichment. In 1509 Pisa was finally subdued by its longtime neighbor and enemy, Florence. Fifty-nine years later the *Gioco del Ponte* was instituted. Though its name means "game of the bridge," there is more of the battle than the game about this. It recalls the days when Pisa was divided into a duo of contentious neighborhoods: the Mezzogiorno south of the Arno River, and the Tramontana to the north. Just before dusk, the battlers begin the proceedings by showing off their sixteenth-century costumes in a riverside historical parade, the *sfilata storica*. Then they mount the Ponte di Mezzo, which spans the river, and launch into a vicious tug-of-war that besmirches those leotards and tunics in a jiffy as throngs of onlookers cheer.

# June 29

## Saint Peter's Day

**P**eter was a fisherman. From the Christian standpoint, he was *the* fisherman, whose deft angling in the Sea of Galilee was rehearsal for his eventual work as a "fisher of men." It is said that Peter's very shadow had miraculous powers, but all for the greater glory of not Peter but Jesus, who had changed his apostle's name to Peter from Simon.

Peter went on to papacy and martyrdom. Now as the patron saint of fishermen and all those who make their living from the sea, the holy angler's feast day is honored at celebrations in port towns all over the Christian world. In Portugal, it is an occasion for fairs, fireworks, fish fries, and bull runs; miniature shrines are erected on the sidewalk. Italian ports (and Italian-American fishing communities, such as the one at Gloucester, Massachusetts) celebrate similarly, with the added attraction of parades featuring decorated boats. A staple snack at Mediterranean Saint Peter's Day festivals is the *romesco*—sardines impaled on wooden sticks, thrust into sand around a little fire. When grilled to a turn, the fish are nibbled like popsicles right off the stick.

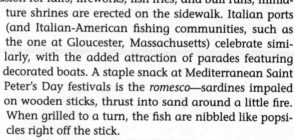

On the Caribbean island of Grenada, Saint Peter's Day is called the Fisherman's Birthday. Various towns celebrate with sober boat blessings and net blessings, which blossom into frenzied minicarnivals complete with boat races and dancing in the streets.

# June 30

## The Burial of Yarilo

**I**n *The Golden Bough,* Sir James Frazer relates a tradition that was, up till the last century, enacted every year on June 30th, and occasionally on the 29th, in the Russian district of Kostroma. He describes how villages selected an old man from among themselves and would entrust him with a miniature coffin enclosing a phallic image known as Yarilo. "This he carried out of town," Frazer writes, "followed by women chanting dirges and expressing by their gestures grief and despair." Outside of town, the villagers dug a grave and lowered the coffin into it "amid weeping and wailing, after which games and dances were begun."

He relates a variation on the rite, practiced in a nearby district, in which Yarilo in his coffin was "carried through the streets after sunset surrounded by drunken women, who kept repeating mournfully, 'He is dead! He is dead!'" The village men, for their part, shook the coffin as if trying to wake Yarilo from the dead. At the burial site outside of town, Frazer tells us, the men "said to the women, 'Women, weep not. I know what is sweeter than honey.' But the women continued to lament and chant. . . . 'Of what was he guilty? He was so good. He will arise no more. O how shall we part from thee? What is life without thee? Arise, if only for a brief hour. But he rises not, he rises not.'" The meaning of this bizarre ritual eludes us today.

# July 1

The unmistakable silhouette of Mount Fuji has inspired countless poems, paintings, proverbs, and corporate logos. But this 12,395-foot, still active volcanic cone is no mere dreamy mountain-in-the-mist. It's climbable, and tens of thousands grapple this hands-on landmark every summer.

July and August comprise the official climbing season, for only during these two months is the peak free of snow. For the average citizen, climbing Fuji is an outing, a workout, a rite of passage. There is an undertone of the pilgrimage about it, too. In the Edo period (1600–1867), Fuji emerged as the focus of a climbing cult. (According to Shinto principle, mountains are the homes of gods, whose permission must be secured before one dares to assail the peak.) White-clad pilgrims flocked to the trails—male pilgrims, that is. Until 1868, women were strictly forbidden to climb Fuji.

The town of Fuji-Yoshida is the main gateway to the mountain. There, the priests at Sengen Jinga shrine officially open the season. A straw rope, flanked by bonfires, spans the entrance to the trail. A crowd of climbers waits beside the rope while a Shinto priest invokes the mountain deity and prays for the climbers' safety on the slope. The priest cuts the rope, and all march onto the trail together. (See August 26 for the climbing season's closing ritual.)

# July 2

## Palio of Siena
### Palio di Siena

**W**hole books have been written about the Palio of Siena, Italy—about why and how an annual horse race that lasts about seventy seconds manages to reduce an entire city's population to a ranting mob. On the one hand, the Palio is just a horse race between Siena's seventeen neighborhoods. (The neighbor-

hoods, each of which boasts its own coat of arms, are named Caterpillar, Unicorn, She-Wolf, Seashell, Tower, Dragon, Forest, Owl, Panther, Tortoise, Porcupine, Giraffe, Leopard, Snail, Ram, and Noble Goose.) On the other hand, the Palio is a cavalcade of curious superstitions and primitive folk customs galloping into the twentieth century.

For weeks in advance, the streets overflow with feasting, chanting, and exorbitant betting. On race day, the horses go to church in the morning and are blessed by priests who personally urge them to win. Then comes a costume parade with Renaissance finery, trumpets and drums, armor and mail, doublets and leggings, and caparisoned beasts. The procession lasts some two hours, at the end of which the spectators lining the town piazza, *Il Campo,* are as thick and excited as ants on honey. The walls of the unusual gibbous piazza have been padded with mattresses to protect the horses and riders. Finally at dusk the jockeys appear, riding bareback, clutching slender whips. The race begins, and. . . .

And scarcely a thundering heartbeat later, it ends.

# July 3

*J*ust after the turn of the century, approximately 10 percent of the Danish population up and left the country in hopes of finding work, wealth, and warmth in other lands. Denmark now boasts numerous genealogical archives and libraries, established to help Danish Americans find their roots.

In this spirit of Danish-American solidarity, Denmark's Rebild National Park is the scene of an annual Independence Day celebration—that's *America's* Independence Day. Land for the park, in northernmost Jutland, was presented to the nation of Denmark by an association of Danish Americans in 1912. Ever since that year, hundreds of thousands from both sides of the Atlantic have gathered to admire the stars and stripes fluttering in the park's natural amphitheater alongside Denmark's red-and-white *Danneborg* flag. Independence Day concerts at the park feature Danish and American music; celebrities present Independence Day speeches. Among the personages invited to speak at past ceremonies are Danny Kaye, Ronald Reagan, Victor Borge, Raymond Burr, Art Buchwald, and Dionne Warwick.

On July 3, the nearby city of Aalborg kicks off its celebration by electing an *American* mayor-for-a-day, who joins the Independence Day parade, which includes musicians in Danish folk costume, marchers in courtly garb, and Danish-born Americaphiles dressed in full Sioux regalia, feathered headdresses and all.

# July 4

## Whalton Baal Fire

Said to date from time immemorial, this annual rite in the Northumbrian village of Whalton takes its name from either the Celtic word *bel,* meaning "bright," the Anglo-Saxon *bael,* meaning "fire," or from the name of the old British sun god, Belenus.

Today the bonfire is lit in the customary corner of the village green at 7:30 P.M., and it blazes hotly while villagers watch, and as morris dancers leap and stamp in the pulsating shadows. In former times the ritual was deeper, more intricate. Reverend J. Walker, vicar of Whalton, wrote in 1903 that "every year on the 4th of July as the sun goes down a huge bonfire is made and lighted." The firewood, he wrote, had been gathered by a select group of youths over the past several weeks in a nearby forest. It was loaded into "a long cart . . . and with much noise and shouting, with the blowing of a horn by one seated on top of the load, it is brought into the village. The pile is carefully constructed. . . . As the twilight deepens, the word is given to 'light her.' Then the children, join-

ing hands, will form a moving circle round the burning pile. . . . As the flame mounts higher . . . it illuminates the whole village, a fiddle is heard and the young people begin to dance. . . . I have heard that it was not unknown for some to leap over the fire."

# July 5

## The Tynwald

The Isle of Man enjoys the world's oldest continuous system of legislature. Called the Tynwald, from the Old Norse *Thingvallr,* "Field of the *Thing*" (a *thing* being an assembly or meeting), this democratic parliament is a Viking legacy. Originally a Gaelic enclave, the island was Christianized in the sixth century. From about 790 onward, a constant stream of Viking raiders came to plunder and finally to settle down. In 1079, midway through the Norse occupation, King Godred Crovan designed the Tynwald, which consisted of representatives from each of the island's districts, or "shealdings." The assembly would meet once yearly, with all freemen in attendance, to discuss old and new laws and to settle disputes, even blood feuds.

The Tynwald still meets. Every July 5, the island's lieutenant governor leads a party of officials from Saint John's Church in the city of Peel to the Tynwald Hill, a twelve-foot circular mound whose terraces are said to have been constructed in days of yore with soil carried from every far-flung corner of the island. The parliamentarians seat themselves upon the tiers, while the lieutenant governor takes the uppermost seat, the one once occupied by Norse kings. From his lofty perch, he reads a summary of all the new laws passed on the island since the last assembly. He reads them in English and then in the island's ancient native tongue, Manx. Following the Tynwald, the list of laws is sent to the Queen for royal approval.

# July 6

## Fiesta de San Fermin (Opening Day)

Érnest Hemingway made this bull-happy Spanish festival famous in his book *The Sun Also Rises*. But Pamplona's *Sanfermines* were flourishing some 450 years before Papa pronounced this "a damned fine show."

The fiesta begins at noon on July 6 and rages nonstop, twenty-four hours a day, until its climax on the 14th. A week of processions, dances, street-band concerts, and enthusiastic drinking are only the white noise underscoring the main event, the daily *encierros:* the "running of the bulls."

Every morning a rocket sounds, announcing that a number of bulls—big and alive and gimlet-horned—have been released from their corral near the Plaza San Domingo. That's the signal for incalculable numbers of virile males in tight white shirts and tighter white pants to come thundering down the street, before and behind and around the animals, who are understandably made nervous by the commotion and tend to run amok, goring people. (Women, for some reason, are officially prohibited from joining the *encierro*.)

The runners wave red handkerchiefs to further excite the bulls. They run until they reach the bull ring, where the beasts are penned up amidst howls and hysteria, and the crowd surges back on itself for more processions, concerts, dancing, and drinking until the next day's encierro with its promise of danger and death.

# July 7

## The Weaver's Festival

### Tanabata

In Japan, a country with a long tradition of arranged marriages, *Tanabata* applauds love at first sight. Both the holiday and the legend from which it derives came to Japan from China. A beautiful sky princess named Shokujo, it is said, lived in the heavens with nothing to do but sit at her loom weaving robes for her father, the sky king. Then along came Kengyo, a heavenly cowherd, driving his beasts across the clouds. Weaver and cowherd fell immediately in love and wanted to marry. The sky king forbade it. In despair, the lovers continued to meet secretly, which affected Shokujo's skill at the loom. Her father forced a confession out of her and vowed that the pair should never meet again. Later he relented, stipulating that they could meet but once a year, on the seventh day of the seventh month. When that date rolled around, the lovers hurried to their trysting place: the heavenly river, the Milky Way. But the river was too fierce to cross, and the herdboy stood sadly on one bank, the distraught weaver on the other. Suddenly, a flock of sympathetic magpies arrived and with their bodies made a living bridge that spanned the river.

On this night, the Weaver Star (aka Vega) and the Cowherd Star (aka Altair) "meet" in the skies above Japan. People celebrate with fireworks and by placing spools of colored thread on little household altars.

# July 8

## Saint Elizabeth's Day
### Santa Isabel

**P**ortugal's beloved saint, the medieval Queen Elizabeth or *Rainha Isabel*, was a virtual dynamo. Married by the age of twelve to the neglectful King Denis, Isabel bucketed about the countryside founding hospitals, "rescue homes" for women in difficult circumstances, orphanages, and convents. When their own son, Alfonso, led an armed revolt against Denis, the cool-headed Isabel plumped for a peaceful reconciliation. Many years later, as a convent-dwelling widow, she followed the selfsame Alfonso—who by that time was king of Portugal—into battle against the Castilians, whose king, strangely, was also named Alfonso. For her good deeds Isabel is remembered with many processions on her feast day. At the *Rainha Santa* or Holy Queen festival at Tinalhas, east of Fatima, chapel services are followed by a dramatic retelling of Isabel's eventful life story.

She is also fêted throughout Latin America, notably in Peru.

# July 9

## Battle-of-Sempach Day
### Sempachfeier

There was a time when the Swiss and the Austrians had a lot to fight about. On July 9, 1386, the two armies clashed near the shores of Switzerland's Lake Sempach, in the region now known as the canton of Lucerne. The Swiss were hugely outnumbered, but thanks to the self-sacrifice of one Alfred de Winkelried, they managed against all odds to defeat the Austrians.

In the land of long memories, the anniversary of this battle is a cantonal holiday, the occasion for an annual pilgrimage. The people of Sempach, some of whom are descended from those brave medieval soldiers, form a procession along with local government officials, school groups, and clergymen. Together they walk from the town to the battlefield, where a chapel now stands. There they perform a memorial service. Afterwards, speakers recite passages from chronicles of the battle, and the party marches back to town. The celebration continues with a feast, concerts, and more speeches.

# July 10

## Lady Godiva's Ride

odgifu—whose name meant "God-given" and was later modernized to Godiva—was a Saxon noblewoman married to Leofric, Duke of Mercia in England. Generous and strong-willed, Godgifu was outraged at a tax that Leofric was planning to levy on the people of Coventry. Leofric offered her a deal: If Godgifu would agree to ride naked on horseback through the town, then he would agree to cancel the tax.

Godgifu was game. "She readily consented to perform a very extraordinary act," wrote historian Paul de Rapin de Thoyras in the eighteenth century. Legend tells how the townspeople, besotted with gratitude, shielded their eyes when the lady rode through town. (The sole exception was a voyeur known to us now only as Peeping Tom; for his rudeness he was struck blind.)

Coventry hosted an annual fair. As part of the festivities, a nude woman would reenact Godiva's ride. From at least 1678 onward, the reenactment—supposedly held on the anniversary of the original ride—was a Coventry staple. The tradition continues to this day, when a partly reverent, partly whimsical procession features the flowing-tressed "Godiva" astride a white horse, flanked by nuns.

# July 11

**M**onks of the Abbey of Disentis in Switzerland's Grisons Oberland annually commemorate the martyrdom of their founder, the obscure Saint Placidus. (Generously, they throw in a simultaneous commemoration of Placidus's friend and cofounder, the equally obscure Saint Sigisbert.) Placidus was a local landowner who in the year 614 donated acreage for the building of the abbey. Then he joined the religious order and lived there as a monk. In later, unhappier times, Placidus was beheaded— on the very land he had owned and given—for having defended the abbey against its enemies. Every year, parishioners and churchmen form a procession that carries the two saints' relics from the abbey to the parish church, through the streets of the nearby village, and then back to the abbey. As they solemnly walk, the participants, many of them dressed in the local folk costume, sing the old and surprisingly extensive "Song of Saint Placidus."

# July 12

**E**ngland's exiled Catholic monarch, James I, attempted to restore Catholicism as England's state religion. This sparked such intense opposition that James's enemies invited William of Orange, the Dutch Protestant, to come to Northern Ireland (where James was exiled) and dispatch the troublesome papist. In June 1690, William set sail with a fleet of ninety ships containing ten thousand men. He landed at Carrickfergus in Ireland's County Antrim. James was waiting with his own army, just as big and just as determined. Tens of thousands of Irish Catholics had pledged to support him. But less than a month later it was curtains for James. A brutal battle on the banks of the Boyne River three miles from Drogheda on July 12 had left him no choice but to flee in shame to France. Ireland's Catholics would in ensuing centuries pay dearly for having supported him.

Thenceforth, Protestant settlers in Northern Ireland sought to cement their solidarity by forming the Orange Order, a protective and political organization whose power grew exponentially with every passing decade. Today the Orangemen head Northern Ireland's exuberant Battle of the Boyne celebrations. They march in bowler hats and sashes while military bands strike up victory tunes. The country's biggest parade is in Belfast, and it ushers in the "marching season," a month of commemorative events.

# July 13

## Feast of Santa Rosalia

### Festino di Santa Rosalia

**B**y 1624 the Black Plague was devastating Palermo, despite desperate pleas to the city's best-loved saints. Then one day a wandering hunter had a vision in which the long-dead medieval hermit, Santa Rosalia, directed him to her cave on the mountain. She gave her word that the city would be saved.

In the cave, Rosalia's relics were found, and when they had been paraded through the streets of Palermo, the plague receded, just as the saint had promised. Thenceforth, Palermo embraced her as its patron. Her annual three-day festival begins every July 13 when multitudes arrive from all over the island to watch the procession as it advances from the cathedral along the Corso to the sea.

The procession's "triumphal cart" was in times past a spectacle as fantastical as any dream, as commanding as a cathedral and nearly as large. A float, a bandstand, and a jumbo votive offering all rolled into one, the cart came in a different shape and design every year. Some years it resembled a ship, others a fortress, or a golden mountain sporting full-sized trees. Other years it resembled a massive dessert. Always it housed an orchestra.

After its eighteenth-century heyday, the festival declined. Recently revived, it now features a gold-and-copper chariot that thousands of pilgrims follow to the sea as their ancestors did in centuries past. Forty musicians in matching uniforms ride inside.

# July 14

**F**rench citizens have not always had *liberté, egalité, et fraternité* at their disposal. During the reign of Louis XVI, the French weren't citizens at all but subjects, ruled roughshod by two small but powerful elites: the callous nobility and the greedy clergy. The national treasury was bankrupt and the populace was seething in its sabots.

The emblem of all that was wrong with France was the Bastille, a grim Paris fortress that had since 1369 been the black hole into which the Crown tossed its enemies. On July 14, 1789, a howling Parisian mob stormed the Bastille, killing the guards. The mob was hoping to seize a store of ammunition with which to battle the aristocrats, but for all their trouble they found little save a handful of puzzled prisoners. Nevertheless, the riot was a springboard for what would become known as the French Revolution.

Bastille Day celebrations erupt in every French city, town, and hamlet, and among French expatriates as well. In Paris, the day begins with a hundred-cannon salute. Then comes a huge parade along the Champs-Elysées, featuring uniformed soldiers, schoolchildren, and marching bands. The tricolor flutters everywhere.

And on the other side of the world, Bastille Day festivities rage in French Tahiti.

# July 15

S within, bishop of Winchester and future saint, asked to be buried "where the feet of passersby tread and the rains of heaven fall." Upon his death, his monks obediently buried him in the churchyard, rather than inside the cathedral as properly befits a bishop.

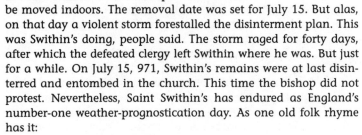

A hundred years later, however, a church official decided that the bishop's remains must be moved indoors. The removal date was set for July 15. But alas, on that day a violent storm forestalled the disinterment plan. This was Swithin's doing, people said. The storm raged for forty days, after which the defeated clergy left Swithin where he was. But just for a while. On July 15, 971, Swithin's remains were at last disinterred and entombed in the church. This time the bishop did not protest. Nevertheless, Saint Swithin's has endured as England's number-one weather-prognostication day. As one old folk rhyme has it:

> Saint Swithin's Day, if thou be fair,
> For forty days 'twill rain no mair [more].

# July 16

The Mother of God . . . you never know *where* she'll turn up. Having worked a miracle or two atop Israel's Mount Carmel, the Virgin was permanently associated with the place. As Our Lady of Carmel, she was the sacred sweetheart of the Carmelite order, a monastic confraternity first organized in 1156. The Carmelites hail her as the Flower of Carmel, the Lily of Paradise. Her main festival is July 16, now a lively holiday in many places. In Puerto Rico, a statue of the *Virgen del Carmen* is mounted on a float and carried down to the sea at Cetano, across the harbor from San Juan. All night she bobs beneficently in the water, while the islanders toast her with regattas, parades, and masquerade balls.

In Naples, they greet *La Madonna della Carmine* with street fairs and a sky asplatter with fireworks. Transplanted Neapolitans and their descendants in Brooklyn's parish of Our Lady of Mount Carmel stage an annual festival that climaxes with the arrival of the *giglio*, "lily," an eighty-five-foot, four-ton, steel-enforced, six-tiered tower that looks like an extremely vertical wedding cake. It takes 120 bearers to half-dance, half-march with it down the street. As the cherub-encrusted spire moves forward with a surprisingly rhythmic grace, a band mounted on a platform at its base launches into *O Giglio e Paradiso*, "The Lily of Paradise."

# July 17

## Aghios Marina

**M**others on Cyprus are careful to remember Saint Marina, patroness of sleeping children. They observe her feast day with candles and prayers, such as this one:

> *Saint Marina, lady who makes children sleep,*
> *Make my child go to sleep; take her for a walk abroad.*
> *And then bring her back for she is my dearest and I want her.*
> *Take her for a walk so that she may see the trees,*
> *Hear the birds chirping and see the pigeons fly;*
> *They go abroad and then come back.*
> *Take her for a walk so that she may see the roses of May*
> *And the red apples of August.*

At one of Marina's shrines on the island, a holy spring is said to flow directly from the breasts of the saint. At another, black snakes that dwell in the nearby bushes are said to be Marina herself in animal form.

It is said that the young Marina, longing to adopt the religious life, entered a monastery dressed in male clothing and calling herself Marino. Her ruse proved so successful that a local innkeeper's daughter appeared at the monastery gate with a newborn baby, naming Marino as its father. Marina/Marino unprotestingly accepted the child and cared for it, all the while maintaining her masculine disguise. When she died, her fellow monks had quite a surprise.

# July 18

## Gion Matsuri

**i**t is said that in the summer of 869, the desperate people of Kyoto built scores of enormous, elaborately decorated floats and staged a procession, hoping that this would tempt the gods to stop a plague then ravaging the city. Apparently the ploy was successful. Today the *Gion Matsuri*, commemorating that event, is probably Japan's most famous festival.

The festival lasts from July 17 to 24, during which time many processions wind their way through the main thoroughfares of the old city. The dozens of grand floats depict historical and mythic scenes and characters, including the sun goddess Amaterasu and the creation god Izanagi. The warrior empress Jingu, pregnant and clad in crimson armor, rides on her ship, bound for Korea. The floats move slowly, preceded by corps of musicians playing flutes and drums. Also in the procession are a number of portable altars—*mikoshi*—carried on the shoulders of straining youths.

# July 19

## Feast of the Redeemer
### Festa del Redentore

i t was 1575, and a plague was ravaging Venice. The people prayed, the plague ended, and Jesus *Il Redentore,* the Redeemer, was credited with saving the city-state. In his name a grand church was erected on the Giudecca, a mini-island across the Giudecca Canal from the rest of the city. And a festival was born: From 1576 onwards, Venetians have annually commemorated the end of the plague.

A row of boats is anchored tip-to-tail across the Giudecca Canal, while another row spans the Grand Canal. This way worshipers, revelers, and worshipful revelers can walk back and forth from town to the church to pay their obligatory visits. All along the waterfront, spectators cluster along decorated balconies and rooftops. Their more restless neighbors pile into boats and meander up and down the canals, hailing other sailors, friends and strangers alike. On board, they tuck into traditional dinners of sweet-sour vinegar-laced sole fillets with pine nuts and raisins—this festival's sine qua non. The boats, like the houses, are wreathed with flowers, twinkling lights, and pastel lanterns. For well over an hour, to the tune of Handel's "Water Music"—penned in 1771 especially for this fête—fireworks vault and scatter across the sky.

# July 20

## The Prophet Elijah's Day

This is the day, they say in Bulgaria, when an abominable chariot roars across the sky and threatens murderous weather. This is the day, they say in Rumania, when the thundering chariot terrifies hidden demons, who leap from their hiding places and run amok. This is the day, they say in Greece, when the chariot trails fire across the sky.

But who is the charioteer? Saint Elias, say the Greeks. Ilinden—that's Saint Elijah, say the Bulgarians. Ilie Profetul—the holy prophet Elijah, say the Rumanians. Orthodoxy has transformed the Old Testament prophet, Elijah, into a saint. And after a life fraught with wonders, so it is said, he ascended to heaven in a flaming chariot. Classical scholars, however, believe that the Orthodox Church's "Elias" is none other than the ancient Greek sun god, Helios. The god's temples, like Elias's shrines, always occupied mountain peaks and other high places, and succeeding generations of worshipers honor the two holies with similar rites.

Now in the midst of the hay-making season, the farmers of Cyprus ask Elias for good weather. They climb up to his lofty shrines carrying sunlike fried eggs as offerings. Folk stories from Cyprus tell how the very faithful can see the prophet himself at the stroke of midnight, floating around his shrines in the form of a blazing basket that bounces, glowing crimson, to the altar and then disappears.

# July 21
## Crawfish Season (Opening Day)

Finland teems with lakes, and Finnish lakes teem with crayfish. Come summer, these freshwater crustaceans (petite cousin to the lobster and second cousin, twice removed, to the cockroach) are officially big enough to eat. July 21 marks the official opening day of the crawfish season. From then on throughout the season, any specimen over ten centimeters long is fair game.

This is the day for festive crawfish feeds. The host adheres to a strict protocol when preparing *keitetyt ravut,* the boiled crawfish. Allowing upwards of ten to twenty crustaceans per guest, the host drops them, fresh-caught and squirming, into a pot of boiling water, head first. Salt, sugar, and dill boil along with the crawfish, which are then set aside to marinate. (Some cooks add garlic and beer at this point.) In the silvery dusk they are served, cold, on a long picnic table overlooking the lake from which they came. Protocol applies to eating as well as cooking. Diners must suck the juice from the leg joints, then pick the white flesh from the claws. Then and only then, according to ritual, can the precious tail be scooped from its shell, spread on buttered toast, sprinkled with extra dill, and eaten. A quick shot of cold beer or schnapps accompanies—"honors," they say—each tail as it goes down. Smart partyers search among the crimson pile for the specimens with especially broad "hips." These are the female crawfish, and it is said that they taste best of all.

# July 22

## Saint Mary Magdalene's Day

### Fête de la Madeleine

**W**hile her sister, Saint Martha, was subduing monsters on the banks of the Rhone (see July 29), Mary Magdalene had her own fish to fry. The sisters, along with their brother, Lazarus, and others, had allegedly arrived on the southern French shore in a little boat not long after the Crucifixion. Still striving to do penance for what she perceived as a life of sin, *la Madeleine* made her way eastward until she came to a forest, where she met some angels who carried her to a high grotto now known as Sainte Baume, "holy cave," after the Provençal word for cave, *bauomo*. There, with only crucifix and psalm book for company (the angels having soon departed), la Madeleine lay fasting, praying, and meditating, nude, for—depending on which account you prefer—seven years, fourteen years, thirty years, or thirty-three years. When at last she died, it is said, her soul took the form of a dove and flew away.

Ever since the Middle Ages, pilgrims have marked her feast day, the supposed anniversary of her death, by climbing up to the grotto, which is hewn out of solid rock. The pilgrimage to Sainte Baume is reputed to be especially beneficial to young couples and to young women hoping to be soon engaged. The old custom was to build little hills of stones along the path to the cave; these announced the builder's desire for a fruitful union.

# July 23

## The Mysteries of Santa Cristina

### I Misteri di Santa Cristina

*C*ristina smashed a roomful of gold and silver statues of gods and goddesses belonging to her father, a Roman prefect at Bolsena, Italy. Then Cristina distributed the precious metal to local beggars. For this, her father threatened her with torture. Cristina scoffed. Cristina was torn with iron hooks, spun on a Catherine wheel, then singed in a roaring oil fire. When she survived even this, she was cast into the sea with a millstone around her neck. Cristina bobbed to the surface, praying. Her father was outraged. Cristina taunted him. He ordered her beheaded. For one reason and another, attempts were unsuccessful. But Cristina was subsequently boiled in pitch and rosin, then locked for five days in a blazing furnace. Then poisonous snakes were draped around her shoulders. Yet Cristina lived. Her breasts were slashed off, as was her tongue, which Cristina saucily threw at one of her persecutors, managing to put out his eye with it. Finally someone shot her in the flank with an arrow, and she died.

Every year on her feast day, the residents of Bolsena perform Cristina's story. The costumed actors proceed from one end of town to the other, pausing at intervals so that the maiden portraying Cristina can be beaten, boiled, and so on. Half the tortures are reenacted on the night of the 23rd; the other half on the 24th.

# July 24

## Mormon Pioneer Day

Via wagon train, Mormons made their way west. Their leader Joseph Smith, who had discovered a cryptic set of gold tablets in upstate New York in 1830, had been arrested for treason and killed by an angry mob while awaiting trial in Illinois. Now headed by church president Brigham Young, a party struck out in 1846 for a new "stake of Zion." Just as the trek began to seem hopeless, Young leaped out of his wagon and delivered the now-famous statement, "This is the place." The place was Utah's Great Salt Lake Valley, which the Latter-Day Saints, as they call themselves, have dominated spiritually and culturally from that day to this.

Pioneer Day, established in 1849, two years after the first Mormons' arrival, is a legal holiday in Utah (a state that, if the Mormons had had their way, would instead have been called Deseret). It is also observed by Mormon communities in Wyoming, Nevada, Arizona, and Idaho. The first Pioneer Day rally featured a huge banner reading Hail to Our Chieftain. Today's festivities include such Western favorites as barbecues, picnics, cookouts, square dances, period-costume parades, rodeos, and cannon salutes, as well as sidewalk variety shows, Pioneer Princess coronations, and reenactments of Mormon pioneer stories.

# July 25

*A*lthough Jesus' flesh-and-blood cousin, the apostle James, was beheaded in Jerusalem, his body was inexplicably "discovered" at Compostela in northern Spain in the year 813. A shrine went up on the spot; it emerged as Europe's primary pilgrimage destination, beloved by kings and queens.

Customs and traditions sprang from James' cult. His emblem, replicas of which even modern-day pilgrims pin to their lapels, is a cockleshell. Hence the reason Coquilles Saint Jacques are called that. In nineteenth-century London, July 25 was "Oyster Day," the opening of the oyster-eating season. As empty shells piled up in gutters, outside restaurants, and alongside vendors' booths, children would collect them and pile them into sidewalk grottoes. They would beg passersby for pennies with which to buy candles that they would then light in honor of the saint.

# July 26

**I**n 1623 Saint Anne, mother of the Virgin Mary, appeared in a vision to a Breton peasant named Yves Nicolazic. She urged him to rebuild a run-down chapel some three miles north of the town of Auray. With some friends, Nicolazic did so. While work was under way, a statue of Saint Anne surfaced inexplicably near the construction site. This discovery sparked devotion that flourishes to this day.

A uniquely Breton form of reverence, *pardons* are annual pilgrimages at which penitents ask the saint to pardon their sins. Saint Anne's pardon is one of the region's largest, drawing over 25,000 worshipers every year. After attending mass in the basilica, pilgrims proceed to climb the *Scala Sancta,* the sacred staircase, that leads up to the cubicle housing Saint Anne's statue. At the altar they light candles, imploring motherly Anne to protect their homes, their property, and all the ships at sea.

Appropriately, Anne's feast day (*Anna Napja*) is celebrated as a kind of Mother's Day in Hungary. In times of yore, wealthy families hosted "Anna balls" and churches sponsored "Anna fairs" where vendors offered pastries and other gifts that people might buy for their mothers.

# July 27

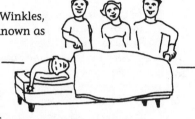

*A* septet of pious Rip Van Winkles, the men who came to be known as the Seven Sleepers had the misfortune of being devout Christians in third-century Turkey in the midst of Emperor Decian's anti-Christian persecutions. The seven fled their homes with the emperor's henchmen in hot pursuit. They ducked into a cave and launched into prayer, preparing for what seemed their imminent martyrdom. They shared what they believed would be their last meal. Then they all lay down to sleep, believing that Decian's men would discover them at any moment. But as miracles will have it, they slept undisturbed for 208 years. By the time they awoke and emerged from the cave, Decian had not only stopped looking for them, he was long since deceased. The current emperor, a Christian, hailed the Seven Sleepers as saints and kissed them, at which point they all lay down and died.

Sleepyhead Day marks the Seven Sleepers' collective feast day in Naantali, southwestern Finland. Soon after dawn, howling revelers fill the streets, headed for the home of the current year's "Sleepyhead": some unsuspecting local celebrity. An official waking-up party is let into the house; the Sleepyhead is roused rudely, hauled out of bed, marched down to the town's harbor, and tossed into the drink.

# July 28

**P**eru, the indigenous home of potatoes and Incas, was distinguished with a high degree of human culture, artisanship, and social welfare by the time the Spanish *conquistadores* arrived in the sixteenth century. One Spaniard, reporting on his first impressions of Peru, marveled, "No one went hungry in that land." The Conquest ensued. On July 28, 1821, Peru—by this time a mixed-blood, mixed-culture land—declared its independence from Spain. This sparked a war, and independence was not entirely won until 1824.

All over the country, Peruvians celebrate with two full days of festivities including bullfights, fireworks, parades, exhibitions, and fairs, often emphasizing national products and indigenous foods and crafts.

In the Misti Indian village of Curahuasi, the people have been known to celebrate Independence Day with greased-pole-climbing contests and bull-and-condor fights.

# July 29

## Saint Martha and the Dragon

### Sainte-Marthe-et-Tarasque

Saint Martha sailed to the south of France, it is said, in the year 48 C.E. in a small boat. She was on hand when a vicious half-lion, half-dragon called the Tarasque began terrorizing the people of Provence, capsizing vessels in the Rhone, and plucking cattle and men from the shore like so many Ritz crackers. Martha, it is said, subdued the monster and tied it up with her belt. Then she stepped aside to let the locals perform the actual slaughter.

In 1400 King René d'Anjou instituted an annual miracle play to commemorate Martha's feat. This would be enacted on Martha's feast day, in the town of Tarascon, where the saint is entombed. Attending a performance forty-four years later, King Louis XI enjoyed himself immensely.

With the passing centuries, the play gave way to a festival in which a mock Tarasque rushed about, stamping and roaring and belching smoke, and finally let itself be led quietly along on a satin-ribbon leash held by a little girl. Today the festival features a fifteen-foot Tarasque, its ivy-green humpback studded with angry red spikes. Above its ravenous mouth is a remarkably human nose and two eyes "redder than cinnabar," as the Provençal poet Frederic Mistral once wrote.

# July 30
## Saints Abdon and Sennen's Day

These two Persians, who were possibly servants, took it upon themselves to attend their fellow Christians who during Diocletian's persecutions had been imprisoned and sentenced to death. Abdon and Sennen, it is recounted, fastidiously went about burying the martyrs as they piled up. Finally they too were arrested and hauled to Rome as prisoners. There they were given the opportunity to save themselves by sacrificing to the Roman gods, but as they chose instead to spit on the gods' statues, they were thrown to wild beasts and finally hewn into pieces by gladiators. Possibly because their own corpses were buried once, disinterred, repackaged, and ceremoniously reburied, they are hailed

as the patron saints of barrel makers, who mark the pair's feast day as do other worshipers, notably in Rome and Florence, where the saints' relics are said to rest.

# July 31

## Saint Ignatius's Day
### San Ignacio

*A*s a young Spanish nobleman dawdling in the court of King Ferdinand, Ignatius was fond of games, chivalry, and military pursuits. He was frustrated indeed when he was struck in the leg by a cannonball and became bedridden.

When he had recovered, however, Ignatius shed his former bravado and embraced the religious life in earnest. Never formally educated, he began taking classes with elementary school children in Barcelona when he was thirty-three. Eleven years later, now a master of arts and nearly a priest, he gathered six like-minded friends around him and together they made a vow of poverty and chastity. This group was to evolve into Ignatius's "Company of Jesus," or in Latin the *Societas Jesu,* which in turn came to be known as the Jesuits. Dedicated to missionizing and education, the Jesuits have attracted more official criticism than any other religious order, having been expelled from more countries more often (five times from Spain alone) than any other.

As a native of the Basque region, Ignatius is beloved by Basques worldwide, who treasure him as their patron. Festivals honor him in the Basque capital, Bilbao, as well as in American towns with significant Basque populations.

# Moveable Feast

**R**amadan is the name of the ninth month of the Muslim calendar—a lunar calendar whose months change in thirty-three-year cycles—so in one year the holiday might fall in one season, the next year another. It is said that on the twenty-seventh day of Ramadan, Allah sent the Koran to Mohammed from Heaven, and at the same time, the tree of Paradise trembled. To mark these momentous events, Muslims fast for forty days. By night they may eat; in fact, they feast. But from dawn to dusk—or in Mohammed's words, "while it is possible to distinguish the white thread from the black"—they abstain from all food and drink, as well as snuff and tobacco.

The days are hard, especially in those years when Ramadan falls during a demanding harvest season. The boom of a gun or a cannon signals the dusk and the start of evening prayers, after which the famished celebrants break the fast with a quick handful of dates or nuts, or a glass of orange juice. The evening meal varies from place to place: in Morocco, the favorite Ramadan dish is *harira*, a hearty vegetable soup made with lamb, noodles, and much red pepper.

# August 1

*A* crucial spoke on the wheel of Europe's agricultural year, Lammas is bittersweet, mingling the joy of the year's first harvest with the inevitable surety that summer will soon be over. As the sheaves are brought in, the harvesters know that the sun blazing overhead is already "dying," descending day by day from its midsummer glory.

Agricultural societies worldwide have their own "first fruits" rites—in which the deities are thanked for a good harvest and ritually offered a sample of the harvest's best. The Celts' version of this was called *Lughnasadh,* after the god of light, Lugh, he of the golden shield and golden hair, in whose honor every August the Celts staged a whole month of postharvest sports and games. Lughnasadh was observed throughout the British Isles and presumably also at Lyon, Leon, Leiden, and Loudun, not to mention Carlisle and even Vienna, all cities named for the golden god. The Anglo-Saxons called their first-fruits holiday *hlaf-masse,* "loaf-mass." They would bring bread made from the newly harvested wheat to church for the priest to bless. By the Middle Ages, this rite, now called *Lammas,* was officially fixed to August 1. At village churches throughout England, sheaves of wheat were offered alongside loaves on the altar, and parishioners brought their own consecrated bread back home. One medieval charm enjoined the faithful to "take from this hallowed bread made on Lammas Day, four pieces, and crumble them on the four corners of the barn."

# August 2

## Porcíngula

While some of the Native American Pueblos of New Mexico, such as Taos, are very well known, others are obscure, and some have even been abandoned postconquest. Pecos Pueblo, abandoned in 1838, was one of these. The refugees came to live at nearby Jemez Pueblo, and they brought their patron saint, Santa María de Los Angeles de Porcíngula, coincidentally the same Virgin after whom Los Angeles, California, was named. To mark her feast day and to honor the Pecos heritage that has by now mingled with their own, the people of Jemez hold a fiesta, preceded by four days of secret kiva rites. The main event of the fiesta is the "Pecos Bull" dance. The dancer portraying the bull wears a black cape with white spots and an expressionistic "bull" head made of sheepskin, with a pendulous red tongue.

Other dancers portray the bull baiters, and they poke and taunt their prey, which fights back heroically, occasionally bowing out for a brief visit to Porcíngula's altar. As the fiesta wears on, a line of white-clad chanters emerges from the kiva; a Catholic priest recites the mass; more dancers appear, then recede. At last all sit down to a feast, wary lest the "bull" mischievously knock over the table.

# August 3

The richness of August has from ancient times been a big deal in Greece. Grapes and figs hang fat and syrup-sweet on the branches; melons lie luminous on the vine. Folklorists tell how Greeks in various parts of the country endeavor to welcome the month. On the isle of Lesbos, for example, bonfires are erected at crossroads, and revelers leap across the flames crying, "August! Figs and walnuts!" Elsewhere, Greeks celebrate with thorough house cleanings, all-night parties in the vineyards, and offerings to the spirits of the dead. All over Greece, August 1 marks the start of a meat-free fasting period that lasts until Assumption Day on the 15th.

The first three days of August (like those of March) are called *Drimes,* and while they usher in a favorite month, they also have a sinister reputation, possibly because August (like March) is a transitional month in the Greek scheme of things. Numerous sayings attest to this: "August has come—the first step of winter"; "Winter begins in August, summer in March." During the  Drimes, people avoid certain activities, such as chopping wood, shampooing hair, swimming in the sea, and (children especially) going out in the noonday sun. The third day of August in particular resonates with meteorological significance. Good weather on the 3rd, they say, assures good weather for the next three months.

# August 4

## Cook Islands Constitution Celebrations

Like gobbets of pancake batter spattered across a griddle, the Cook Islands' 93 square miles of land occupy a whopping 850,000 square miles of Pacific Ocean. Rarotonga, the main island and home to half the Cook Islands' total population of 20,000, was "discovered" by Captain James Cook in the late eighteenth century.

Bounced back and forth between various absentee chaperones, the Cooks were annexed to New Zealand in 1900 and finally achieved their independence on August 4, 1965. The self-governing islands now celebrate the date every year with two weeks of festivities. These Constitution Celebrations are a time for reinforcing traditional island culture—and each of the Cooks, no matter how small, has its own. Song-and-dance concerts are a festival favorite: the flower-decked, raffia-skirted, whirling-hipped men and women, keeping time to percussive rhythms on drums and woodblocks, keep alive a musical tradition that is a cousin to Hawai'i's hula. On Constitution Day itself, agriculture expos showcase local produce, and prizes are awarded in many categories, such as to "the small farmers' best beast." Handicraft shows, rugby matches, and traditional island sports round out the two weeks.

# August 5

## Grasmere Rushbearing

The floors of old stone churches can get pretty cold, a fact well known among churchgoers obliged to kneel upon them. Several centuries ago, the sensible Britons hit upon a solution: They could insulate the chilly floors with coatings—"strewings," they called them—of fresh-cut rushes, straw, or hay. By the early nineteenth century, rushbearings and haystrewings had become lively annual rituals throughout northwestern England. At such an event, a team of costumed men would pull the heavily laden "rushcarts." These were adorned with dazzling silver ornaments and had ropes ingeniously braided from rushes. Morris dancers capered down the street, heralding the cart's approach.

The region's best-known and longest-lived rushbearing is the one at Grasmere, Cumbria, held in honor of Saint Oswald (cousin of saints Oswin and Oswy), a seventh-century king of Northumbria. At the festival, girls in green pinafores carry the rushes on a broad, handwoven linen sheet. Other townspeople bring "bearings," woven rush emblems in the shape of Oswald's crown, his hand, and other designs. These are later used to decorate the altar while the rushes from the sheet are spread across the floor. After the service, with its "Rushbearing Hymn," parishioners line up for slices of "Saint Oswald's gingerbread," a sort of gingery shortbread.

# August 6

## Hiroshima Peace Ceremony

### Genbaku Kinenbi

The atomic bomb, whose makers had puckishly named it Little Boy, fell on Hiroshima at 8:15 A.M. on August 6, 1945, and within minutes wiped out some 75,000 lives. Thousands more perished in the fires that swept the ruined city, and tens of thousands more died of radiation sickness afterward, and of bomb-related cancers. Even in thriving, reconstructed Hiroshima, where the Peace Memorial Park with its origami-draped  Children's Peace Memorial and its grisly A-Bomb Museum stands like a beacon of optimism directly over Ground Zero . . . even here and now, Little Boy continues to pluck off its victims one by one.

An arched cenotaph in the park bears the names of all those known to have died from the bomb and its effects. As part of the peace ceremony, a sheaf of new names is added to the roster every year. People from all over the world gather for the city-sponsored ceremonies, which begin with an 8:15 A.M. memorial service in the park. Silent prayer vigils and peace rallies sustain the anniversary's pacifist, sad-but-hopeful aura. After dark, the crowd performs a traditional Buddhist rite, placing on the waters of the Ota River some ten thousand tiny paper lanterns, each on its own delicate bamboo raft. The lanterns light the way for the souls of those killed by the bomb, keeping them company as they flow from this world to the next.

# August 7

U p and down the streets of Aomori, Japan, rages an annual week-long bacchanal, as urgently hilarious now as when it was instituted 1,200 years ago. Exactly how the *Nebuta* began remains a mystery. The festival's centerpiece is a collection of floats—enormous paper, bamboo, and wire constructions illuminated from within like outsize lampshades. These travel on wheeled carts. The floats bear stylized, Kabuki-ish images of ancient warriors' faces, eyes ablaze and eyebrows flailing, and the faces of mythical monsters, all fang and flared nostril. Thousands of people descend on the town, and with the help of free saké distributed on street corners they dance for days and nights on end, chanting the traditional "*Ra-se, ra-se, ra-se, ra-a-a-a!*" This festival is especially popular with the young.

The general consensus is that during the ninth century, Japan's "barbarian-quelling shogun," Sakanoue Tamuramaro, used floats like these to terrify his enemies (who were probably, in fact, the aboriginal Ainus). Today's festival retains the giddy bravado of a victory march. But some folklorists suggest that *Nebuta*—also celebrated in nearby Hirosaki under the name *Neputa,* with a *p*—stems from the old rite of *neburi-nagashi,* "casting away sleep," in which the spirits of sleep were symbolically set adrift on a body of water. Late summer's drowsy, paralytic heat was considered dangerous.

# August 8

By Japanese reckonings, the 7th and 8th days of August are the "dog days": the year's hottest, fraught with pestilence, lethargy, and fever. In times past, the dog days were loathed and dreaded, inspiring such lines as the poet Soseki's:

> *Dreaming of shouting cicadas*
> *I waken, parched. . . .*

To stay healthy through this brief but perilous time, it was customary to eat lots of eels: believed to be highly nutritious, refreshing, and in their slippery fishiness evocative of a deep and placid cool.

Today, eels are popular in summer, either canned or fresh. In small towns, the eel peddler still makes his rounds with a sloshing tubful of live eels, on a wheeled cart. As per tradition, he kills and cleans them for his customers, who take them home and cook them.

# August 9

## Genbaku Kinenbi

Were it not for cloudy weather on the morning of August 9, 1945, a 4.5-ton atomic bomb would have dropped on the city of Kokura in far northeastern Kyushu. Instead, it dropped on Nagasaki, the American bombardiers' secondary target. The city lost a third of its buildings and about a third of its population as well. While Little Boy was the name its designers had given the bomb dropped on Hiroshima three days earlier, the one that hit Nagasaki had been named Fat Man—and rightly so; the latter bomb was nearly twice as big, and twice as explosive, as its predecessor. Everything within a half-mile radius of the Nagasaki target was flattened. Soon fires had eaten their way across another two miles.

The epicenter was Nagasaki's Urakami suburb, once the site of Asia's largest Catholic church. Ironically, Urakami's cathedral, a smug outpost of Western culture, was leveled in the August 9 bombardment. Urakami now has a four-story A-Bomb Museum, the *Kokusai Bunka Kaikan*. Nearby is Hypocenter Peace Park, with its Nagasaki Peace Statue. Peace Park is the scene of the annual memorial ceremony and prayer vigil. An anti-nuclear demonstration draws thousands of sympathetic participants from far and wide.

# August 10

## Saint Lawrence's Day

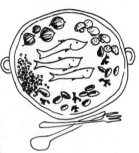

"**T**his side is done now," Saint Lawrence reportedly said to the Roman soldiers who were roasting him alive on a red-hot iron grid. "You can turn me over." The third-century archdeacon was quick with quips. In fact, sarcasm is what landed him on the griddle. Perversely, Lawrence is now revered as the patron saint of cooks. A custom in Spain and Italy is to avoid eating roasted or grilled foods on his feast day, substituting raw dishes such as *gazpacho*.

At a morning mass held in the cathedral at Pointe-a-Pitre on the Caribbean island of Guadeloupe, a priest blesses the food that will later be used at the annual chefs' festival, the *Fête des Cuisinieres.* After church, Saint Lawrence's statue heads a whimsical procession in which cadres of dancers march to a *beguine* beat with spatulas and other cooking implements dangling from their calico turbans. When the party reaches the town's assembly hall, the *cuisinieres*—island women who annually present and even pay for the event—go inside and start cooking. They prepare vast quantities of local dishes such as wine-stewed rabbit, *saucissons,* a fish-stuffed bread, French pastries, rum punch, and—since they are not as squeamish as their Mediterranean counterparts—grilled clams. Late in the afternoon, the doors swing open and the islanders come in to eat, five hundred at a time. Saint Lawrence's statue occupies the place of honor at the head table.

# August 11

**M**odern-day revelers can only guess at the meaning of King Puck, the virile (but tame) male goat that presides over the annual Puck Fair in Killorglin, just west of Killarney, Ireland. King Puck stands on a lofty platform overlooking the proceedings. His whorling horns frame a shiny gold crown; regal purple robes drape hairy shoulders. City officials take turns sweeping the platform and refreshing the fodder trough as the beast mildly munches its way through the three-day event, a Killorglin institution since 1613.

August 10 is "gathering day," on which the crowned goat is paraded through town and installed on the royal platform. The 11th is fair day proper, on which livestock dealers from all over the region arrive for vigorous buying and selling. On the third day, "scattering day," the goat is ceremoniously disrobed, dethroned, and sent back into the fields at sunset.

Although modern fairgoers look on King Puck with a humorous eye, the animal may well be the descendant of some ancient pagan goat god. Or perhaps it is an homage, as some suggest, to the herd of goats that once warned the people of Killorglin that an invading army was on its way. But why "Puck"? No one knows for sure.

# August 12

**L**ong before a Spanish boot ever scuffled across American soil, the native people we now call Pueblo Indians—in their settlements along what we now call the Rio Grande—were celebrating their own festivals in their own ways, at the same times every year. Upon arriving in a native village, the Spanish priests, bent on conversion, scoured their Catholic calendars for a saint whose feast day corresponded with the date of that village's primary festival.

Hence Santa Clara Pueblo, whose original name was K'hapoo—"where the wild roses grow near the water." On Saint Claire's feast day, after a morning mass in the village church, everyone retires to the plaza for the corn dance. In Pueblo culture, corn is both symbol and staple. Now, at the peak of the dry season, this dance is a prayer for rain, evoking the planting, sprouting, maturing, and harvesting of the corn crop—all phases entirely dependent on adequate rainfall.

As the corn dance begins, four runners head off in the cardinal directions, then return to the center. Double lines of dancers, men and women both, stamp to the rhythm of a big willow drum. The men wear tufts of pine lashed to their arms, and they stamp hard and quick. The women move across the dust more subtly, their wooden headdresses cut and painted to represent sky and cloud. They carry the heavens on their heads.

# August 13

**O**-*bon*, Japan's three-day version of Day of the Dead, is not spooky but dreamy, warm, and poetic. Celebrated by some people from July 13 through 15 and others from August 13 through 15, O-bon gets its name from the Sanskrit word for "to hang upside down." It refers to a legend about a Buddhist monk who, deep in meditation, was able to "see" his long-dead mother hanging upside down in the Buddhist version of hell. This was her punishment for having eaten meat during her lifetime—a Buddhist taboo—and refusing to repent of it. The monk was holy enough to go to hell and buy his mother's passage to Nirvana with some of his own excess goodness.

On the first day of O-bon, people decorate their loved ones' graves with fruit, cakes, and lanterns. On the second day, spirit altars, *tamadana,* are assembled at home: Atop a woven rush mat stand the ancestors' memorial plaques, tempting vegetarian dishes, and cucumbers carved to represent horses on which the spirits are invited to ride. On the third day, whole communities gather—often in the middle of the street—for the *bon-odori,* a hypnotic, slow dance that moves in concentric circles or multiple lines. Hundreds of people often dance together. As evening falls, tiny paper lanterns are set adrift on river or sea: These *omiyage* gently light the spirits' way back to the "other shore."

# August 14

*A*ssumption Day squats in the middle of *Ferragosto,* Italy's traditional mid-August holiday, which takes its name from the Roman Emperor Augustus's own personal *feriae augustae.*

Assumption Eve finds the people of Cortona, Tuscany, celebrating with a gargantuan cookout. Masses of local beef sizzle on what has been identified as Italy's largest grill. The same day finds Sardinians in the town of Sassari carrying a series of 800-pound wooden towers down the street in honor of the Virgin. And Messina, on the eastern tip of Sicily, celebrates *Ferragosto* with a three-day festival that features a procession with a sixty-foot wooden pyramid from which, in times of yore, live children swung, impersonating angels and saints. In *Celebrating Italy,* Carol Field notes that a local girl dressed as the Virgin Mary used to free a real-live prisoner from jail every year to complete the festivities. Today the revelers haul out *I Giganti,* a pair of twenty-seven-foot papier-mâché giants that represent Messina's legendary founders, Mata and Grifone. Motherly Mata is golden blonde; her swashbuckling Saracen husband, Grifone, is black.

# August 15

Compared to the hullabaloo surrounding her son's death, the demise of the Virgin Mary is cloaked in eternal mystery. While history—and the Bible—fails to record exactly where she died, or when, how, or what happened afterwards, apocryphal legend tells how her body, too holy for the humiliating process of postmortem putrefaction, simply ascended, whole, to heaven.

The anniversary of Mary's assumption was being celebrated in Roman churches as early as the sixth century; it was a major festival by the ninth century, and by now it has taken hold as the year's most prominent Marian rite. Assumption Day is celebrated by Catholics worldwide, especially in Europe where, historians have pointed out, it supplanted harvest festivals including a Mediterranean rite in honor of the goddess Diana that had been observed on the middle day, the *ides*, of August.

Assumption Day is the year's biggest holiday on the Greek island of Kefalonia, where in the town of Markopoulo thousands of harmless little snakes with cross-shaped black markings on their heads come writhing in from the hills. The serpents make directly for the church, where the faithful hug them and include them in the day's religious service. The snakes time their arrival perfectly every year.

# August 16

Saint Roch—aka Roche, Rock, Rocke, Roque, and Rocco—is hailed as a miraculous healer. Born to noble parents in Montpellier, France, in the fourteenth century, Roch turned pilgrim as a young man and traveled south to Italy, where the bubonic plague was raging. In the town whose Latin name was Aquapendus—"hanging water"—Roch vowed to serve the sick, against the protestations of a kindly local official who "dreaded lest Rocke, which was a young flowering man should be smitten with the pestilence," as Caxton's *Golden Legend* tells us. Roch cured people, then went on to cure sufferers in Rome and other cities. He was, of course, courting disaster: He caught the plague himself, "and he thereof gave thankings to our Lord ... saying, O Jesu ... I thank thee that thou puttest me to affliction like thine other servants." He was not to die of the plague, however. A friend's dog nursed him back to health.

Florence's San Rocco procession features marchers in fourteenth-century costume. Bread bakers in Villa Santo Stefano in the Abruzzo region used to produce a bread for the occasion called *pagnata de San Rocco;* now the town's festival features a spicy chickpea soup instead. The healer is honored in Tarija, Bolivia, where feather-bedecked revelers at the *San Roque fiesta* welcome dogs to join the festivities.

# August 17

**O**ne thing is certain: On this day every year, at the bridge called Pons Aemilius, the Romans celebrated the *Portunalia* in honor of their god, Portunus. Millennia being what they are, however, the thing we don't know is exactly what sort of god Portunus was. Nor do we know much about his rites, or where the bridge was.

Portunus did have his own priesthood, and his own *flamen* or high priest, who may (or may not) have been a plebeian, and who did something or other with grease. (An ancient text makes an oblique reference to *unguit*.) Yet another citation, which classicist W. Warde Fowler calls "a curious but mutilated note," hints that Portunus may have been a god of gates (that is, portals), and, by extension, keys: specifically the keys that secured the official grain storehouses. "We can hardly avoid the conclusion," Fowler asserts, "that something was done to keys on this day." Possibly, important keys, which were very old and made of hardwood, were repaired on this day.

This was the Romans' harvest time. Naturally people would be thinking much just now about their gates and the locks and keys that would safeguard the fruits of their labors. "It is not unlikely," Fowler concludes, "that the word *portus* originally meant a safe place of any kind, and only as civilization advanced became specially appropriated to harbors"—that is, ports.

# August 18

**B**orn of humble parentage, Helen married an emperor—Constantius—and then gave birth to yet another emperor, Constantine. But when her son was still a teenager, Helen's husband abandoned her—for political reasons, we are told. Constantine gallantly stood by his mother, who converted to Christianity, traveled to the Holy Land, did a bit of exploratory spadework around the hill of Calvary, and, we are told, discovered the cross on which Jesus had been crucified. This she endeavored to bring back to Constantinople. Subsequent centuries found shards, chips, and slivers of the so-called True Cross (aka *Santa Cruz, Santa Croce, Saint-Croix,* and Holy Rood) enshrined in churches all over the Christian world. As the discoverer of the cross, Saint Helen has enjoyed much veneration. (See May 3 and September 14, which are both celebrated as Holy Cross Day in different parts of the world.)

On her feast day, all of her countless Mexican namesakes—all the Elenas—reserve the right to throw themselves a name-day party, with serenading mariachis, a *piñata,* and streams of well-wishers in and out of the house all day. Similarly, all the French Helenes are entitled to special treatment on their namesake's feast day.

# August 19

The *Vinalia,* aka the *Vinalia Rustica,* was everything its name suggests—a rustic alfresco rite, the vineyardman's holiday, the vintage, the Roman vintner's first fruits. On this day every year, the priest called the *Flamen Dialis* performed the *auspicatio vindemiae*—that is, he plucked the year's first ripe grapes and prayed and sacrificed to the gods, asking that they protect and bless the entirety of the crop. This was, after all, the start of the two diciest weeks in the vintner's year: The grapes hung ripe and fully formed on the vine, but a sudden storm or outbreak of blight could demolish them before they were harvested, thus ruining the grower's months of hard work.

Historians are undecided as to how this wine festival came to be linked with the love goddess Venus. Her dominions were of an emotional and venereal nature rather than an agricultural one. Nevertheless, documents attest that the Vinalia was held in her honor and that she was invoked on this day. Was it mere coincidence that Venus's temple in the Circus Maximus (built with funds extracted from Roman matrons who had been fined for adultery) was officially dedicated on August 19, in the year 295 B.C.E.—the date of the Vinalia? Some suggest that as an extension of her ripe and voluptuous charms, Venus also ruled growing plants.

# August 20

## Szent Istvan Napja

Saint Stephen of Hungary, one of Christendom's half-dozen Saint Stephens, was well connected. The son of a duke, Stephen was baptized by a future saint, and married to the sister of both another future saint and an emperor. In 1001 Stephen was himself crowned Hungary's first king; his son, Prince Imre (aka Emeric) died young and then was sainted anyway.

Born at Esztergom circa 975, Stephen is credited with the Christianization of Hungary. His conversion methods were often characterized by the charmless brutality of his era; nonetheless, they proved successful. As a result, Stephen's feast day is one of Hungary's oldest and most beloved national holidays. Hundreds of years ago, the roads would be jammed with pilgrims from all over the countryside. Everyone was bound for Buda, where the saint's preserved hand in its gold-and-glass reliquary was carried in procession amidst regal splendor from the Chapel of the Royal Palace—where it had been installed in 1083—to the Coronation Church.

Twentieth-century Saint Stephen's Day celebrations also feature sporting events, folk music concerts, fireworks, parades, military bands and revues, flower shows, and performances of folk theater. Festive meals often center around chicken *paprikas* and end with *gesztenyekrem*—a blend of chestnut puree, egg yolk, rum or brandy, sugar, and whipped cream.

# ✿August 21

*Consualia*

**i**n Rome's Circus Maximus, the sacred altar of the god Consus was buried underground. As the deity of sowing, the lord of seeds, to whose efforts are owed every harvest, he would naturally inhabit a subterranean domain; his potency lurked below the surface of the earth.

The altar was uncovered on only two days every year, Consus's festivals on August 21 and December 15. The August festival was a harvest rite, the chronicler Tertullian tells us. A sacrifice was performed over the altar by the high priest of the god Quirinus, since Consus did not have a priesthood of his own. The Vestal Virgins were also in attendance.

The *Consualia* was a horses' holiday. Horses and mules, beasts of burden who had worked hard all throughout the agricultural year, were now freed from chores. They were unbridled, garlanded with flowers, and raced in the Circus Maximus.

# August 22
## Feast of the Queenship of Mary

The Virgin Mary has many nicknames—Star of the Sea, God-bearer, Our Lady, and so on. One of the most popular of these (stolen, unquestionably, from Isis, whose adherents called her that long before Jesus was even a twinkle in his father's eye) was Queen of Heaven. In the summer of 1954, Pope Pius XII decided to make that moniker official. In a document titled *Ad Caeli Reginam,* "To the Queen of Heaven," the pontiff decreed that thenceforth, August 22 would be recognized as the Church's Feast of the Queenship of Mary, to be "celebrated throughout the world yearly."

On this holiday, he hoped, "there [will] be renewed the consecration of the human race to the immaculate heart of the Blessed Virgin Mary." Church services on the Queenship festival include relevant liturgies, such as the one that begins, "The Queen stands at your right hand arrayed in cloth and gold," and goes on to exhort, "Our Queen and Mother: with the support of her prayers may we come to share the glory."

# August 23
## Paper Costume Parade & Holy Bath
### Cortejo de Papel e Banho Santo

*A* paper suit is a risky thing to wear to the beach. It's even riskier if you plan to go into the water. But that doesn't matter to the people of Oporto, northern Portugal. Every year on the eve of Saint Bartholomew's Day they happily don their colorful paper outfits and swarm down to the strand en masse. One costumed man, designated Neptune-for-a-day, presides over a sprawling mock battle between paper-clad "pirates" and equally paper-clad "landlubbers." (Rr-r-r-ip!) Afterwards, "Neptune" rides his carriage straight into the waves and everyone piles in after him.

The procession starts in Oporto's Foz do Douro district and winds up at Ourigo Beach. Locals maintain that their festival, flimsy garb and all, is of ancient origin, and that the communal dip taken this day is a "holy bath," worth seven ordinary baths in its power to cleanse the swimmer of evil and sin.

# August 24

Although Saint Bartholomew's Bun Race takes place on Saint Bartholomew's Day at Saint Bartholomew's Hospital (near Sandwich on England's Kentish coast), Saint Bartholomew himself has virtually nothing to do with the proceedings. The race happens on this day because on August 24, 1217, a sea battle took place offshore from Sandwich, in which British ships beat back a French invasion headed by a piratical sorcerer called Eustace the Monk. The battle was so important that its anniversary, coincidentally Saint Bartholomew's Day, gave its name to the local hospital, which was not a hospital in the modern sense but an almshouse, a place of charity. Now it is a senior citizens' community centered around a thirteenth-century chapel.

Every August 24, Sandwich's mayor pays a ceremonial visit to the residents, then attends a service in the old chapel commemorating the great battle. Afterwards, local children gather for the "race," which really isn't a race since all they have to do is run around the chapel once in order to "win" a currant bun. Every child gets a bun; the senior citizens hand them out. The custom is at least eighty years old and is possibly descended from the almshouse's old custom of offering a "Saint Bartholomew's Dole"—that is, bread, cheese, and beer—to all who asked for it.

# August 25

**O**ps was a Roman goddess of the fertile earth, of sowing and reaping. Not dissimilar to the generous Greek earth mother Rhea, she who "sends up fruits," Ops came to embody the abundance immanent in all the state-owned crops and fields and orchards. One of Italy's oldest deities, she was a kind of divine treasurer, the holder of the goods—the *opulence*—on which the civilization thrived.

Her shrine was located at the Regia, a building in the Forum that was believed, as its name implies, to occupy the site of the home of Rome's first kings, who did double duty as sovereigns and high priests. In the Imperial Romans' version of "once upon a time," the king's daughters performed sacred functions in and around the Regia. Later, the Vestal Virgins, a team of irreproachable priestesses chosen from among the cream of Roman womanhood, were trained to be the spiritual descendants of those holy daughters. A pontifex, who assumed the priestly duties of the long-ago kings, dwelt in the Regia and supervised the Vestals.

On the day of Ops's festival, priest and virgins squeezed into the goddess's sanctum sanctorum. It was very small and the rites were secret. As the goddess truly lived within the earth, the celebrants evoked her while sitting on the ground and touching the soil with their hands.

# August 26

## Climbing Mount Fuji
## (Last Day)

**M**ount Fuji's official climbing season is short and fervent. July and August are the only two months when the summit is completely free of snow—the result, it is said, of a curse. According to legend, a demon once asked Fuji's resident deity for a night's lodgings, and was refused. The vengeful demon swore to keep the peak frozen nearly all year 'round: If *he* was not permitted to enjoy the mountain, then no one else should, either.

A Shinto ceremony ritually opens the season on July 1. The same shrine, Sengen-jinja in Fuji-Yoshida, one of the mountain's primary trailhead towns, hosts the season-closing ceremony every August 26. The July ceremony starts at dawn with the cutting of a straw rope that spans the mountain path. The August ceremony, appropriately, is a nighttime event, a fiery spectacle for which towering torches, ten feet high and several feet in diameter, are erected all along the streets of town. Thousands gather to watch as, in the gathering dark, the Shinto priest gives a signal and all the torches are lit simultaneously. The flames leap and crackle atop their high perches until well past midnight.

# August 27

## Saint Phanourios's Day

**P**hanourios is revered on Cyprus as a re-
vealer of future husbands, a reuniter of
separated lovers, and a finder of missing objects. His name echoes the Greek for "reveal."
On his feast day, Cypriot women bake special
breads—Saint Phanourios's *pittas*—to express
their thanks for the saint's help throughout the
previous year. The pitta requires seven ingredients:
flour, olive oil, sugar, blanched almonds, rose water, cinnamon,
and spring water that the baker has carried home without uttering
a word to anyone. Once out of the oven, the pitta is divided among
seven women friends, all of whom have been married only once. As
they nibble their slices, the women must offer up prayers not to
Phanourios himself, but to his mother, whose miserly habits, it is
said, caused her much suffering during her lifetime.

The saint's shrine is located in a grotto above the surf at Kyrenia.
It is said that Phanourios settled here after crossing the sea on
horseback, having fled a band of angry Saracens in his native land.
(Splinters of horse bone found in the cave have added fuel to the
legend.) To this shrine the faithful women come, carrying leftover
chunks of *pitta*. These they leave behind, after paying respects to
the saint. But again, the bread isn't meant for Phanourios. As an
act of faith, the next person who comes to the shrine must eat the
bread she finds there. She in turn leaves bread of her own for the
next visitor.

# August 28

*A*ugustine, later to gain fame as one of Catholicism's most prolific writers, was the child of a mixed marriage: His father was a staunch pagan; his mother was Saint Monica. Undecided for the first thirty-three years of his life, Augustine had an epiphany while reading Saint Paul's epistles in a Milanese garden. After that, there was no turning back for the scholarly Algerian. Baptized a Catholic in 387, he was ordained a priest a mere four years later. Five years after that, he was a bishop. Passionate about many issues, Augustine authored more than 113 books and treatises, hundreds of letters, and hundreds of sermons. To this day, numerous monastic orders follow the Augustine rule.

The Augustine convents of Puebla, Mexico, were long known as cultural matrixes, especially in the area of cuisine. It was here that a dish was developed to honor Saint Augustine's feast day. *Chiles en nogada,* "chiles in walnut sauce," starts with large green peppers, into which go a stuffing made of ground meat, tomatoes, onion, garlic, raisins, chopped almonds, saffron, peaches, pears, cinnamon, cloves, sugar, and eggs. Dipped in a cinnamon-tinged egg batter, the peppers are deep-fried, then doused with a sauce made of ground walnuts, cream cheese, spices—and one hard dinner roll, which has been soaked in milk and crumbled.

# August 29

*A* hydrophiliac itinerant preacher, John the Baptist ran into trouble when he upbraided Herod Antipas for sexual peccadilloes. (Herod was sleeping with his own half-brother's wife, Herodias.) John landed in prison, where he languished, communicating with his friend Jesus via helpful messengers. But then Herod indulgently promised to give Herodias's daughter, Salome, anything her heart desired. After a quick conference with her mother, Salome asked for John the Baptist's severed head. She got it, too, on a platter.

John went on to an illustrious sainthood; nearly twenty churches in Constantinople alone were dedicated to him. His June 24 birthday is widely celebrated, having supplanted pre-Christian midsummer festivals (see June 23). The anniversary of his beheading is a holiday, too, in some places. On the Isle of Wight, an old saying warns against stepping on the red-spotted flower called Saint Johnswort. To do so on this day, it is said, is to risk being dragged off to oblivion on the back of a phantom horse. In Greece, people mark *Apotomi tis Timias Kephalis to Prodromo* with strict fasting. Pious Cypriots scan the clouds to see if amidst the billows they can discern the silhouette of John's head on a platter. (Only the truly honest, it is said, can see it.) Also on this day, conscientious Cypriots refrain from slicing onions. To cut an onion, they say, would too closely resemble cutting off someone's head.

# August 30

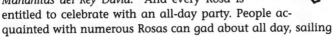

**M**any Mexican children and adults hold fiestas to mark the feast days of the saints for whom they were named. As August 30 is the feast day of Saint Rosa, every Mexican named Rosa has the right to expect that a mariachi band might arrive beneath her bedroom window at dawn to sing the name-day standard, *"Estas son las Mañanitas del Rey David."* And every Rosa is entitled to celebrate with an all-day party. People acquainted with numerous Rosas can gad about all day, sailing from party to party.

Saint Rosa is an especial favorite in Mexico because she was the first American ever canonized. A Peruvian of Spanish descent, Rosa lived in her parents' backyard from the age of twenty until her death at thirty-one in 1617. There she grew flowers, did needlework, and performed mortifications such as sleeping in a coffin and wearing a hair shirt as well as a belt lined with sharp metal spikes. Also she dragged a heavy wooden cross around and starved herself. She was sainted as much for her care of the local sick and poor as for her vigorous self-abuse.

Rosa is also honored with festivals in many countries, notably the Caribbean islands of Saint Lucia and Trinidad.

# August 31

## Malaysian National Day

They say it was Great Britain's idea. That the British government urged Malaysia—then called Malaya—to forge its own independence. Into the breach strode Tunku Abdul Rahman, a prince from the Kedah territory. Joining with leaders of the Malayan Chinese Association and the Malayan Indian Congress, he created a multiethnic bond, which was essential for the running of a polyglot nation.

On August 31, 1957, Malaysia officially achieved independent status, *merdeka,* within the British Commonwealth. Tunku Abdul

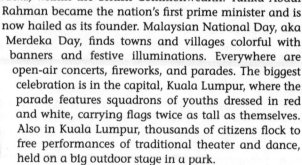

Rahman became the nation's first prime minister and is now hailed as its founder. Malaysian National Day, aka Merdeka Day, finds towns and villages colorful with banners and festive illuminations. Everywhere are open-air concerts, fireworks, and parades. The biggest celebration is in the capital, Kuala Lumpur, where the parade features squadrons of youths dressed in red and white, carrying flags twice as tall as themselves. Also in Kuala Lumpur, thousands of citizens flock to free performances of traditional theater and dance, held on a big outdoor stage in a park.

# Moveable Feast
## The Feast of the Tabernacles

### Sukkot

"You shall dwell in booths for seven days," the Old Testament exhorts. So in preparation for this holiday, many Jews erect three-sided makeshift huts—*sukkahs*—in their backyards or in synagogue courtyards. They dine and sometimes even sleep for seven consecutive nights inside the sukkah, whose walls are hung with the jewel-bright produce of early autumn. The sukkahs are meant to recall the tents in which the ancient Hebrews slept during their desert wanderings, as well as the temporary shacks in which farmers dwell in the fields when the work of the harvest is at its peak.

Following on the heels of the ascetic *Yom Kippur,* or Day of Atonement, Sukkot is a rich, happy feast, and important Biblical wanderers as well as the diners' own deceased ancestors are symbolically invited to the spicily sweet meals. In the hauntingly earthy Ritual of the Four Species, the *ethrog* or citron (which looks like a bumpy, muscular lemon) is joined with the *lulav,* a spiky and fragrant bouquet of palm frond, myrtle, and willow. On the last of the seven nights of this holiday—whose roots lie in thirsty desert lands—celebrants pray for rain.

# September 1

**E**ven if it hadn't been for a certain churchly decree, circa 313, naming September as the beginning of the religious calendar, the people of Greece would still have hailed this as their New Year's Day. And many Greeks still do, for this date marks the start of the Greek sowing season, a time of hope and promise.

To start things off right, farmers' families take plates of seeds to church for the priest to bless. On the island of Kos, people fashion first-of-the-year wreaths of pomegranates, grapes, quinces, garlic bulbs, and plane-tree leaves—all of which are traditional symbols of abundance. Just before dawn on September 1, island children carry their households' wreaths down to the shore, the old year's wreaths and the new ones, and they throw the old ones out to sea. They briefly immerse the new ones, for luck. Then they carry seawater and pebbles home in a jar, to serve, along with the new wreath, as protective devices. Tradition calls for exactly forty pebbles and water collected from the tops of exactly forty waves.

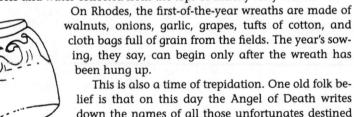

On Rhodes, the first-of-the-year wreaths are made of walnuts, onions, garlic, grapes, tufts of cotton, and cloth bags full of grain from the fields. The year's sowing, they say, can begin only after the wreath has been hung up.

This is also a time of trepidation. One old folk belief is that on this day the Angel of Death writes down the names of all those unfortunates destined to die within the coming year.

# September 2

## Saint Mamas's Day

The industrious Mamas befriended lions, milked lionesses, and made the milk into cheese, which he then distributed among the poor. It is said that Mamas escaped murderous pursuers by hiding in a Turkish cave, where he was fed and cared for by a pair of mountain sheep. When at last his enemies discovered him, they threw him to wild beasts that tore him to shreds (ironic, considering his Dr. Doolittle-like friendship with lions and sheep). Mamas's parents scooped his mangled remains into a wooden casket, which they tipped into the sea. The box floated across to Morphou on Cyprus, where it was hauled ashore, amazing the locals with its sweet fragrance—a sure sign of saintliness—and its seeming ability to cure abscesses.

At least two of Cyprus's Saint Mamas shrines share the legend that on the saint's feast day, a number of mountain sheep appear on the rocks overhead as if inspecting the rite. (At one of these shrines, it used to be the pilgrims' custom to shoot one of the tasty beasts every year while letting the others go free. But one year the pilgrims shot them all.) Near the Morphou chapel is a pair of saltwater springs. As the priest performs the mass on Mamas's day, the springwater bubbles up as red as blood. Or so say the faithful, who collect bottles of the water to use as sacred medicine throughout the year.

# September 3
## San Marino Founder's Day

Like an island afloat in the midst of Italy, the independent Republic of San Marino sits, wrapped in a not entirely faux medieval ambience, smugly governing its twenty-three-square-mile self. This country-inside-a-country mints its own coins (to the delight of numismatists worldwide) and prints its own postage stamps (to the delight of philatelists).

The republic was independent by the year 885 C.E. But general consensus is that San Marino goes back all the way to the fourth century, when a Christian stonemason—later to be known as Saint Marinus, aka San Marino—established a hermitage here, on Monte Tirano. Hagiographers agree that Marino was fleeing something; they differ on whether it was a strange woman claiming to be Marino's wife or whether it was Emperor Diocletian's persecutions in Marino's native Dalmatia. Today the cute republic swarms with tourists, who clamor for its reconstructed medieval buildings and the green-and-red-clad soldiers of San Marino's little army. A pair of captains regent presides over the nation's Grand Council, a lawmaking body whose members have the power, among other things, to confer titles of nobility. San Marino's photogenic Founder's Day celebrations feature military parades and much impassioned chanting of the official motto: "Honor to you, O ancient republic." The festivities also recall Marino, the hermit, whose relics lie in the basilica that, like the country itself, bears his name.

# September 4

## Los Angeles's Birthday

In the beginning, there were not so many K-Marts. When in 1769 Captain Gaspar de Portola came upon the site with his team of Spanish explorers and missionaries, it was an Indian village named Yang-na. Portola didn't stay. But twelve years later an expedition set out from Junipero Serra's San Gabriel Mission, nine miles to the northeast, bound for Yang-na. On September 4 they arrived: a government official, some soldiers, a few priests, and some Indian converts. Invoking God's blessing, they marched around the would-be plaza of El Pueblo de Nuestra Señora La Reina de Los Angeles.

It took the bumbling settlers three years just to build a simple adobe church. The Mexican government officially declared Los Angeles a city in 1835. In 1846 the American flag was planted here, and the first annual birthday celebration was held in 1894. The one held in 1931 was a ten-day extravaganza. After a massive dance contest and an equally massive cake-cutting ceremony, the grand parade featured stagecoaches, covered wagons, Franciscan monks, pioneers, hundreds of horsemen in eighteenth-century Spanish garb, a Fiesta Queen with thirty ladies-in-waiting, and a ten-year-old girl who had been selected from among the city's orphanages to be *la Princesita*. A coronation ceremony and a rodeo followed, as well as mass for 105,000 in the Olympic Stadium and vesper services for 35,000 in the Hollywood Bowl. The city still celebrates, but in smaller ways.

# September 5

## The First Labor Day

The Industrial Revolution changed a lot of things forever. Chiefly, it spawned a new "working class," a huge international community of men and women (and, unfortunately, children) who labored in plants and factories. In time, the world's workers found ways to organize, to represent themselves to their bosses, and to improve working conditions and wages.

In 1882 labor leader Peter J. McGuire announced to New York City's Central Labor Union that a holiday ought to be established to honor the toiling masses. The tenth child in an Irish-American family, McGuire had himself been working in piano and furniture factories by the age of eleven. The Central Labor Union favored his suggestion and staged the first annual Labor Day parade and ceremonies on September 5 of that year. Over ten thousand workers marched in New York's Union Square and afterwards disported themselves with dances, picnics, fireworks, and speech making. The idea caught on, and plans were made to create a national Labor Day. In 1887 Oregon became the first state to officially adopt Labor Day. New Jersey soon followed suit; then New York and, by 1893, thirty others. By 1928 Wyoming was the only holdout. Today it is observed—as per a later suggestion from Peter McGuire—on the first Monday in September.

# September 6

## The Virgin of Remedies

### Fiesta de los Remedios

When Cortez's men had finished smashing and melting all the sacred objects in the Aztecs' great temple, they placed something of their own on the now-denuded altar: a wooden madonna just a bit larger than a Barbie doll. One of the *conquistadores* had brought her with him from Spain, and now here she stood, blandly mocking the gods whose thrones she had usurped.

But not for long. On the night of July 20, 1520, the infuriated Aztecs drove Cortez and his minions out of town. The Spaniards would thereafter refer to this as *la noche triste,* the "sad night." They barely escaped with their lives, a miracle that they attributed to the little *Virgen de los Remedios.* Somehow, the statuette disappeared in the tumult. (Some of the Spaniards reported having seen the Virgin come to life that night and take up arms to viciously fight the Aztecs.) It stayed missing for twenty years, at which point the Virgin appeared to an old Indian and told him where to find the statue. He found it, and a sanctuary was eventually built on the site. The Spaniards loved her and nicknamed her *la Conquistadora.*

Today her fiesta draws thousands of worshipers to the sanctuary at San Bartolo for fireworks, dances, food stalls, and elaborate church services.

# September 7

lorence and Siena, now a pair of well-preserved Renaissance heirlooms, used not to be so genteel. Throughout the Middle Ages, the neighboring city-states were forever at each other's throats. One of the high points of the ongoing skirmish came in 1230, when the Florentines crouched outside Siena's walls, catapulting quantities of human excrement and putrid donkey corpses over the top, in hopes of starting a plague. In 1260 the Florentine troops launched another fierce attack; in response, the Sienans begged the Virgin Mary for protection and then tore into their enemies with a brutal fury.

Three hundred years later, Florence's Cosimo de Medici once and for all annexed Siena. He became the first Grand Duke of Tuscany. To celebrate his victory, Florentines initiated the *Rificolone* festival. In times of yore, people came from all over the surrounding region, carrying picnic lunches of cheese, bread, fruit, and anise- and fennel-spiked sweets. At night, they carried colored paper lanterns down to the banks of the Arno River and set them afloat. Today's celebrations also include picnics and lanterns—as well as floats, folksinging, and street dancing.

# September 8
## The Virgin Mary's Birthday

Although the Bible itself has little to say about Mary, countless apocryphal legends have taken liberties with her life story. Christians have celebrated the Virgin's birthday ever since the mid-fifth century, when Saint Romanus the Melodist, a Byzantine composer, wrote a hymn that popularized the concept. "Our Lady's Nativity" was an important event in sixth-century Rome and among the Anglo-Saxons in seventh-century England. By the tenth century, chroniclers all over Europe were recording elaborate birthday celebrations.

For example, Naples's Piedigrotta, now defunct, was a vast outpouring of music, food, and fervor, which used to attract hundreds of thousands of revelers. Today many places all over the world hold fairs and festivals on this day. On the island of Malta, September 8 is the year's major national holiday. The archbishop celebrates a requiem mass in the cathedral at Valletta, the capital city. Afterwards, the crowd spills into the streets, which have been brilliantly decorated for the event. Colorful *dghajsas*—gondola-like Maltese boats—compete in a regatta in Valletta's Grand Harbor, while *festas* erupt at many villages around the island. Greased-pole climbing is a standard feature at these celebrations.

# September 9

## Chrysanthemum Festival
### Choyo no Sekku/Kiku no Sekku

*J*apan's Edo period was a time of rigidly enforced national seclusion; any Japanese who dared travel outside the country faced the death penalty if and when he or she tried to return. Arts, literature, and other cultural activities flourished in this hothouse environment. During this period the *go-sekku,* the five seasonal festivals, were developed and came to be cherished. Along with the still-popular Doll Festival (see March 3), the Boys' Day (see May 5), and the Weaver's Festival (see July 7), these included January 7's *Wakane no Sekku,* "Day of the Young Herbs," and September 9's Chrysanthemum Festival.

A complex and showy flower, the chrysanthemum is associated with Japanese emperors; a mum appears on the imperial family's crest. As *Choyo no Sekku,* "double-ninth day," this was once the time when all feudal lords were expected to pay their annual visits to the shogun. In later years, the emperor held state banquets on this day. Now, renamed *Kiku no Sekku,* literally "Chrysanthemum Day," the festival enjoys only limited attention. Mainly it is a focus for local chrysanthemum exhibitions and gardeners' competitions. At this time of year, the old city of Nagoya in central Honshu is renowned for its displays of chrysanthemum plants arranged in humanoid shapes, dressed in costumes, and placed in historical tableaux.

# September 10

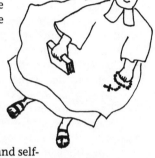

S alvi was the son of a noble family. He became a monk, then an abbot. One day he said good-bye to his monks and shut himself into his cell. Having not seen or heard from Salvi in a disturbingly long time, his monks went to investigate and found the abbot sprawled out apparently dead. They prepared his body for burial. Just as he was about to be interred, Salvi leaped up, red-cheeked and refreshed, and went back to his daily routine of hard work and self-imposed starvation. Naturally the brethren were deeply curious. Salvi's mother was persuaded to come to the abbey and drag the story out of her son. Against his better judgment, Salvi revealed that he had had an out-of-body experience. He had taken ill in his cell and his soul had flown to heaven, amidst incredibly bright light. But then he had heard a voice saying, "Let this man return to earth; the Church needs him." As soon as he reported this, Salvi's tongue swelled to enormous size and erupted into lesions. He took this as punishment for having revealed too much. In 574 he was elected bishop of Albi in the south of France.

Hailed as a visionary and a liberator of slaves, Salvi is fêted in his native France. Several towns, including Coulommiers and Oissel, host processions on his feast day; his own Albi hosts a *fête patronale* on the Sunday following September 10.

# September 11

## Coptic New Year

With their racial homogeneity, their liturgy in an obsolete language, and their (some say heretical) beliefs regarding the exact degree of Jesus' divinity, Egypt's Coptic Christians have always been unusual. Not exactly outcasts, certainly not outlaws, definitely outnumbered, the Copts endure on the outskirts of orthodoxy, practicing their archaic rites.

Just as followers of other Christian sects celebrate the feasts on different dates, the Coptic Church too has its own calendar, based on its own regional geography, cosmology, and meteorology. The Coptic New Year is based on the reappearance of Sirius, the dog star (*Sothis,* to Egyptians) in the skies over Egypt. From time immemorial, the star has presaged the annual swelling of the Nile and the subsequent flooding of the Nile Delta, which in turn marks the start of a new agricultural year.

Copts observe the New Year with memorials to Coptic martyrs. Altar dressings and officiants' vestments are bright red on this day, to represent the martyrs' spilled blood. Also it is customary to eat red dates. The hard pit, they say, is as solid and unbreakable as the martyrs' faith.

# September 12

## Nichiren's Pardon

*W*hile not exactly Zen's evil twin, the Buddhist sect now known worldwide as Nichiren Shoshu is certainly its rowdy younger brother.

Nichiren (1222–1282) was a zealous priest, considered the most vehement Japanese Buddhist of his time. Significantly, his time was the turbulent Kamakura period, during which the reigning shogun moved the nation's capital from Kyoto to Kamakura, near present-day Tokyo. Also in this era, three contrasting Buddhist schools emerged and began competing—in a firm-yet-gentle Buddhist way—for adherents. Nichiren broke from his conservative background and espoused a discipline based on the supremacy of the Lotus Sutra. His devotees chanted (and still chant) *Nam myoho renge-kyo,* which means "Hail the miraculous law of the Lotus Sutra." When Nichiren began denouncing other sects and the government that condoned them, he was sentenced to death. He received a last-minute stay of execution when lightning—an omen, people said in awe—struck the execution site. The priest was instead exiled to Sado, the prison island where many a troublesome Japanese intellectual had been sent.

In 1271, on the lunar date that corresponds to September 12, Nichiren was officially pardoned and his followers rejoiced in the streets. To this day, the anniversary of Nichiren's pardon is an occasion for massive celebrations, with thousands of devotees chanting en masse.

# September 13

## The Gods' Banquet
### Epulum Jovis

**G**uess who's coming to dinner? The guests of honor at this annual *epulum*, this sacred Roman banquet, were a crucial triad of deities: Juno, Minerva, and Jupiter, whose great temple on the Capitoline Hill had been dedicated on this date. Originally a matronly goddess of marriage and childbirth, Juno developed into the kindly protectress of the whole Roman state. Minerva, worshiped mainly as a goddess of wisdom, also ruled business, music, artisanship, war, and medicine, thus making herself indispensable. Sky god Jupiter was a thunder-wielding warrior, and some say the *Epulum Jovis* was a thanksgiving meal in the wake of the summer battle season.

Deciding what to serve the gods seems an even knottier problem than what to do when Bob brings the boss home for dinner. But an ancient chronicler reported that he saw tables in the sacred hall spread with very basic foods, served on rough earthenware dishes. The three deities' statues were anointed and dressed up in finery. On their heads rested curly wigs framing faces specially made up for the occasion. Jupiter's statue was laid on a couch, the goddesses' on thrones. Following a sacrifice (the victim, we are told, was almost certainly a white heifer), the faithful sat down to eat, keenly aware that the gods were dining among them.

MINERVA

# September 14

## Holy Cross Day

*A*fter his mother, the adventurous Saint Helen, returned from a trip to Jerusalem reporting that she had found there the cross on which Jesus was crucified, Emperor Constantine hurried to the Holy Land. He built two churches there, it is said. On September 14, 335, the supposed anniversary of Helen's discovery, Constantine dedicated these two shrines, thereby instituting an annual pilgrimage. Enormous crowds arrived every September to venerate what had become known as the Holy Cross. In time, the corporeal relic's importance mingled with that of a vision Constantine once had on the eve of a battle. The cross had appeared to him, luminous, inscribed with the message, "Conquer with this!" Historians now suggest that the Church's eager touting of Holy Cross Day was an effort to uproot an important September rite that generations of Europeans had been performing in honor of the grain goddess, Demeter, and her daughter, Persephone.

In Greece, Holy Cross Day inspired the seamen's proverb about lying low for the season: "On the day of the Cross, cross your sails and tie your ropes; rest in harbor. On St. George's Day rise and set sail again." Meanwhile in Britain, this Holy Rood Day was an outdoorsy affair, an occasion for nut gathering.

# September 15
## Respect-for-the-Aged Day
### Keiro no Hi

**P**aper lobsters are standard New Year's decorations in many a Japanese house. This is because the lobster's curved back resembles that of an elderly person, and every New Year's greeting includes a wish for longevity. Similarly inspired, people eat noodles on their birthdays; the long noodles symbolize long life.

All this passion for longevity entails a deep respect for the aged, who have lived long enough to know much about the world. A national holiday in the country with the world's longest life expectancy, *Keiro no Hi* thanks the aged for, as a Japanese government missive puts it, "their years of service to society." Schools, civic organizations, and the media all offer programs emphasizing old people's great value to family and community. For the occasion, small-town women's groups organize the presentation of gifts to all citizens over the age of seventy. At this time of year, many Buddhist temples offer special amulets said to protect the wearer from becoming incontinent.

# September 16
## Mexican Independence Day

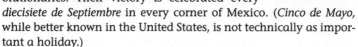

The Mexican Revolution, they say, began with *un grito,* "a shout": On September 16, 1810, a humble but determined priest, Father Hidalgo, cried out from his pulpit in Dolores, Guanajuato, *"¡Viva la Virgen de Guadalupe!"* This was tantamount to saying, "Down with Spanish rule! Let Mexicans rule themselves!" As the grito echoed though the countryside, Mexican *insurgentes* clashed with royalists. For his act of patriotism, Hidalgo was shot, along with three companions, in Chihuahua. The quartet's severed heads festered atop poles for quite a while, an indignity that only served to infuriate the revolutionaries. Their victory is celebrated every *diecisiete de Septiembre* in every corner of Mexico. (*Cinco de Mayo,* while better known in the United States, is not technically as important a holiday.)

In Mexico City, the festivities begin just before midnight on the 15th. Then Independence Day erupts with military parades, clanging church bells, banners, flowers, bullfights, cockfights, masses, memorial services, fireworks, dances, and concerts. Street musicians strike up favorite revolutionary songs, of which "La Cucaracha" is an honored specimen. And everywhere is heard the grito: *¡Viva la Virgen!*

# September 17

## Von Steuben Day

**B**aron Von Steuben was a brilliant young military strategist, already distinguished and decorated in his native Germany, by the time the American colonists approached him asking for help with their Revolution. He came and, although his English was very minimal, swiftly earned the respect of his peers and the soldiers who fought under his command. He is known for having engineered many important battles. After the war, he made himself even more popular by becoming an American citizen.

German-American communities all over the country, notably those in Pennsylvania's larger cities, celebrate Von Steuben's birthday to show their pride in Teutonic contributions to American history and culture. Usually these celebrations take the form of a daytime parade followed by a nighttime banquet featuring, of course, German dishes.

In his book *Conduct Unbecoming*, author Randy Shilts identifies Baron Von Steuben as one of the United States' first gay heroes.

# September 18

## Dr. Johnson's Birthday

The son of a Lichfield bookseller, Samuel Johnson lived to become one of the English language's most profound influences. His 1755 dictionary was the most thorough lexicon of its time, remarkable for its previously unheard-of use of famous literary quotes to illustrate words' meanings. But Johnson, aka "Dictionary Johnson," wore other hats, too. No mere egghead, he was at various points in his life a travel writer, a hack writer, an Oxford dropout, and a hypochondriac. He also experienced poverty and was married to a woman twenty years his senior.

He was born September 18, 1709. Every year on that day or the Saturday nearest, members of the Johnson Society gather in the author's hometown where at noon the Lichfield mayor ceremoniously lays a wreath at the foot of Johnson's statue. Meanwhile, the cathedral choir sings hymns and the "Johnson Anthem." After a visit to the house where the author was born and other Johnsonian diversions, the group sits down to its annual Johnson Supper in the Lichfield Guildhall. This features the old valetudinarian's favorite comestibles: steak and kidney pie, with apple tart and cream for dessert. On the following Monday, the nearby town of Uttoxeter performs its own Johnson memorial. A wreath is laid on the spot where, in a fit of tardy remorse, Johnson did public penance for having hurt his father's feelings—all of fifty years previous—when he fled the county rather than be a clerk at the old man's bookstall.

# September 19

**Festa di San Gennaro**

*J*anuarius, bishop of Benevento, was hard to kill. During Emperor Diocletian's anti-Christian persecutions in the early fourth century, Januarius was seized and tossed into a fire-belching furnace. This, legend tells, he survived. Then he was cast into an amphitheater full of hungry wild animals. The animals acted as if he wasn't even there. He survived an attempt at beheading but then finally was felled by a sword at Pozzuoli, near Naples. His elderly nurse, legend says, ran forward to collect Januarius's spilled blood as it poured from his death wound. Now enshrined in a flagon-shaped vial inside a glass reliquary mounted on a jewel-encrusted stand in Naples's cathedral, the saint's dried blood liquefies every year on September 19, the anniversary of his death.

Multitudes gather in Naples every year to witness the patron saint's *miracolo.* A sisterhood of Neapolitan women who call themselves *I Parenti,* "the relatives," are said to be the descendants of Januarius's nurse. On this festival day, they beg and harangue the blood not just to liquefy but to liquefy redly and wetly. (Some years the blood is gluey and black or yellowish, which is considered a bad omen.)

Transplanted Neapolitans and their descendants celebrate the *festa* in New York's Little Italy. The faithful bear a golden statue of the saint down Mulberry Street amidst music, lights, and stalls selling calzone, sugar doughnuts, seafood, and the festival's sine qua non, *torrone:* soft, white, honey-and-almond-flavored nougat.

# September 20

This Roman military officer underwent a conversion and upon his
baptism changed his name from Placidus
to Eustace. His wife, too, was baptized,
and changed her name from the eu-
phonious Tatiana to the less cheer-
some Theopista. Eustace's conversion
came about thusly, they say: One day he
was hunting deer in the forest when he
encountered a stag with a glowing crucifix between its antlers. The stag looked
into Eustace's eyes and intoned, as legend tells, "Placidus, Placidus,
why persecutest thou me? I am Jesus Christ."

Following a particularly successful battle campaign, the Roman
Emperor Trajan invited Eustace to join him in thanking the gods.
Eustace refused. Irked, Trajan ordered him, his wife, and their two
sons, Agapistus and Theopistus, to be thrown to starved lions. The
lions, it is reported, merely frisked about their would-be prey and
didn't take so much as a mouthful. Infuriated, Trajan had the family locked inside a hollow bull made of brass. A fire was laid under
the bull and the quartet were cooked to a turn.

Because the stag incident echoes similar tales in other saints'
legends as well as in various Asian folktales, many modern hagiographers are inclined to dismiss Eustace and family as entirely ficti-
tious. Nevertheless, as Saint Eustace he is still honored on his feast
day in the French town of Valenciennes, and elsewhere.

# September 21

## Christ's Hospital Founder's Day

For one reason or another, England's historical who's who sports more than its share of benefactors—kind and/or generous and/or egomaniacal types who found it in their hearts to finance hospitals, foundling homes, libraries, schools, almshouses, and annual charities or "doles." With such a charitable act, the benefactor not only helps the less fortunate but also earns him- or herself a slice of eternal fame. Literally thousands of founder's day events take place all over Britain every year.

Edward VI would have been famous anyway; he was king. But he enriched his portfolio by founding numerous schools, including two London institutions "for necessitous children." One of these, the grimly titled Christ's Hospital, endures in the mutated form of a prestigious school for boys at Horsham in Sussex. The school commemorates its founder every year by sending three hundred representatives to London. They wear the school's official Tudor uniform: a priestly-looking navy blue cassock, sunny yellow stockings, white neckbands, and buckled shoes. In formation they march from the tube station to the church of Saint Sepulchre's-without-Newgate, which is near the school's original site. Members of the school band, also in uniform, march and play as well.

After a midmorning commemorative service in the church, the students march to the Mansion House, where London's Lord Mayor graces each boy with the gift of a newly minted coin.

# September 22

## Saint Maurice's Day

**S**ometime in the third century, it is said, Captain Maurice and his legion of six thousand soldiers marched from Thebes to Gaul, where they went about their soldierly work. One day, while stationed at Agaunum (now Saint-Maurice-en-Valois in Switzerland), they received orders to turn their swords against the local Christian population. The men of the Theban Legion, as it came to be known, were Christians themselves, and they refused. Emperor Maximian, who had sent the orders, became incensed and sentenced the entire legion to death. Other soldiers were sent to massacre them, at which the Thebans, it is reported, gleefully welcomed death, offering their throats to the assailants' swords. After a series of bloodbaths, every last one of the six thousand had been butchered.

While all of this may never have actually happened, the story of the military martyrs has enjoyed enduring popularity. When in 1489 two hundred bodies were unearthed near Lucerne, they were immediately claimed to be those of Theban troops. Maurice shares a common feast day with his men, which is celebrated heartily throughout Switzerland as well as in France.

# September 23

## Autumn Equinox
### Shubun no Hi

Equinoxes are like bridges. As the sun crosses directly over the equator, night and day are of exactly equal duration. According to Buddhist thought, these conditions allow the dead to cross the mythical waters between their world and the world of the living: to travel to and fro between here and *higan*, the "far shore." The spring and autumn equinoctal weeks are thus called *Higan*, and the central day of these weeks, the *shubun*, "equinox," is an official holiday on which people are expected to pay respects to the dead.

The custom of *ohakamairi*, "grave visiting," came to Japan via China. On *Shubun no Hi*, people bring food offerings, incense sticks, fresh-cut flowers, and vases to the cemetery. At the grave site, water is sprinkled over the gravestone to symbolically cleanse it. Then the flowers are arranged in the vase, the food is set around the vase, and the incense is left to burn in a little sand-filled china cup. Some families, who have traveled far into the countryside to ancestral graveyards, make this an all-day affair and sit down to leisurely graveside picnics.

The autumn equinox serves as a seasonal bridge as well as a spiritual one. While it is said that the spring equinox marks the end of winter, in September Japanese recite the saying, "No summer heat lingers beyond this equinox day."

# September 24

## Schwenkenfelder Thanksgiving

The Schwenkenfelder sect takes its name from its founder, Caspar von Schwenkenfelder, who had been an important personage in Germany's Catholic Church before he discovered Martin Luther and all the lures of Protestantism. Schwenkenfelder gathered a group of evangelical followers around him, and all went well until after his death in 1582, when the leaderless group faced much persecution and ridicule. Yet they persisted.

A party of Schwenkenfelder Society members sailed to America in 1733 and settled comfortably in the Philadelphia area. They wrote letters urging the rest of the society to come too; and on September 22, 1734, 184 of them did. Two days later, on the 24th, they marched downtown to the State House and swore their allegiance to the English king, which is what people did in those days. Then they launched into a full day of prayer, thanking God for delivering them safely to the New World. Their descendants, who live in the various Pennsylvania Dutch counties, still observe this as their annual thanksgiving day.

# September 25
## The Dolls' Memorial Service
### Ningyo-kuyo

The unhappily childless in Japan appeal to Kannon, aka Kwannon. A Boddhisattva, or Buddha-to-be, Kannon turned down a well-deserved ticket to nirvana eons ago, deciding instead to remain human until every last sentient being on earth attained enlightenment. So now this tower of compassion devotes her life to answering every prayer that comes her way. And she can be compassionate to people of all kinds, having been, at various times in her life, both male and female.

In China she is sometimes addressed as *Sung-Tzu-Niang-Niang*, "she who brings children." In Japan, too, where childless couples make offerings of dolls at her shrines and temples, Kannon is renowned for her power to grant fertility. In Ueno, one of Tokyo's oldest parks, is the temple of Kiyomizu-do, where Kannon presides. Many Tokyoites offer dolls here in hopes that Kannon will help them conceive. *Ningyo-kuyo*, "doll offering," is a memorial service for all the dolls left at the shrine during the past twelve months. Spectators watch as the temple priests assemble all the dolls into a towering pile, which is then set on fire. As the dolls burn, the priests chant sutras in thanks for the dolls' self-sacrifice.

# September 26
## Saints Cyprian and Justina's Day

**O**nce there was a lusty young pagan who lived near the grove of Daphne at Antioch. But this is not his story; he is merely a pawn. For when this pagan approached the sorcerer Cyprian, asking him for help in winning the heart of the Christian maiden Justina, the sorcerer himself fell in love with Justina and strove to get her for his own. In the middle of the night Cyprian conjured up a demon, which he sent to Justina's bedroom. She "saw the hideous demon," Butler's *Lives of the Saints* tells us, "and blew in his face. Thereupon he fled howling." Three nights in a row Cyprian sent her demons, and each she repelled in the same clever way.

Assessing the pitiful impotence of his magic, Cyprian went to the bishop of Antioch, confessed his sins, and begged to be baptized. At this point, we come to a fork in the hagiographical road. Some say that the reformed magician and Justina were wed at Nicodemia. Others attest that they were not wed but boiled in pitch together, and when instead of dying they sat amidst the bubbles singing gaily, they were beheaded.

Two bodies alleged to be theirs are entombed in the Vatican; another pair similarly labeled lies nearby at Piacenza. A head said to be Justina's rests at Lucca, and yet a fourth is enshrined in Luxembourg. Because their story is such a resonant and clear-cut moral tale, Cyprian and Justina are fêted on their feast day in various French towns.

# September 27
## Saints Cosmas and Damian's Day

osmas and Damian were a pair of saintly brothers, Arabians with a knack for medicine and leechcraft. They also had a knack for annoying people. A story tells of how Damian cured a woman who then gratefully tried to pay him. When he refused, insisting that he worked for the love of God and not for money, she cussed him out most viciously. Later, during Diocletian's anti-Christian persecutions, the brothers survived being burned in a fire, stoned by a crowd, and thrown into the sea with heavy chains looped around their necks. They did not, however, survive being beheaded.

The late Cosmas and Damian were said to appear in pilgrims' dreams, diagnosing and curing ailments and injuries. It became the custom for sick Christians to spend the night in the brothers' shrines, hoping for miraculous cures. One pilgrim in Rome, legend tells, had a cancerous thigh. He dreamed that the martyrs approached him with surgical instruments. They removed so much of his leg, however, that they endeavored to replace the missing parts with those of a certain Ethiopian who had been buried that day in a nearby cemetery. When the dreamer awoke, he jumped for joy and told his tale to church officials, who hastened to the cemetery and found an Ethiopian corpse sans thigh.

On Cosmas and Damian's feast day, Sicilian bakers offer special bread, *pane rimacinato*, shaped like the saintly brothers, hand in hand.

# September 28

## Confucius's Birthday

The scholar whose name was Latinized from K'ung Ch'iu—Master K'ung—is today hailed by millions as "China's great teacher." A conservative and an intellectual in a time of political upheaval, Confucius taught his disciples history, poetry, ethics, politics, and ancient ritual and ceremony.

Not religious or even philosophical, his teachings were social, aimed at forging a rigidly formalized, feudalistic system, with its members in awe of authority. Confucius felt that he had been sent to earth from heaven to achieve this task, but other than that, he left divinity out of the curriculum. Nevertheless, when he died in 479 B.C.E. in Shantung province, his disciples mourned as they would have for a dead god: for three solid years. A temple was built alongside the tomb, at which annual sacrifices became the custom.

Today Master K'ung's birthday is celebrated every September 28 in Taiwan, where it is a national holiday and where the master's teachings are still influential. While Confucian temples throughout the island hold ceremonies, the biggest is at the main temple in Taipei; people buy tickets well in advance. Beginning at dawn, the celebration features classical Chinese music performed on ancient instruments and three-thousand-year-old rites that the master himself esteemed, taught, and practiced.

# September 29

## Lord Mayor's Election

**M**ore than just a mayor, London's lord mayor, newly elected every September 29, is devastatingly prestigious. In the powers allotted him, he is practically an earl. He is also the admiral of the Port of London, master of the Tower of London, and the city's "chief citizen." His election is riddled with pompous medieval novelties, as is his installation, which takes place some weeks hence (see November 8 and November 9).

The lord mayor is not elected by the populace but by the liverymen of London's eighty-one guilds: the goldsmiths, gunmakers, vintners, spectacle-makers, haberdashers, ironmongers, grocers, drapers, skinners, needlemakers, joiners, smiths, 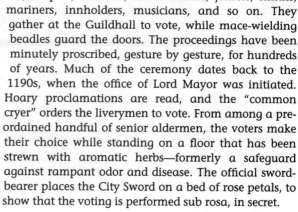 mariners, innholders, musicians, and so on. They gather at the Guildhall to vote, while mace-wielding beadles guard the doors. The proceedings have been minutely proscribed, gesture by gesture, for hundreds of years. Much of the ceremony dates back to the 1190s, when the office of Lord Mayor was initiated. Hoary proclamations are read, and the "common cryer" orders the liverymen to vote. From among a preordained handful of senior aldermen, the voters make their choice while standing on a floor that has been strewn with aromatic herbs—formerly a safeguard against rampant odor and disease. The official sword-bearer places the City Sword on a bed of rose petals, to show that the voting is performed sub rosa, in secret.

# September 30

## Saint Jerome's Day

**C**urmudgeonly Saint Jerome (aka Hieronymous, aka Geronimo) would be horrified to see the jolly way his feast day is celebrated at Taos Pueblo in New Mexico. The learned scholar *cum* hermit *cum* linguist *cum* priest *cum* hospice administrator *cum* biblical translator would hardly have approved of a pole climb.

Yet that's the main event at Taos's San Geronimo fiesta, another of the Southwest's many native traditions that have, through the vicissitudes of colonization and missionization, been tagged with saints' names. The pole climb is purely pagan, an ancient sun rite. Pueblo residents as well as visitors from outside the village gather to watch the antics of the *koshares,* the black-and-white-striped clowns who delight in miming people in the crowd, friends and strangers alike. The day's festivities at this most traditional of pueblos include various dances, exhilarating relay races, and the climb: The koshares take turns attempting to shinny up a towering stripped pine, some fifteen inches in diameter and shiny-smooth (although not greased). A bundle of food and other prizes is attached to the top.

# Moveable Feast

## Mid-Autumn Festival

### Zhong Qiu Jie

In the Chinese cosmology, the moon—not the sun—is the dominant orb, and not only has its radiance inspired countless poets, priests, and peasants alike, but its waxings and wanings have inspired the calendar according to which most of Asia plots yearly events. It's only natural that a lunar year should include a holiday set aside for appreciation of the moon. The Mid-Autumn Festival, aka Moon Festival, a Chinese staple since the Sung dynasty, is just that. The moon is said to be at its loveliest on this night: its roundest, brightest, and most magical.

Outside their homes, families erect altars that are stocked with wine, tea, incense sticks, and fruits, including the huge grapefruit-like pomelo, whose Chinese name, *yow,* is a homophone for "to have." Also on the altar is a stack of the holiday's ubiquitous mooncakes—thick pastries shaped like corrugated drums. The cakes are filled with sweet bean paste or lotus seed, and at the very heart of each is a boiled egg yolk to symbolize the moon.

The Chinese tradition of moon-viewing parties long ago carried over to Japan, where this holiday is called *Tsukimi.* Friends gather for the evening beside lakes or in special moon-viewing pavilions, having first enjoyed bowls of "moon-viewing noodles": thick white *udon* in broth with a perfect egg yolk floating on top.

# October 1

## The Godless Month

### Kami-nazuki

According to Shinto belief, October is the month during which the gods hold their annual convention. Come October 1, all of the eight million *kami* take leave of their shrines all over the islands and converge on the great temple of Izumo in western Honshu. There they relax, compare notes, and make crucial decisions about humankind. The second oldest sanctuary in Japan, Izumo is also the largest. On its grounds are *juku-sha*, long dormitories in which the visiting gods reside.

At the end of the month, all over Japan, people make special visits to their neighborhood Shinto shrines to welcome the resident gods back home. But until then, it is understood that all Japanese shrines are empty except Izumo. The poet Basho captured the desolation of an October shrine when he wrote:

*The god is absent;*
*the dead leaves are piling up,*
*and all is deserted.*

# October 2

## Old Man's Day

One day during the reign of the Virgin Queen, the people of Braughing, Hertfordshire, solemnly gathered for the funeral of Matthew Wall, a local farmer. Pallbearers collected the casket, with Wall inside it, at the farmer's home on Fleece Lane. But en route to the churchyard, the pallbearers slipped on some fallen leaves—remember, it was autumn—and they lost their grip on the coffin. To everyone's horror, the casket crashed to the street and broke open. Imagine the villagers' surprise when the "corpse" dazedly stood up: Matthew Wall had never been dead at all, only comatose, and the fall had revived him. He lived on to a ripe old age.

In his will, Wall provided for an annual charity. Every October 2, villagers—each of whom receive a few pence from Wall's bequest—retrace the pallbearers' route from Fleece Lane to the churchyard. They sweep dead leaves as they go, which is ironic, considering that such leaves saved Wall's life. Church bells peal sonorously as for a funeral. At Wall's grave, the rector retells the story of his adventure, and all assembled pray for the Old Man's soul. At this point, the bells change their rhythm from morbid to joyous.

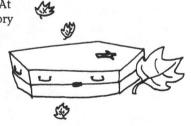

# October 3

## National Foundation Day

### Tangun

According to Korean legend, there were once two friends, a tiger and a bear, who asked the Supreme Being to make them human. The Supreme Being agreed, but warned that they would first have to undergo an ordeal. In order to properly become human, the pair must sequester themselves inside a cave for a hundred days. They would be able to talk, sleep, and play in the cave all they wanted, but they must not leave. And they must not eat anything save what the Supreme Being provided, namely, garlic and wormwood.

This ordeal was easy for the bear, who was accustomed to cave dwelling. The restless tiger, however, gave up after a few claustrophobic weeks. When the hundred days were up, the bear was transformed into a magnificent woman. She was lonely, so the Supreme Being paid her a visit, after which she gave birth to a son whom she named *Tangun.*

National Foundation Day commemorates this Tangun, who grew up to found Korea. It is said that he ruled as king from 2333 to 1122 B.C.E. He called the country not Korea but *Choson,* meaning "land of morning calm," in memory of the bright, peaceful morning on which his mother first emerged from her cave into the sun.

# October 4

## Saint Francis's Day

One of Christendom's most popular figures, Francis of Assisi was a wealthy medieval youth who stunned and angered his dear ones by tearing off his finery and embracing what he termed "the fairest of all brides, my lady poverty." He is renowned for his buoyant happiness. Francis heard statues talking; he lived in a hut; he had supernatural rapport with animals. He wrote cozily of "Brother Sun," "Sister Moon," "Sister Death," and so on. Today, Francis's simpering plaster statue overlooks many a backyard garden, and he is the patron saint of environmentalists.

Because of Francis's associations with animals, his feast day has in some places become an occasion for annual "pet blessings" at which the priest sanctifies his parishioners' beasts. A 1961 Saint Francis's Day gathering of this type at New York's Saint John the Baptist Church, attended by Shetland ponies and horned lizards, received much media attention at the time.

At New Mexico's Nambe Pueblo, twenty miles from Santa Fe, Francis is the patron saint. The native Tewa people mark his day with a series of dances in the plaza.

# October 5

### Nuestra Señora de Zapopan

ighting the native Chimalhuacanos in Jalisco, the *conquista-dores* had reason to worry. They enlisted the help of their compatriot, a friar who had been in the area a while and had won the Indians' trust. This priest wore a carving of the Virgin Mary around his neck, and as he ran onto the battlefield brandishing the figurine, the Chimalhuacanos abruptly surrendered, so deeply did they esteem their Franciscan friend and his ten-inch "goddess." Ten years later, the monk donated his statuette to the now-converted Chimalhuacanos, who had settled in the village of Zapopan. Installed in the church, the statue came to be regarded as an arbiter of weather.

In 1734 church and state authorities declared her *la patrona de los aguas,* "the patroness of rains." In order to ensure adequate rainfall in the region, it was determined that from June 13 to every October 4 the statue should "visit" all the different churches of Guadalajara, Jalisco's capital. She would dwell a few days in each church, and afterwards she would be carried the three miles back to her home in Zapopan. Today one sorrowful but resigned fiesta bids the Virgin farewell in June. The one that greets her return in October is ecstatic. As many as 450,000 worshipers, many of them dancing and singing, accompany the statue all along the three-mile route from Guadalajara to Zapopan. Church bells peal as the figurine is replaced on its altar, and for two full days the faithful celebrate.

# October 6

## Dedication of the Virgins' Crowns

**F**ew things are sadder than a child's death, few rituals more pathetic than a child's funeral. In England well into the twentieth century it was customary for a dead youth's pallbearers to be not the usual black-suited elders but his or her own peers. These tender coffin bearers would wear white sashes, gloves, and armbands to symbolize innocence and purity. To drive the point home even further, in some parts of the country a "maiden's garland" or a "virgin's crown" made of real or imitation white blossoms would rest atop the casket throughout the church service.

In the village of Abbots Ann, Hampshire, one of the last places where this custom is still current, the garlands are hung up in the church, high on the wall, along with the pallbearer's white gloves. There they stay permanently. Every October 6—the feast day of Saint Faith, the village's patron—a special dedication service recognizes the young people who have died throughout the previous year. Then the gloves and the garlands, which are dome-shaped helmets rather than simple circlets, are affixed to hooks on the wall. Beside each hook is a plaque inscribed with the name of the deceased and a set of dates.

# October 7

## Twyford Bell-Ringing

**D**avies was almost home. At least he thought he was. But suddenly a thick fog rose over the barren downs, and what had moments ago been a familiar landscape now melted away into blinding grayness. Lost, the man wandered, steering his horse this way and that. Suddenly, out of the fog came the sound of church bells—the bells of his own village's church! Now if he could just get his bearings, he could guide himself home with the bells' aid. Pulling his horse up short so as to better hear the bells, Davies discovered to his horror that he had been just about to wander over the edge of a chasm. Had the bells not stopped him in his tracks, he would have steered his horse right over the verge.

HARK!

All the rest of his life, Davies felt beholden to church bells. When at last he died in 1754, his will revealed that he had bequeathed one pound a year to his village's bell ringers. The money was to be awarded every year on the anniversary of his near escape, "provided they ring on that day forever." In Davies's village of Twyford, Hampshire, every October 7 at 6:30 A.M. and again at 7 P.M., the bells still ring. Afterwards, the bell ringers and their friends toast Davies at a banquet commemorating his adventure.

# October 8

Nagasaki's most important spiritual event lasts for three full days, culminating on October 9. On the lunar calendar to which Japan long adhered, the equivalent of that date had strong seasonal connotations, marking the official beginning not of autumn itself but of the autumn festival season.

A parade features big umbrella-topped floats, borne by teams of sweating youths, who twirl and whirl their burdens while grunting mightily. But the most striking part of the festival, held at Nagasaki's four-hundred-year-old Suwa-jinja shrine, are the lion dances, in which a caterpillar-like row of dancers marches and lunges down the street, concealed within the folds of the lion's flowing "body." The carved wooden head with its goggle eyes, jaunty beard, and snapping jaws is deftly manipulated from inside by the lead dancer. Said to bring luck to all who see them, *Okunchi's* "lions" are an idea enthusiastically borrowed—like so much else—from China, and they clearly resemble those seen at Chinese New Year and other celebrations.

# October 9

For the first few hundred years of Korea's history, Koreans had a spoken language of their own but no alphabet. They were constrained to write in classical Chinese, which was daunting because the thousands of Chinese characters—each representing a distinct meaning—were unwieldy when applied to a foreign tongue. Few Koreans outside of government and academia were able to master them. In 1446, Korea's King Sejong became exasperated with the situation. He assembled a team of scholars to come up with a system of written Korean. After the team had spent three years working in the palace's Hall of Talented Scholars, Sejong publicly announced that "being distinct from Chinese, the Korean language is not confluent with Chinese characters. Hence, those who have something to put into words are unable to express their feelings. To overcome such distressing circumstances, I have designed . . . letters that everyone may learn with ease and use with convenience in their daily life." The twenty-four letters in *Han-gul,* the Korean alphabet, express sound, not meaning.

At first, many in the upper echelons opposed Han-gul, fearing the power of the masses. During World War II, however, Han-gul emerged as a symbol of Korean resistance and patriotism, and in 1945 the alphabet at last became official. The anniversary of King Sejong's declaration is celebrated with children's and adults' calligraphy contests. The latter often entail large cash prizes.

# October 10

## Taiwan National Day

### Shuangshi Jie

China's last dynasty, the Ching, was over-thrown in 1911 by a band of rebels in the wake of a nationwide uprising. Proclaiming China a new republic was the leader of these rebels, the modest Dr. Sun Yat-sen. Sun went on to serve as the republic's first president, and he is still hailed as a hero—especially by Taiwanese and many Chinese expatriates.

Also called Double Tenth Day because it falls on the tenth day of the tenth month, National Day is Taiwan's greatest civic holiday. Every hotel room in Taipei, the capital, is packed, and the airport is jammed all during the previous week as tens of thousands of overseas Chinese pour into town from all over the world. On the 10th, the crowds assemble to watch the festivities, most of which take place in the broad plaza fronting the Presidential Mansion. Folk dancing, sword fighting, martial arts demonstrations, and military revues transpire on the ground, while in the sky air force planes perform daring airborne acrobatics.

# October 11

U ttering sacred phrases about "old things" and "new things" and perhaps invoking a goddess called Medetrina (who may or may not have actually existed in the Roman pantheon), Romans on this day sipped the *mustum,* the "new wine"—that is, the product of the most recent vintage, not yet fully fermented.

Plutarch wrote about the wholesome, medicinal, and nonintoxicating nature of new wine. But we know little of this festival. While at least one account refers to "the goddess Medetrina who lends her name to this day," more recent scholars have doggedly attempted to prove that there was no goddess called Medetrina. Some are inclined toward the theory that the deity invoked at the new wine feast was actually Jupiter.

95- MEX
DIA DE LA RAZA

# ☀October 12

*Fiesta de Nuestra Señora*
*del Pilar*

**H**aving made the decisive career move from angler to apostle, Saint James (see July 25)
strove to make himself useful to his chosen cause.
After the Crucifixion, he traveled (say the Spaniards)
to Spain, then back to the Holy Land, where Herod
beheaded him.

While still in Spain, however, James (say the
Spaniards) had an interesting adventure. He
was one day strolling along the banks of the
River Ebro when the Virgin Mary appeared to
him, mounted on a post. Surprised to see her so
far from home, James greeted her quizzically. Mary explained that
she wanted a shrine erected in her honor on the spot where they
now were standing. To further encourage him, she handed James a
miniature replica of herself, post and all, carved of wood and jasper.

Today the basilica at Zaragoza on the banks of the Ebro is
Spain's primary Marian shrine. Mary's post—*el pilar*—rests here still
and serves as the namesake for women in Spanish-speaking countries worldwide. The shrine's annual festival on October 12 features
bullfights, a parade, fireworks, and a battle of the bands.

# October 13

**I**n their sultry Mediterranean clime, the ancient Romans had good reason to be thankful for fresh drinking water. No wonder that, at summer's end, they held this rite, of which the chronicler Varro writes: "*Fontinalia:* to the fountains, because this is their festival day; and then [worshipers] throw flowers into them, and crown them with flowers."

There probably was (but possibly wasn't) a Roman fountain god named Fons or Fontus, to whom this day was sacred. Rome had a *delubrum Fontis* (a Fontus sanctuary), an *ara Fonti* (Fontus altar), and a *porta Fontinalis* (Fontus gate).

Water worship was prevalent all over pagan Europe. Healing wells, springs, rivers, and their sources were hailed as the homes of gods. The sixth-century English monk, Gildas, wrote describing what he believed to be the defunct heathen custom of his country: "Fountains . . . or rivers . . . to which the blind populace paid divine honor." But water worship was—and is—far from extinct, a fact evinced by Europe's prodigious number of "holy wells," now usually named after saints. Ireland alone has three thousand of them.

# October 14

## Mega-kenka Matsuri

**W**idowed and pregnant at the beginning of a long-awaited campaign to conquer Korea, Japan's legendary Empress Jingu dashed into battle undaunted. Wielding her sword as well as a bow and arrows, she staved off labor and childbirth (some say for three entire years) by the ingenious method of tying a stone around her middle. Circa 201 C.E., it is said, she accomplished her goal, subduing all of Korea's three kingdoms. Afterward, she gave birth to Ojin, soon to be emperor and later to be deified as the war god, Hachiman. (So Japan concedes that its warrior spirit has feminine origins. Or does it? Some insist that the embryonic Ojin, fully conscious, directed all the battle operations from the inside of his mother's womb.)

Appropriately warlike is this festival, held in the shadow of Himeji-jo castle, near Kyoto. At the Matsubara Hachiman shrine, teams of men shoulder portable minishrines, *mikoshi:* One represents Jingu, another represents Ojin; the third represents a spirit, a *kami.* While spectators clamor for a good view, the three teams rush forward and batter each other's shrines. Back and forth they clash, sometimes bloodily as befits a war rite, until at last one of the mikoshi is smashed to bits.

# October 15

**T**wo chariots, each one hitched to a pair of horses, waited side by side every October 15 on the Rome's Campus Martius alongside the Tiber. At the signal, they were off. When the chariots clattered across the finish line, the right-hand horse of the victorious team was led away and ritually slaughtered. Its tail was cut off and rushed to the Forum, where the blood spattered across the goddess Vesta's sacred hearth while still warm and fresh. Later, priestesses distributed the congealed tail-blood among farmers, who used it as a protective charm. Meanwhile, back in the Campus Martius—war god Mars's field—the horse's head was cut off. Draped with loaves and cakes, the head was affixed to the side of a house or a tower, the *turrus Mamilia*, where it hung for quite some time.

The rite of the October horse, as classicists call it, is one of the most mystifying on the whole Roman calendar. No doubt extremely primitive, this kill-the-winner horse race has been labeled, of all things, an agricultural festival. In *The Golden Bough,* Sir James Frazer asserts: "The alleged object of the sacrifice [was], namely, to procure a good harvest." Frazer suggests that "the horse was killed as one of those animal representatives of the corn-spirit of which we have found so many examples. The custom of cutting off the horse's tail is like the African custom of cutting off the tails of oxen and sacrificing them to obtain a good crop. In both the Roman and the African customs the animal apparently stands for the corn-spirit, and its fructifying power is supposed to reside especially in its tail."

# October 16

## The Lion Sermon

*i*t's not every day that wealthy London merchants find themselves face to face with savage beasts. Yet that's exactly what happened in 1630 to Sir John Gayer. He traveled regularly to the Near East in search of spices, rugs, and other export items. On one of these business trips, Gayer somehow became separated from his party in the midst of the Arabian desert. Out of nowhere a lion appeared, gnashing its teeth as it circled him hungrily. Gayer fell to his knees in prayer. All he could think of, he later reported, was the biblical story of Daniel in the lion's den. Amazingly, the lion lost interest in Gayer and trotted peaceably away.

Having made this one miraculous escape, Gayer was soon to make another. Back in England, Gayer's royalist leanings landed him in the Tower of London after the Civil War. This too he survived, living on to become sheriff, then lord mayor.

Feeling many times blessed, Gayer made a special endowment in his will. This provided for an annual service to be held every October 16 in his neighborhood church, London's Saint Katherine Cree. The "Lion Sermon" has been performed every year since Gayer's death in 1649. The sermon always includes a section from the Book of Daniel, as well as material concerning Saint Peter's adventures in prison, and then a retelling of Gayer's own lion story.

# October 17

**M**argaret Mary was a misfit. Even in the rarefied world of the convent, where she was known as a conscientious if dour nun, this Frenchwoman managed to alienate her peers. She did this by experiencing, between 1673 and 1675, four separate visions in which Jesus revealed his ventricles and exhorted her to promote worldwide veneration of what he called the Sacred Heart, the *Sacre-Coeur*.

Her fellow nuns balked. Throughout almost all the rest of her life, they thought Margaret Mary was delusional. Only as she approached death in 1690 did she manage to earn a touch of credibility. The long-suffering Margaret Mary had the last laugh, for she was later canonized and the cult of the Sacred Heart is now a major Christian phenomenon. On Margaret Mary's feast day, pilgrims flock to her convent at Paray-le-Monial in Burgundy, a historic structure that today is France's third most popular pilgrimage site, behind only Lourdes and Lisieux.

# October 18

## Brooklyn Barbecue

For years, Brooklyn's great barbecue was an annual event. It commemorated what is said to be the nation's first official barbecue—a stunt the Republican party staged as part of the 1876 presidential campaign. On Tuesday, October 18, 1876, the Republicans paraded a pair of enormous oxen through the streets of New York and then around Brooklyn. Finally they reached Brooklyn's Myrtle Park, where the oxen were tethered. By 11 P.M., the smaller of the beasts, at 983 pounds, had been slaughtered and was roasting over a spit above a coke fire. The spit had a peaked iron roof and vast pans to collect the drippings, with which the meat was repeatedly basted. When at last the ox was done to a turn, several thousand hungry New Yorkers were clamoring for the free meal they had been promised. Working their way methodically through the first ox and 800 loaves of bread, the Republicans handed out thousands of sandwiches. The Republican candidate had been politicking nonstop, while the smell of roasting meat held his audience spellbound. Then the second ox was slaughtered.

# October 19

## Our Lord of Miracles
### Nuestro Señor de los Milagros

**P**eru is earthquake country, and between 1655 and 1687 the people of Lima were beside themselves—literally and figuratively. A spate of violent temblors had wiped out nearly every structure in the city, killing thousands. Despite the survivors' prayers, the quakes continued.

In the aftermath of one spasm, it was discovered that in the neighborhood where most of Lima's black people lived, every single structure had collapsed with the exception of an adobe wall on which some anonymous muralist had painted a dark-skinned Jesus. Almost immediately, people started venerating the image. The adobe wall was carefully freed of its moorings and carried bodily through what was left of the city, as penitents loudly confessed their sins and flagellated themselves with leather thongs. Soon somebody pointed out that the earthquakes had stopped.

Lima's annual procession is organized by a purple-robed brotherhood rooted in the neighborhood where the wall was discovered. The original painting, framed in silver, stands in Lima's Las Nazarenas church. All through October, the church is filled with purple-ribbon-wreathed candles. Local dignitaries are offered chances to help carry the wall during the procession. Thousands follow the procession; many walk backward so as not to turn away from *el Señor*.

# October 20

## Colchester Oyster Feast

For nearly two thousand years, people have been cultivating the common British oyster, *Ostrea edulis,* in the lower reaches of England's Colne River—ever since the town now known as Colchester was a Roman fortress called Camulodunum. The Romans exported boatloads of Camulodunum oysters to Italy; Pliny is said to have loved them.

Colchester's oyster harvest is still a big event. On opening day in late September, the mayor and city council members don ceremonial regalia and travel via fishing boat to the "oyster-fattening beds" at Pyefleet Creek. There the town clerk reads aloud a 1256 proclamation stating Colchester's right to the beds "from time beyond where memory runneth not to the contrary." The mayor dredges the season's first oysters and immediately eats one. As is customary in this rite, he chases that with gin and gingerbread, toasting the queen's health.

The second oyster ceremony, the Colchester Oyster Feast, has been an institution since before the seventeenth century—and always on October 20, the eve of the day formerly dedicated to Saint Denys, which in times of yore was a major occasion for trade fairs. Originally the oyster feast was a literal free-for-all, with everyone hauling bucketfuls of oysters from the river. Today the feast is a genteel, controlled function at the Colchester Moot Hall. At the formal evening banquet, some four hundred diners, often including a Royal or two, consume upwards of twelve thousand oysters.

# ☼ctober 21

t Portobelo, Panama, the people on the beach were squint-ing: A huge wooden crate was bobbing in the water off-shore, too far out for them to reach but certainly too tempting to ignore. With the help of some fishermen, the box was towed in. To everyone's amazement, inside was a life-size statue of Jesus, carved of a very dark wood, dressed in contemporary—that is, seven-teenth-century—clothing. The statue's dark eyes were rolled back as if in agony, and daubs of red paint across the forehead created an effectively punctured effect.

This enigmatic jetsam was hurried into town, where a cholera epidemic was in full swing. As soon as the statue was installed in Portobelo's church, the epidemic faded. Not one more person, it is said, took sick. Today, *El Jesus Nazareno* is the town's patron. It takes eighty men to carry the statue, later determined to be carved of ex-otic cocobolo wood. In unison the bearers take two big steps forward, then two lit-tle steps back. In this hypnotic fashion they proceed through the streets, accom-panied by women with smoking censers. All chant mournfully as befits the statue's tortured visage.

# October 22

## Festival of the Ages

### Jidai Matsuri

**K**yoto's beloved history-on-parade pageant features a cast of thousands. And tens of thousands come to watch. After a Shinto service in the morning at which the spirits of deified emperors are invoked, the procession winds its slow and sumptuous way between Kyoto's Imperial Palace (for a thousand years the capital of Japan) and the Heian-jingu shrine, passing through the shrine's massive red *torii* gate.

Characters of every class and profession march along, representing historical periods including the Enryaku (782–805), the Kamakura (1185–1333), the Edo (1615–1868), and the Meiji (1868–1912). Peasants, priests, and merchants are here, as are shoguns with their trademark *hitatari* pants flopping down over their slippers and dragging along behind like a bride's train. Archers, fishwives, warriors, warlords, middle-class townspeople, scholars, smiths—all of history goes by, but it goes in reverse. The parade *starts* with the twentieth century.

# October 23

## The Swallows' Departure

**M**uch fuss has been made about the swallows' annual return to Southern California's Mission San Juan Capistrano. At least, much *used* to be made of it, enough to inspire the 1939 hit song, "When the Swallows Return to Capistrano." In 1776 mission-meister Father Junipero Serra founded Capistrano, the seventh in what would be California's chain (some would say garrotte) of Catholic missions. In 1812 the stone church collapsed in an earthquake, never to rise again. Flocks of swallows, however, continued to "worship" at the mission, nesting amid the ruins from spring till autumn.

The swallows always arrive, thousands at a time, on Saint Joseph's Day, March 19. Throngs of sightseers gather at the mission every year to welcome them. Less well known is the swallows' annual departure from their picturesque lodgings. Like other migratory birds, Capistrano's swallows fly south for the winter, traditionally departing the mission every October 23, which is the death anniversary of Saint John Capistrano, the fifteenth-century Italian saint for whom the place was named. Urbanization, industrialization, and pesticides threaten the natural marvel, as insect-eradication efforts have been steadily killing off the swallows' main food sources.

# October 24

## United Nations Day

*A*s World War II raged on with no end in sight, the United Nations was conceived as a way to help prevent future world wars. As early as 1943, government officials from the United States, Great Britain, and the Soviet Union agreed to meet to discuss plans for an international peacekeeping organization. A year later this organization already bore the name United Nations. Its members agreed to fight against the Axis powers, and under its auspices the U.N. Relief and Rehabilitation Administration began offering aid to people in war-torn countries. The U.N. Organization for Educational and Cultural Reconstruction was formed a year later for similar purposes.

The U.N. was formally established October 24, 1945, in San Francisco. Since then, its membership has risen to over 140 nations. According to a 1947 declaration, each member nation is encouraged to observe October 24 as United Nations Day. Towns and schools sponsor fairs, exhibitions, concerts, essay contests, and banquets—all with an international theme. Some communities host a whole United Nations Week. In New York, U.N. delegates attend the formal United Nations Day Ball and in Washington, D.C., diplomats attend the annual U.N. concert.

# October 25

## Saint Crispin's Day

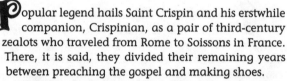

**P**opular legend hails Saint Crispin and his erstwhile companion, Crispinian, as a pair of third-century zealots who traveled from Rome to Soissons in France. There, it is said, they divided their remaining years between preaching the gospel and making shoes.

Crispin's feast day is remembered by shoemakers and leather workers, of whom he is patron saint. In the Apulia region of the saint's native Italy, one town celebrates the day with a huge *calzone* feed. And in *King Henry V*, Shakespeare wrote about the Battle of Agincourt, which took place on October 25, 1415, on the banks of the River Somme in France. Henry's exhausted soldiers were victorious, although outnumbered five to one by the leaping, fresh-as-a-daisy French army. The battle was a bloodbath. Shakespeare wrote:

> *This day is call'd the Feast of Crispian:*
> *He that outlives this day and comes safe home,*
> *Will stand a-tiptoe when this day is nam'd,*
> *And rouse him at the name of Crispian:*
> *He that shall live this day and see old age,*
> *Will yearly on the vigil feast his neighbors,*
> *Then he will strip his sleeve and show his scars,*
> *And say, These wounds I had on Saint Crispin's Day.*

## Quit Rent Ceremony

**P**roof that the Middle Ages was a time of boisterous wit, quit rent ceremonies entail the payment of symbolic or token "rents"—instead of real money—for pieces of real estate. Medieval landlords perfected the practice as a way of "giving" land to friends or to those who had done them favors. But by demanding annual compensation in the form of peppercorns or roses or pork pies, the landlord was able to keep at least nominal title to the land.

London has for over seven hundred years been involved in a pair of annual quit rent ceremonies. The city solicitor still dutifully "pays" these to the queen's remembrancer every October 26 (or as near as possible) at the Law Courts in the Strand. One of these began in 1211 when King John (of Magna Carta fame) granted the city some moorland near Shropshire. No one today is sure why he did this or where it was. In exchange for the land, the king demanded the annual payment of two knives. One of these had to be sharp enough to cut through hazelwood, the other so dull that it would, King John stipulated, "bend in green cheese." Sometime after 1521, the city started substituting a hatchet and a hook for the knives. Because of the hazelwood reference, this payment is called the Faggot Service.

On the same day, the solicitor "pays" the remembrancer for the site of a now-defunct forge in London's Saint Clement Danes parish. Payment for this, proscribed since the year 1234, is half a dozen old horseshoes and sixty-one nails.

# October 27

## Feast of the Holy Souls
### Fiesta de las Santas Animas

This is the time, say the Tzeltal people of Chiapas in Mexico, when the dead are afoot, and so they stay for thirteen days. For the first few days of their visit, the dead are unintrusively left to fend for themselves—looking for meals in the old accustomed places, reacquainting themselves with things loved and remembered. On the 25th, celebrations begin in earnest. They last for many days thereafter, not ending at any one conclusive moment but gradually, bit by bit, as gaggles of ghosts stagger graveward.

Families begin the fiesta by cleaning their relatives' graves and adorning them with pine needles and flowers. They assemble makeshift graveside altars, stocking them with candles and all kinds of food: meat, beans, chiles, salt, tortillas, fruit, and sometimes liquor. Then each person takes a turn talking to the departed spirit, offering it the food and assuring it, often tearfully, that it is loved. The ceremonies go on for several days, as every family has more than one grave to attend to.

# October 28

In April 1936, Greece's recently restored King Yiorgiou ("George") II appointed General Yannis ("John") Metaxas prime minister. This was considered a highly suspect move (as, in fact, the king's own restoration had been, just one year earlier). Various factions protested the appointment of this clearly militaristic new leader. The king responded by dissolving Parliament. Greece settled into several years of dictatorship under Metaxas. So what's to celebrate, you may wonder. Metaxas was a great admirer of both Benito Mussolini and Adolf Hitler, yet he drew the line at actually having them in his own backyard. In October 1940, the Italian ambassador demanded permission to build Italian military bases on Greek soil. Without a moment's hesitation, Metaxas gave his famous reply: *Ochi,* meaning "no." One legend has it that the ambassador showed up on Metaxas's doorstep in the middle of the night and that the prime minister answered the doorbell in his pajamas. A less imaginative school of chroniclers holds that the pair communicated via telegram. War between Greece and Italy erupted within hours. Inflamed with the spirit of resistance, the poorly armed and ill-prepared Greeks managed to rout the invaders.

Today on this national holiday honoring Greek resistance, military parades march through Athens and Thessaloniki. Smaller towns throughout the country are decked in blue and white, the colors of the Greek flag.

# October 29

## Lost-in-the-Dark Bells

*A* surprisingly large number of English villages share the tradition of "lost-in-the-dark bells." In each case, local legend (in some cases, fact) tells of a person who, lost in the dark (in some cases, fog) and headed for certain disaster, was guided toward safety by the reassuring sound of church bells. The lucky survivor, ever after besotted with gratitude, leaves money in his or her will providing for the preservation of the bells (see October 7).

BONG
BONG

At Saint Mary's, Kidderminster, Worcestershire, the story is told of Pecket, who became hopelessly lost in the dark while en route home from Saint Luke's fair. Suddenly, Pecket stopped short: He could hear church bells ringing. The sound told him he was heading the wrong way; in fact, he had been just on the verge of plummeting over the unseen lip of a ravine. In his memory, they still ring every October 29, pealing across the darkness.

# October 30

## Meiji Festival
### Meiji Reidaisai

*A*fter a long period of self-imposed isolation from the rest of the world—and most emphatically from the West—Japan found itself less and less able to fend off foreign visitors. By the turn of the nineteenth century, the Russians were coming, and the British, and then the Americans. In 1853 the U.S. Navy's Commodore Perry arrived with his now-famous contingent of "black ships," demanding that Japan open its doors to international trade. The populace was churning with discontent. In 1867 the reigning shogun stepped down, and governmental control fell into the hands of the emperor, Meiji.

Under what is now known as the Meiji Restoration, which lasted from 1868 to 1912, the shogunate was dissolved completely, the capital was moved from Kyoto to Edo (Tokyo), and Japan underwent climactic industrial revolution and unprecedented Westernization. In the years since then, as many buildings, institutions, and products have been named after Emperor Meiji as things in the United States are named after Washington. Commemorating the decisiveness of the Meiji period is this festival, held at Meiji-jingu, a Tokyo Shinto shrine erected in memory of Emperor Meiji and Empress Shoken. The event features five days of performances—*noh* dramas, martial arts, classical court dancing, concerts, and horseback-archery contests. The affair climaxes on November 3, Emperor Meiji's birthday.

# October 31

The Celts knew this day as the eve of their great festival Samhain. This was the time for leading livestock home from summer pastures to the winter shelters. Samhain Eve was a time when the veil between the worlds of the living and the dead grew especially thin, and ghosts ventured toward the warmth of people's hearths and homes. On Samhain Eve the Celts built bonfires in memory of their departed ancestors and left food and drink on their tables overnight for the nourishment of the ghosts.

Odile, the tenth-century abbot of Cluny, changed Samhain's name to All Saints' Day. October 31 became All Hallows' Eve or Hallows' Even, and eventually Halloween. Never having lost its haunted quality, Halloween has fallen into the hands of children, whose practice of trick-or-treating has its roots in the English custom of "soul-caking." From medieval times onward, poor people would beg door-to-door for spiced cakes that the householders would award as payment for prayers the beggars promised to say for the householders' ancestors. The soul-cakers sang:

> *Soul, soul, for a souling cake,*
> *I pray, good missus, a souling cake.*
> *Apple or pear, a plum or a cherry,*
> *Any good thing to make us all merry.*

# Moveable Feast
## Cluster-of-Lights Festival

**Diwali**

**P**eople travel enormous distances just to be home with their families for this happiest and most important of Hindu holidays. And the homes look inviting, too, throughout the late-autumn week of *Diwali,* especially at night, as celebrants line window sills, porches, and garden walls with long rows of tiny earthenware oil lamps, whose cotton wicks give off a soft, pulsating glow. Diwali (aka *Divali* or *Deepavali*) is a sort of New Year, at which time people strive to settle old feuds and quarrels and, if they can afford it, buy brand-new clothes in which to celebrate. In the mountain regions, bonfires devour the year's accumulation of combustible garbage; in many cities, fireworks dance across the sky.

The festivities honor the victory of Rama—an avatar and manifestation of the love-god Vishnu—over the ten-headed demon who had stolen Rama's wife, Sita. Devotional music and lamp-lighting ceremonies give way to vegetarian feasts, games of chance, and the exchanging of gifts, usually fruit or sweets. For the occasion, some Hindu temples display towers of pastries fifteen feet high.

# November 1

Children in Sicily go to bed on November 1 well aware that outside, in all the graveyards, the dead are rising from their tombs and coming like Santa Claus to deliver candies, cookies, and gifts.

Across the globe in Mexico, All Saints' Day is specially devoted to *los angelitos*, the little angels—that is, all the dead children. This is a prelude to November 2's *Día de los Muertos,* Day of the Dead, a national holiday on which all the grown-up ghosts will be arriving in full force. The littler specters get a head start. To help them find their way back to the homes where once they lived, parents and still-living siblings often shoot off firecrackers. In some parts of the country on this night, for the same purpose, they strew a path of flower petals from the graveyard to the front porch.

In chilly Estonia, meanwhile, folktales tell of unsuspecting persons who wander into village churches on this night only to find all the pews filled with ghosts who sit and kneel attentively while a ghostly priest celebrates mass at the altar. The nearness of the dead is keenly expressed in the All Saints' Day customs of England, Belgium, Hungary, France, and other countries.

# November 2

## All Souls' Day
### Día de los Muertos/I Morti

**M**exico's *Día de los Muertos* (Day of the Dead) calls for jolly all-day picnics beside the graves of dead relatives—during which Mexican cemeteries become as crowded and colorful as marketplaces. At home, people assemble little altars called *ofrendas,* stocked with the departed loved ones' favorite foods and drinks, their photographs, and other memorabilia, as well as candles and pungent marigolds, a flower long associated with death. In the spirit of the holiday, shops and markets are overflowing with death-themed toys and novelties: wooden skeletons on sticks, toy coffins complete with pop-up skeletons, papier-mâché skeletons wearing doctors' (or policemen's or bandleaders' or clergymen's) uniforms. Confectioners sell shiny-eyed sugar skulls and *panes de muertos,* anise-tinged egg-breads baked in the shapes of well-dressed men, women, and animals. The Mexican custom of erecting Day of the Dead altars has caught on north of the border, where the altars serve as the focus for ancestor rituals and memorials.

Sicilian chefs have similar ways of marking the holiday—with almond-flavored "bones of the dead," bone-shaped biscotti, with molded-sugar dolls, and with *fave dei Morti,* little Venetian cookies in the shapes of fava beans, a legume associated since ancient times with rites of the dead.

# November 3

## Saint Hubert's Day
### Saint-Hubert

**B**loodhounds in the basilica, barking: The priest doesn't mind—at least, not on the feast day of Saint Hubert, patron saint of hunters. In his honor, many churches in the eighth-century saint's native Belgium host a special hunters' mass. It is said that while still a heathen, this fun-loving sportsman went hunting in the Ardennes forest one Good Friday, only to meet a giant stag with a golden cross gleaming between its antlers. (Saint Eustace [see September 20] is said to have had an almost identical hunting experience.) Instantly converted, Hubert lived on to become bishop of Tongres-Maestricht and bishop of Liege. His feast day marks the official opening of the hunting season.

The hunters' mass celebrated in the town of Saint Hubert, southeast of Brussels in the center of the Ardennes, draws hundreds of pilgrims every year. Red-jacketed, velvet-capped huntsmen wail away on spiraled hunting horns, while ranks of dogs stand by, waiting for their masters to present them to the priest, who blesses them one by one.

# November 4

## Mischief Night

*A* time of misrule, when every principle is turned on its head, is a tempting thing indeed. Halloween is one of these, as was ancient Rome's *Saturnalia* (see December 17). Some sociologists have theorized that such festivals-of-chaos are necessary for the running of a decent culture.

From time immemorial, British children have celebrated a Mischief Night. This is the time for plugging neighbors' chimneys, whitewashing enemies' windows, and setting fire to piles of dogdoo on doorsteps so that the unfortunate householder gets an unpleasant surprise while stamping out the flames. Until relatively recently, different regions celebrated their Mischief Nights at different times of year. In Cornwall and Devon, where it was called Nickanan or the sinister-sounding Dappy-Door Night, Mischief Night fell on Shrove Monday. Other regions preferred May Day; others Halloween. But during this century, Mischief Night has attached itself to November 4, Guy Fawkes Eve. Especially popular in Lancashire, Yorkshire, and the northern Midlands, as well as New Zealand and Australia, Mischief Night is loud with firecrackers and bright with bonfires.

# November 5

## Guy Fawkes Night

On November 5, 1605, one Guy (short for Guido) Fawkes, a Catholic Yorkshireman, was arrested in the cellar of the House of Lords. With him were thirty-six barrels of gunpowder with which he had planned to blow up King James I and the entire Parliament. Parliament had refused to temper its repressive anti-Catholic policies and promptly declared the anniversary of Fawkes's arrest a national holiday of thanksgiving, to be celebrated with church services every year. Within seventy-five years it had become a thrilling "bonfire night," when people made effigies of the pope and burned them. As the *Portsmouth Daily Evening Times* reported in 1892, "The chaps . . . dance in fantastic glee," chanting jingles like "A rope, a rope, a rope to hang the pope," and "Please to remember the fifth of November: gunpowder, treason and plot." And

> *Here is the pope that we have got,*
> *The whole promoter of the plot.*
> *We'll stick a pitchfork in his back*
> *And throw him in the fire.*

Today the biggest celebrations are in Lewes, a Sussex town that has never forgiven the Catholic queen, "Bloody Mary," for having executed seventeen of its Protestant citizens. Beginning at dusk in Lewes, countless leaping fires gobble effigy after effigy, as mock "archbishops" and "prelates" deliver solemn death sentences.

# November 6

## Leonard's Ride

### Leonhardi-ritt

**B**avarians living in villages along the bend of the Isar River have been paying homage to Saint Leonard, patron of cattle and horses, for hundreds of years. Leonard's popularity has diminished much since the days when medieval Crusaders adored him. (He may or may not have been a hermit, and may or may not have founded a French monastery, and may or may not have worked a few miracles.) From all over the surrounding countryside, farmers' families ride into the village of Bad Tolz on the morning of Leonard's feast day. They ride *truhenwagenen,* special wagons that they have decorated with scenes from the saint's life—a considerable challenge, since no one knows much of anything about him.

They have spent weeks on the decorations. The horses drawing the wagons have their tails, manes, and harnesses wreathed in ribbons, flowers, and green herbs. Everyone steers toward Kalvarien, or "Calvary," a hill on the outskirts of town. A sprawling, ancient tree once stood here and may have been the focus of rituals. In 1722 a chapel supplanted the tree. Members of the clergy and the city council head the procession, riding in a wagon of their own, drawn by white horses. The wagons go around the chapel three times, and then the priest performs mass. Later, back in the village, the festival transmutes into a songfest and a whip-cracking contest.

# November 7

**W**hile all of Mexico devotes the first two days of this month to the care and feeding of the dead, the Maya people of the Yucatan peninsula afford their deceased an entire week. The first ghosts to arrive, it is said, are those of the children, *los angelitos*. They come in the morning and are treated to breakfast—usually boiled corn on the cob. Prayers are said for them in church; candles are lit at their graves. Then comes lunch: squash, chicken, *atole*, chocolate, biscuits. When the little ones have eaten their fill, the adult ghosts arrive. The living have cleaned and decorated their loved ones' graves for the occasion; and throughout the day living and dead share a rich meal, usually featuring a stuffed meat dish.

For the rest of the week, the ghosts disport themselves in customary fashion, and on November 7 they depart. The living bid them farewell with a banquet.

# November 8

## Swearing in the Lord Mayor

 ertainly lordly, London's lord mayor enjoys an earl's privileges and an admiral's as well. His is a title that was established over eight hundred years ago. In many civic ventures, he takes precedence over everyone except the queen; wherever the lord mayor goes, pomp follows.

In the weeks following his pomp-encrusted election, the nascent lord mayor lies low, save one official visit to the House of Lords, for which (according to medieval decree) he dresses "discreetly," in a long purple gown.

Then comes his admission ceremony, his swearing in. For hundreds of years, this was held every November 8 (it was recently reassigned to the second Friday in November). At the Guildhall, he offers his formal Declaration of Office, after which the entire proceedings are carried out in total silence—a practice that has earned this ceremony the alternate title "the Silent Change." In silence, the old and new lord mayors exchange seats. Then the old passes to the new all the paraphernalia of the office: the city scepter, the sword, the Elizabethan city purse, the seals and keys of mayoralty, and the crystal mace, whose medieval shaft and fifteenth-century head sport gold and pearls. When the new lord mayor has these in hand, trumpets blare and the bells of all the nearby churches begin to peal.

# November 9

## The Lord Mayor's Show

This first annual public appearance of London's lord mayor has grown increasingly rococo since it was initiated in 1215. Londoners throng the sidewalks to watch the parade as it passes. Among the paraders are uniformed marching bands, decorated floats, red-coated musketeers, armored pikemen, footmen, and trumpeters, all going in solemn procession from the Guildhall to the law courts. Towering wickerwork giants representing mythical characters were part of the procession until 1708, when they were replaced by less breakable wooden giants. In the position of honor at the rearmost of the parade is the newly elected lord mayor in a gilt-and-glass coach, used for this purpose only, whose side panels are bright with golden encrustations and paintings of angels. Waving from inside is the "chief citizen" in flowing red robes, fur-and-lace collar, and all the regalia of his office. These include the "Cap of Dignity," the jeweled lord mayor's badge, and the five-foot-long sixteenth-century mayoral chain, which comprises interlinked silver roses and double *S*'s (standing for *souvent me souviene*, "remember me often," motto of the House of Lancaster). For centuries a November 9 standby, the Lord Mayor's Show is now held on a movable date early in November.

# November 10

## Martin Luther's Birthday/
## Saint Martin's Eve

### Martinsfest

*C*atholic Germans, on November 11, celebrate Saint Martin's Day with torchlight processions and abundant thanksgiving-style feasts. Their Protestant compatriots, however, celebrate a wholly different Martin on the preceding day. Martin Luther, founder of Protestantism, is the operative Martin in this *Martinsfest*. Lantern-light processions honor him, too, especially in Erfurt, where Luther attended university. A longtime tradition at this event has been for the thousands of participants, once they reach the plaza facing the cathedral, to arrange their flickering lanterns into the "Luther rose," Martin Luther's insignia.

A time for family reunions and goose-and-sauerkraut feeds, Saint Martin's Eve—Catholic, again—prompts harvest-home celebrations in traditional Latvia. In Belgium the day was long considered a sort of mini-Christmas, on which Martin himself arrived bearing fruits and candy for good people, whip lashings for bad ones.

# November 11

**F**easting at this time of year is such a steadfast French tradition that it is called *faire le Saint-Martin*, "doing the Saint Martin." Here in the land where the Hungarian-born Martin converted the Gauls and became the cherished patron saint of kings, roast goose is the meal *de rigeur* on his day, as it is in Latvia, Sweden, England, and elsewhere.

In memory of his kindness to a drunken beggar who had stumbled and fallen down in front of him, Martin is hailed as the patron saint of drunks and beggars as well as of tavern keepers. Thus many French and Italian towns, where the year's new wine is just now ready to drink, sieze the opportunity to mark Saint Martin's Day with wine-tasting extravaganzas.

In centuries past, *San Martino* was one of the most important days in the Italian year, on which governmental sessions and schools reopened, and leases were traditionally signed. Now it is not so significant, but special pastries are still made for this day. These include a Venetian butter-horn, honey-drizzled Sicilian potato fritters called *sfinci*, and thrice-baked Sicilian *biscotti di San Martino*.

*Marten Gas* parties in the goose-rich province of Skane, southern Sweden, feature prune-stuffed geese, cabbage dishes, and a visceral blood soup in which bob bits of the goose's neck, heart, liver, and wings, along with ginger, pepper, vinegar, sugar, apples, and wine.

# November 12

## Tesuque Feast Day

**T**esuque is now a relatively obscure Pueblo Indian village just north of Santa Fe, New Mexico. But once—when its name was the pre-Spanish Taytsoonghay—this was a place to be reckoned with. The Pueblo Revolt of 1680 started here, touched off when villagers killed a Spanish civil servant. The very next day a Spanish priest arrived to say mass; he was promptly dispatched too.

Today the villagers observe both Christian rites and their own ancient ones. On the annual feast day, they emerge from church to witness the buffalo dance. One of the Pueblos' three great wintertime dances, this celebrates the nature and the mysteries of wild game, the hunting of which fed these people's ancestors through the cold, fruitless months. The buffalo, winter's herald, is said to "bring" the snow. The dancers portraying buffaloes wear huge shaggy headgear, made either from real buffalo heads or from other animals' fur with cow horns attached. The masks sport long black beards that slap rhythmically against the dancers' white-daubed chests as they shuffle side by side in orderly, hypnotic lines.

- CHILDREN'S DAY — HONORS INDIA'S FIRST PRIME MINISTER, JAWAHARLA NEHRU B. 11/12/1889 — CELEBRATES CHILDREN, FEATURES ART CONTESTS

# November 13

**N**ovember was a quiet month in ancient Rome. The one bright light was the *ludi plebeii,* the plebeian games. From the year 220 B.C.E. onwards, these tournaments and other diversions took place every November 13 in the Circus Flaminius.

While with the passing years the games came to extend over a longer period, their original day remained sacred to the goddess Feronia. Coincidentally the mother of a three-headed, three-souled demon who was murdered three times over, Feronia was a goddess of fertility and plenty. Originally Etruscan, she is linked with the *plebs*—the common people—and she was known as a liberator of slaves and a protector of freed slaves. Some addressed her as Libertas, as in "liberty," and the chronicler Livy reports that in the year 217 B.C.E., a great sum of money was raised as an offering to Feronia by a group of *libertinae,* Roman freedwomen. Her festival in the midst of the *ludi* probably dates back to an ancient Etruscan fair.

# November 14

## The Little Carnival

The true Carnival ushers in the dreariness of Lent. In Cyprus and parts of Greece, the Little Carnival ushers in the Advent season, which, for purists, is also a time of abstinence. Many observe a forty-day fast, and generally no meat, sweets, or fats are eaten from November 15 until Christmas. So the Little Carnival is a last fling, a binge. Throughout the preceding week, Cypriots travel into the towns from all over the countryside, just to shop for tonight's feast. Nobody wants to be, as the saying goes, "caught barefooted and naked" when the Little Carnival arrives. For many country people, this constitutes a rare visit to town, so this has also become known as the time for replenishing household supplies, clothes, and shoes. An essential item at the feast is a type of sesame-seed-studded pastry, which is baked in the shapes of men and women, animals and farm implements, each with a little dough cross superimposed on top. One of these cookies is hung from a beam or placed before a household icon and left there for good luck until the next year's Little Carnival.

In southernmost Greece's Mani region, feasters gorge on *lalangia,* deep-fried knots and twists of sourdough. These are appropriately rich and have the added bonus of warding off a certain kind of Christmas demon that populates the earth in this season. The *lalangia* are eaten with roasted meat, sprinkled with cheese, or drizzled with honey. Their very fragrance, it is said, signifies the start of the Christmas season.

# November 15

**I**n 1215 this humble Austrian prince refused to even be *considered* as a candidate for the imperial throne. Nevertheless he was ambitious enough to have sired eighteen children. As Austria's patron saint, he is most beloved for his generosity, having founded three of the country's most prominent abbeys: Klosterneuberg, Heiligenkreuz, and Mariazell.

In Austria, Leopold's feast day marks the start of the *heurigen,* the new wine season. People celebrate with outdoor wine tastings and wine picnics, often accompanied by live music. This too is the day for a pilgrimage to Klosterneuberg Abbey, home of the eminent wine called Leopoldsberg, which the vintner-monks have been making for centuries. (Even in medieval times, this beverage was a major pilgrim draw.) The Leopold's Day custom called *Fasselrutschen,* "sliding down the cask," involves an elephantine 12,000-gallon wooden barrel, commissioned by the abbot for Klosterneuberg's wine cellar in 1704. One by one, pilgrims climb to the top of the cask and slide down its smooth wooden side for good luck. The rougher the slide, they say, the better the luck. (They land on a padded platform.) The Fasselrutschen enjoys a reputation as Austria's "great leveler": The hundreds of pilgrims standing on line for a turn run the gamut of classes and types.

# November 16

An ancestress of the current British royal family, Margaret was born in Hungary, in exile. Then her father, Edward d'Outremer ("the Exile") brought her to the court of the Scottish King Malcolm, where she and the king hit it off and were married in 1070 at Dunfermline Castle. The virtuous and talented Margaret is said to have polished her husband's manners as well as promoting art, education, and culture in her adopted country. In private life she was religious to the point of austerity, eating and sleeping hardly at all. She observed two Lents every year, went to church daily at midnight, and daily washed beggars' feet. In a surprise attack in 1093, the English King William Rufus slew Malcolm. Four days later Margaret too was dead.

Of her eight children, three lived on to become kings, one became queen, and one became a saint. Since 1673, when Margaret was officially declared patroness of Scotland, her feast day has taken on national significance.

# November 17

## Queen Elizabeth's Day

English Protestants saw Elizabeth I's accession to the throne as a victory; her queenship launched a whole new wave of religious persecution. Queen Elizabeth's Day, celebrated in English towns for over a hundred years, marked the anniversary of her accession and was a major holiday on the Protestant calendar.

It was a happy occasion, typically celebrated with a mummers' procession that rollicked through the streets bearing a makeshift sedan chair on which sat the pope, the devil, and the Catholic pretender to the throne. Pretending to speak in the voices of Satan and the Catholics, revelers shouted out mock plots to assassinate the queen. In the crowd, men dressed as monks wielded big knives. Musicians underscored the satire.

With all the confidence of a moral majority, the party marched to a field where a huge bonfire crackled hungrily. As the effigies were cast into the flames, the throng chanted songs such as this one, penned by a Protestant bishop:

> *Three strangers blaze amidst a bonfire's revel:*
> *The Pope, the Pretender, and the Devil.*
> *Three strangers hate our faith, and faith's defender:*
> *The Devil, and the Pope, and the Pretender.*

# November 18

## Saint Plato's Day

**D**eliciously obscure elsewhere, Saint Plato is well respected in Macedonia along the Greek-Serbian-Bulgarian border, where he is formally known as Saint Plato the Martyr. His feast day, like that of many other saints, is alleged to be crucial for meteorological prognostications. Especially along the coast, it is held that the weather that prevails at sundown on Saint Plato's Day is going to last all the way through the Advent season. Locals used to tell stories about how Saint Plato's Day was the real reason Napoleon Bonaparte's Moscow campaign failed. They said that the Russian czar, having noted the weather on Saint Plato's Day, planned his defense accordingly and thus was able to outwit the Corsican.

# November 19

Two Spanish ships carrying human cargo from Nigeria to the American colonies were wrecked off the coast of the Caribbean island of Saint Vincent. Some of the Africans managed to flee the wreckage and swim to shore. Here they came to live among the Carib people for whom the region is named. (The Caribs are also the source of the word "cannibal.") Within a few years a mixed-race people, the "black Caribs," was thriving on the island, to the annoyance of European colonists who feared a slave revolt lest their own servants discover a free black colony on the island. The black Caribs were rounded up and deported to a small isle off what was then called Honduras and is now called Belize. There they came to be known as Garifunas. Some immigrated to Nicaragua and Guatemala, and in 1832 the bulk of them settled in southern Honduras, where the locals passed rumors that the Garifunas worshiped devils and stole babies for culinary purposes.

A national holiday in modern Belize, Garifuna Day (current rumors concern polygamy and a "secret language," passed from Garifuna mothers to daughters and unintelligible even to Garifuna males) draws thousands to the Garifuna town of Dandriga for a day of folk dancing, outdoor food stalls, and *punta* rock music, the local specialty. The main event is a reenactment of the Garifunas' arrival on these shores via dugout canoe.

# November 20

## Commerce God Ceremony

### Ebisu-ko

Ebisu, the Japanese commerce god, is a happy deity, beaming confidently as he oversees all aspects of business and ensures that mortals give each other fair deals. After the January 10 rite during which business owners ask the god for his New Year's blessing, the 20th day of every month is designated as Ebisu's *ennichi,* his "special day." This tradition rose to prominence during the Edo period and is less commonly practiced today. In its heyday, these banquet/meetings were so elaborate that the expression "like *Ebisu-ko*" came to denote any especially sumptuous meal. Ebisu merits twelve ennichi every year because his good graces are so essential. (See December 20.)

At a typical Ebisu-ko, guilds or tradesmen's organizations would gather for their monthly meetings. These took the form of lavish luncheons at which a statue of Ebisu stood over an altar. Or sometimes a *kakemono,* a painted scroll depicting the god, hung in the banquet hall's *tokonoma* alcove. Upon arriving, each guest would place an offering in front of Ebisu's image. Before sitting down to eat and talk, members of the group would conduct a mock business deal, complete in every detail, purely for the god's enjoyment.

# November 21

## The Presentation of the Virgin Mary

*A*t the age of three, it is said, Mary was brought to the great temple of Jerusalem, where the precocious tot insisted on climbing the monumental marble staircase all by herself. At the top, she was embraced by the head rabbi, who personally led her—presented her—to the temple's high altar.

Thereafter, she lived in the temple under the tutelage of holy women, all the while receiving (one apocryphal gospel tells us) daily visions and angels' visits. On Mary's fourteenth birthday, the head rabbi led her into a roomful of men and promised that he would give her in marriage to whichever one of them could make his walking stick burst into blossom. Joseph, as it happens, was that lucky man.

During the Middle Ages, the anniversary of the Presentation became an occasion for mystery plays, sacred dramas halfway between ritual and reenactment. Philippe de Mézières recorded the details of such a play which he attended at Avignon in 1372. Nine angels, he wrote, stood on a staircase and sang a Marian hymn, which cued others in the cast to sing acclamatory verses of their own. One character complained and was shoved downstairs by two archangels. Lucifer howled and was also hurled downstairs. Mary's parents led her to the rabbi, who embraced her. Then the whole cast celebrated mass, a white dove was released into the air, and Mary was carried bodily out of the church.

# November 22

## Saint Cecilia's Day

Cecilia, it is said, demonstrated her true faith by silently singing hymns all through her wedding. Later that night, when she told her pagan bridegroom that she was a Christian and had taken a vow of celibacy, he politely converted on the spot. Some time later, they were both martyred, but not before Cecilia had distinguished herself by singing charmingly to angels and (so it is said) inventing the pipe organ. Thus she emerged as the patron saint of music, and as such was beloved of medieval musicians' guilds.

In 1683 the British Musical Society began staging annual Saint Cecilia's Day concerts. Every November 22, the society's London members attended a service, usually at Saint Bride's Church, at which the priest pointedly lauded the glories of religious music.

After the service, the society enjoyed the Cecilia anthem, a new one of which was composed every year. Samuel Dryden's "Song for Saint Cecilia's Day," presented in 1686, told of "divine Cecilia . . . inventress of the vocal frame; the sweet enthusiast." Alexander Pope's "Ode for Music on St. Cecilia's Day" was 1707's offering. The celebrations continue to this day. After the service and anthem, the society sits down to a luncheon and a concert of modern and traditional English music.

# November 23

## Saint Clement's Day

Clement's martyrdom, it is said, came about when he was lashed to an iron anchor and thrown into the sea. Thus he became patron saint of ironworkers and blacksmiths. On November 23, blacksmiths in the south of England used to fashion bearded effigies of the saint, tongs in hand, that they would settle into chairs and carry around the neighborhood. It was traditional for master blacksmiths to honor the day by awarding each of their employees a "wayz-goose," not a goose at all but a leg of pork, stuffed with sage and onions. Another English custom was that of "clemmening," in which children went door to door on Saint Clement's Day, begging for treats as at Halloween. One Staffordshire jingle implored:

*Clemany! Clemany! Clemany mine!*
*A good red apple and a pint of wine,*
*Some of your mutton and some of your veal:*
*If it is good, pray give us a deal.*

# November 24

## Serra Pageant

In California, Father Junipero Serra (pre-monastic name: Miguel José Serra) is famous for founding the state's Catholic mission system. In the name of God, Serra gallivanted from one gorgeous locale to another. Mallorcan-born, he taught philosophy in his native island's capital, Palma, before sailing to Mexico in 1749 with his best friend. From there he accompanied an expedition to San Diego in 1769; from there, he junketed up the coast in search of Monterey. When he found it, Serra dug in his heels. As president of the Alta California missions, he was headquartered in what is now Carmel. In the ensuing years, the priest founded missions at San Luis Obispo, San Juan Capistrano, and elsewhere—twenty-one of them in all. He often enlisted the local natives to do the hard labor.

At Mission Carmel, annual Father Serra birthday celebrations were instituted in 1948. These usually took the form of a pageant reenacting Serra's many adventures, including his 1769 arrival in San Diego.

# November 25

## Saint Catherine of Alexandria's Day

The "Catherine wheel" on which this saint was tortured bears some vague resemblance to a spinning wheel, which helps to explain Catherine's status as patron of lacemakers, seamstresses, and unmarried ladies—that is, spinsters.

For hundreds of years, women in the sewing professions enjoyed a festive day off in Catherine's honor. It was a party day, too, for unmarried Frenchwomen over the age of twenty-five. These so-called *catherinettes* would don paper caps on their patron's day and march through the streets of Paris. The expression "she's putting on Saint Catherine's hat" meant that a woman was on the way to becoming an old maid. Unmarried Irishwomen used to fast on this day in hopes of finding husbands. Their English counterparts celebrated by "Catherning": going door-to-door begging for apples and pennies. English Saint Catherine parties often featured a warm rum-and-beer mixture thickened with beaten eggs. Another delicacy was "lambswool": spiced ale or cider flecked with the soft pulp of roasted apples. "Kattern Cake," the Bedfordshire specialty, was a round yeasted loaf made with butter, eggs, and caraway seeds, cut into wedges and served with tea.

When the Industrial Revolution put an end to commercial hand-sewing and hand-lacemaking, it also put an end to most Saint Catherine's Day celebrations.

# November 26
## Saint Peter of Alexandria's Day

**P**eter was bishop of Alexandria during the reign of Emperor Diocletian, a time when dozens of Christians were being hunted down and persecuted and usually killed. A very old man himself, Peter worked hard to guard the members of his flock from arrest. At the same time, he coached them on how not to fear death if they were in fact captured and tortured. The secret, Peter said, was to die to the self, renounce self-will, and detach from all earthly things. He followed his own advice when in the year 311 he himself was executed.

As the last Christian put to death by public order at Alexandria, Peter earned saintly distinction. The Egyptian Copts, who embrace him as their own martyr and regularly mark his feast day, call Peter the Seal and Fulfillment of the Persecution.

# November 27

## Saint Maximus's Day

**i**f it were up to Maximus himself, this Provençal bishop would not be famous at all. He avoided public recognition with incredible zeal. When in his youth it was discovered that Maximus had a knack for reviving people on their deathbeds, crowds surged from far and wide to visit him. Maximus sneaked away and hid in a forest. Learning that the community of Fréjus on the Côte d'Azur wanted him to serve as its bishop, Maximus stayed away, living in penance, prayer, and poverty in the woods all through the rainy season. When at last he reentered society in the year 434, his superiors demanded that he take over the bishopric of Riez, in Provence.

Hearing this, Maximus tried to get away in a boat. He was brought back, however, and forced to assume the position. Saint Hilary himself ordained him. Against his will, Maximus served, exhibiting great care for his monks as well as the radiant humility that had always made him such a compelling figure. He is renowned as one of the most prominent prelates of his time as well as patron saint of the dying.

# November 28
## Ascension of 'Abdul-Baha

*A* Persian-born offshoot of the now-defunct Muslim sect called Babism, the Baha'i faith now has adherents and temples all over the world. Its founder was Baha'u'llah, aka Mirza Hessein Ali (1817–1892). He preached that God can appear to humans in human form—Abraham, Moses, and King David were examples of such a manifestation, he said, as were Jesus, Mohammed, and others, including himself. For this, and for his faith in widespread education and the equality of the sexes and of the world's religions, he was imprisoned in Baghdad, Constantinople, Adrianople, and finally in Acre, where he died. Baha's successor was his son, 'Abdul-Baha Bahai, aka Abbas Effendi. He too was much imprisoned, and exiled as well. Finally settling in Haifa, he was knighted in 1920 and went on the lecture circuit in the United States. There Sir Abdul, as he was called, laid the cornerstone of a grand Baha'i temple in Chicago.

November 28 is a Baha'i holy day marking the anniversary of Sir Abdul's death, which Baha'is call his ascension—that is, the rising of his spirit to heaven.

# November 29

## Saint Andrew's Eve

**i**n many parts of Europe, this was long considered *the* night for fortune telling. In Poland, where the holiday is called *Noc Swietego Andreja,* a favorite method involved drizzling melted candle wax into a bowl of cold water. The shapes of the hardened wax globules could then be interpreted. People were especially vigilant for blobs resembling hearts and ships. Also, young women would snap bare branches off cherry trees. They would "plant" these in wet sand on Saint Andrew's Eve and water them diligently in hopes of forcing them to blossom before Christmas—an omen, it was said, that the planter would marry within the next year. Other divination techniques included the analysis of shadows and the floating of walnut-shell "boats" to see which ones bumped into each other.

In Rumania, the night called *Ajunul Zilei de Sfantul Andrei* was not fun but fearsome. This and only this was the night when *strigoii,* vampires, rose from their graves and roamed around, bent on violence, balancing their coffins on their heads. Generally they headed for the houses where they had once lived. People carefully rubbed their doorknobs and window latches with fresh-cut garlic to repel the strigoii.

# November 30

## Saint Andrew's Day

Legend says that this Galilean fisherman-turned-apostle was martyred circa the year 70 on an *X*-shaped cross in Greece. Some of his relics now rest in Saint Andrews, Scotland, where Andrew is patron saint; the *X*-shaped cross is the country's national symbol. Once a major Scots holiday, the popularity of Saint Andrew's Day, aka Andermess, had dwindled much by the late 1800s but is enjoying a comeback, especially among expatriates. No Saint Andrew's Day banquet is complete without a singed sheep's head, which serves as the main course. It is carried aloft into the banquet hall to the accompaniment of wailing bagpipes and shouts of "Here's tae us." The haggis, too, often makes an appearance.

This day has matchmaking connotations as well, possibly because the saint's name evokes the Greek *andros,* meaning male. Martin Luther recorded an invocation current in the Germany of his time: "God, my God! Holy Andrew, give me a pious manliness, and send me a wife today." An English verse illuminates:

> *To Andrew all the lovers and the lustie wooers come,*
> *Believing, through his ayde, and certaine ceremonies done,*
> *While as to him they presentes bring, and conjure . . .*
> *To have good luck, and to obtaine,*
> *Their chief and sweete delight.*

# Moveable Feast

## The Feast of Lights
### Chanukah

**O**n the Jewish calendar, this midwinter rite is a relative light-weight. And yet it remains one of the best-loved. Like Purim, Passover, and others, Chanukah sprang from a tale of anti-Semitism. In the second century B.C.E., the Seleucidan king, Antiochus IV, strove to convert all Jews forcibly to the polytheistic Greek religion. As the Roman historian Tacitus later wrote, Antiochus barred the Jews from their temple on Mount Zion and insisted that they "sacrifice swines' flesh, and . . . leave their sons un-circumcised"—under penalty of death. Seleucidan troops raided the temple and installed a statue of Zeus on the altar, outraging the Jews. After much bloodshed, Jewish guerrillas, 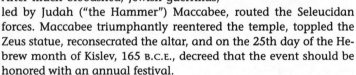 led by Judah ("the Hammer") Maccabee, routed the Seleucidan forces. Maccabee triumphantly reentered the temple, toppled the Zeus statue, reconsecrated the altar, and on the 25th day of the Hebrew month of Kislev, 165 B.C.E., decreed that the event should be honored with an annual festival.

With this, it is said, he lit the *menorah,* the candelabra. Tales are told of how the temple's depleted oil supply, while technically enough for only one day's burning, miraculously lasted eight days. Thus celebrants today light their own menorahs, adding another candle on each of Chanukah's eight nights before sitting down to a festive meal. The holiday's standby is *latkes,* fried potato pancakes, usually topped with applesauce or sour cream.

# December 1

Unlike most Japanese rulers before him and certainly all who would come after, Toyotomi Hideyoshi (1536–1598) was of plebeian blood, having been the adopted son, it is said, of a farmer. He was of such slight build and had such distinctive features that his associates nicknamed him *Saru-san*, "Mr. Monkey." His generosity made him a favorite with the populace, as did his vivid lifestyle.

One of the things Hideyoshi loved was the tea ceremony. He studied under Sen no Rikyu, Japan's greatest tea master, and he commissioned artisans to make him a solid gold portable tea arbor, so that he might enjoy his tea even on battle campaigns. To celebrate an important military victory in October 1587, Hideyoshi threw a tremendous tea party at a Kyoto temple, to which all citizens were welcome, regardless of class or station. Commemorating the ruler who is credited with popularizing the tea ceremony, *Kencha-sai* is an annual all-day reenactment of Hideyoshi's party, held at the same shrine, Kyoto's tenth-century Kitano Tenjin.

# December 2

## Saint Bibiana's Day

This young Roman is said to have lived in the mid-fourth century with her father Flavian, her mother Dafrosa, and her sister Demetria. The family came to the attention of the anti-Christian Julian the Apostate, who had them all arrested and sentenced to death. Flavian was branded in the face with a red-hot iron and died shortly afterwards of his wounds. Dafrosa was beheaded. Demetria simply fell down and died, presumably of stress. Bibiana was tied to a column and beaten to death with lead-weighted scourges. The entire family was soon canonized. During the Middle Ages, Bibiana's story was popular reading material, especially in Germany and Spain, where many churches were named after this romantic figure.

Bibiana and her kin were stripped of their saintliness by papal order in 1969, possibly because they never existed. Still, Bibiana's feast day is observed at the basilica on Rome's Esquiline Hill where a Bernini statue of the maiden rests on the altar. Frescoes depict her adventures, and her stout death-column is on display.

# December 3
## Saint Francis Xavier's Day

**F**rancis sailed eastward in 1542. His first stop was the Portuguese-influenced Indian city of Goa. Francis established his headquarters there, then went on to evangelize Ceylon, the Moluccas, the Malay peninsula, and finally Japan, where as an official representative of the Portuguese king he was well received. Two years later he was waiting for a boat to China when he fell ill and expired in a hut.

By this time, Francis had been in Asia for ten years. He is credited with hundreds of thousands of conversions, although the original figures have since been disputed. Some time after his death, Francis's body was disinterred and brought back to Goa.

The body was laid out in Goa's Chapel of Saint Paul. Soon afterwards, an ecstatic pilgrim bit off one of Francis's toes and ran off with the relic proudly clamped in her jaws. A few years later, another toe was nabbed, and then in 1614 the pope himself asked for, of all things, Francis's right arm. Thus dismembered, the body was finally enclosed in a sarcophagus, which was opened amidst much

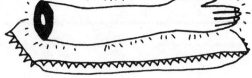

rejoicing every year on the saint's feast day. In 1974, deterioration having set in, the corpse was exposed for the last time. Francis's feast day remains Goa's most important annual festival.

# December 4

**B**arbara's legend starts out like a fairy tale and ends like a snuff film. Her father, Dioscurus, kept the lovely girl locked in a tower to shield her from the eyes of plebes. Then, when princes came begging for her hand, Dioscurus offered Barbara her choice among them, at which point (here the snuff film commences) she announced that she was a Christian and had no intention of marrying anyone except Jesus. Dioscurus grew enraged. Barbara transformed a herd of sheep into a plague of locusts; Dioscurus dragged Barbara around by her hair. Caxton's *Golden Legend* goes on to tell how Dioscurus's henchmen "unclothe[d] her and beat her with the sinews of bulls, and frot her flesh with salt." Then she was "hanged between two forked trees," where her tormentors "burn[ed] her sides with burning lamps, and . . . made her strongly to be beaten, and hurted her head with a mallet." Finally she prayed for death and so expired.

In Poland, her feast day, *Dzien Swietej Barbary,* was long considered an important weather harbinger. If it rained on Saint Barbara's Day, the farmers said, then there would be ice by Christmas. If Saint Barbara's Day came with ice, then it would rain on Christmas Day. As *'Id al-Barbarah,* the holiday prompts parties among Syrian Christians, who host colorful candlelit meals complete with special desserts and Barbara hymns.

# December 5

They say in the Netherlands that Saint Nicholas comes not on Christmas but on the eve of his feast day, and that he comes from Spain, in a boat, dressed in bishops' robes. Every year on the Saturday nearest this day, a man dressed as Saint Nicholas rides a white horse through the streets of Amsterdam while, all along the canal, thousands welcome him. *Sinterklaas*'s companion is Zwarte Piet, "Black Peter," dressed as a Moor in blackface, plumed hat, doublet, and hose. (In recent years, the centuries-old Black Peter tradition has prompted discussions of racism in the Dutch media.) Here as in Belgium, Germany, and Hungary, children set out empty shoes today for Nicholas to fill with cookies and toys during the night. Some leave hay or carrots for the horse.

Come nightfall every December 5, Saint Nicholas arrives in the Swiss village of Küssnacht, on the shores of Lake Lucerne, only to be chased down the streets by dozens of white-gowned villagers. For this *Klausjagen*, "Santa Claus hunt," the careening participants balance enormous, intricately perforated cardboard mitres on their heads. Often nearly as tall as the wearers themselves, the mitres or *iffelen* are candlelit from within and make for an eerie spectacle. Admittedly a pagan holdover, the *Klausjagen* persists despite governmental attempts to quash it.

# December 6

## Saint Nicholas's Day

mericans associate Saint Nicholas with Christmas, but the bishop's actual feast day is December 6, which in many places is a holiday in its own right. In France it is said that the Virgin Mary gave Nicholas the province of Lorraine as a present, and that he spends the day touring the region.

Germany's Saint Nikolaus arrives today with his associate, the black-faced Knecht Ruprecht, who brandishes a chain and threatens to tie up bad children in burlap sacks. Austria's Saint Nicholas, like the rest of his Teutonic counterparts, brings gifts for those who deserve them, while his sinister sidekick doles out punishment to those evil reprobates who have not been studying the Bible. In some parts of the country this sidekick is a pronghorned monster called Klaubauf; in others it is a female demon called Krampusweibl, and sometimes a sinister three-legged goat called the Habergeiss.

Pious Syrian Christians go to church and listen to recitations of Nicholas's adventures. Meanwhile, seamen light candles before Nicholas's icon on board every Greek vessel. It is hoped that the sailors' patron, this guardian of ships and rescuer of persons imperiled at sea, will grant them another year's worth of safe voyages.

# December 7

## Burning the Devil
### La Quema del Diablo

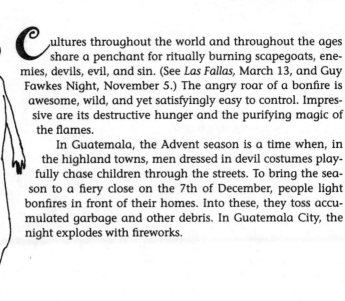

Cultures throughout the world and throughout the ages share a penchant for ritually burning scapegoats, enemies, devils, evil, and sin. (See *Las Fallas,* March 13, and Guy Fawkes Night, November 5.) The angry roar of a bonfire is awesome, wild, and yet satisfyingly easy to control. Impressive are its destructive hunger and the purifying magic of the flames.

In Guatemala, the Advent season is a time when, in the highland towns, men dressed in devil costumes playfully chase children through the streets. To bring the season to a fiery close on the 7th of December, people light bonfires in front of their homes. Into these, they toss accumulated garbage and other debris. In Guatemala City, the night explodes with fireworks.

# December 8

## Feast of the Immaculate Conception

**W**hen the Virgin Mary tells you, "I am the Immaculate Conception," she isn't talking about how she birthed Jesus. She means that she herself was immaculately conceived in the womb of her mother, Saint Anne. By the late sixth century the anniversary of this amazing event was already being celebrated in Byzantium. Through the centuries the holiday grew increasingly popular all over Europe. Reportedly, cannons roared and crowds cheered in Seville when Pope Paul V issued a papal bull in July 1615 that officially instituted the commemoration of the Immaculate Conception.

The holiday is in many places still the year's tenderest renewal of dedication to the Virgin. At Mexico's Lake Patzcuaro, the fiesta opens with the antics of white-gowned stilt dancers, *monigotes,* continues with church services honoring la Virgen de la Salud, and climaxes with fireworks. A street fair marks the occasion at San Juan de los Lagos, a Mexican town where, among other local miracles, the Virgin herself is said to have brought a dead acrobat child back to life. In Uruguay, the holiday doubles as *Día de las Playas,* Beach Day, the official first day of the southern hemisphere's swimming season, on which priests go down to the sea and bless the waters.

# December 9

## Saint Leocadia's Day

This high-born maiden of Toledo was summoned before the governor of Spain in the year 304 to defend her faith. Apparently she said the wrong thing because the governor sentenced her to death. Languishing in prison, Leocadia meditated on her compatriot, Saint Eulalia of Merida, who had recently found herself in the same situation. The twelve-year-old Eulalia was tortured and burned to death, at which point—as a popular Spanish poem recounted—a white dove seemed to fly out of her mouth and a mysterious snow seemed to fall upon her sizzling corpse. Leocadia prayed fervently that she too would expire soon. By the time her executioners arrived for her, they found Leocadia dead in her cell.

Leocadia's feast day was already much celebrated in her native Toledo by the fifth century. In the seventh century at least one Toledo church was named after her. She has been fêted elsewhere, notably in Spanish-influenced Flanders, where she is known as Locaie.

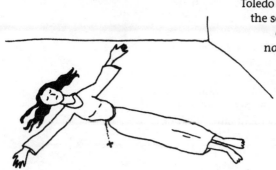

# December 10

*A*lfred Nobel, the nineteenth-century industrialist and inventor who lends his name to the much-lauded annual prizes, was a Swede. And so it is in Stockholm that the prizes, founded with the money Nobel made from the invention of dynamite, are awarded in a very formal, very pompous-and-circumstantial ceremony every December 10. Presenters and recipients stand at attention in tuxedoes and flowing gowns; an orchestra plays jubilantly; and under a furled blue and gold banner, Alfred Nobel himself—or at least his sculpted bust—looks on.

In 1968 a prize in economics was established in Nobel's memory. The categories now include physics, chemistry, medicine or physiology, literature, and peacemaking. The peace prize is awarded in Oslo, also on December 10.

After the awards ceremony, the whole entourage proceeds in its fancy clothes to the Nobel ball, which constitutes the most significant annual event in the Swedish aristocrats' social calendar.

# December 11

The tiny village of Tortugas, three miles south of Las Cruces in southern New Mexico, is a thousand miles north of Mexico's Tepeyac Hill, where in 1531 a wandering Indian met with the dark-skinned stranger who would later be known as the Virgin of Guadalupe. Still, the Tortugueños, the people of Tortugas, feel a keen allegiance with Guadalupe: She is patron of Mexico's native peoples and mixed-race *mestizos;* and by the mid-nineteenth century over 90 percent of Tortugueños boasted a mixture of Spanish blood and that of at least one (often several) of the Pueblo Indian groups.

The three-day annual pilgrimage, climaxing on Guadalupe's feast day, begins on the 10th with a *velorio,* a ceremonial firing in the air of twelve-gauge shotguns. All that day, the people serenade the Virgin with violins, maracas, and ancient Pueblo chants. Before the sun comes up, a group of pilgrims perform the *alva,* the dawn dance. Thus begins the candlelight procession to a shrine on Tortugas Mountain, seven miles east of the village. Drumming, dancing, singing, and praying, the hundreds of worshipers walk, many of them barefoot, pausing now and then to fashion little crowns from cactus, bear grass, and desert flowers found along the way. At the shrine, each pilgrim pays respects to the Virgin. (It is a tradition that local men just back from war make this pilgrimage in thanks for having survived.) At dusk the descent begins, and the pilgrims reenter the darkened village triumphant, candles held high.

# December 12
## Pilgrimage to Guadalupe
### Nuestra Señora de Guadalupe

One day in 1531, on a hill long sacred to the corn goddess Tonantzin, an Indian called Cuatitletoatzen—aka Juan Diego—met a mysterious woman "as radiant as the sun," who coaxed him to convince the authorities that a shrine must be built on the hill called Tepeyac. But the local bishop merely scoffed at the poor Indian's story, and Juan Diego returned shamefacedly to Tepeyac, where the lady urged him to try again. This time the bishop demanded proof. Juan Diego went once again to Tepeyac, where the lady filled his cloak with out-of-season roses and promised to cure his sick uncle, to boot.

The roses wowed the bishop, as did the inexplicable image of the Virgin that he found firmly imprinted on Juan Diego's cloak. News of the cloak-and-roses miracle spread far and wide, and Indians were converted by the thousands. Mexico—then called New Spain—embraced the mysterious stranger, now dubbed the Virgin of Guadalupe, as its patron and protector, a role made official by papal bull in 1754. Today tens of thousands, including many barefoot and bloody-kneed penitents, make the annual pilgrimage to the cathedral near Mexico City that houses Juan Diego's *tilma*—his cloak—a relic of which Pope Pius XII once said, "Brushes not of this world painted this most sweet icon." Native *conchero* dancers leap for hours at a time in the church's atrium.

# December 13

## Saint Lucy's Day
### Lucia

**C**rowned with glowing candles, the Swedish Lucia-girl walks, bearing sweets and coffee, and sometimes *glögg,* fruity mulled wine. From bedside to bedside in her family's home Lucia walks, just before dawn on December 13. Sometimes she makes her rounds at a factory, office, or school. White-gowned, she offers *pepparkakor,* ginger cookies, and swirly little saffron rolls called *lussekatter,* "Lucy-cats." Trailing behind her are other girls with glitter in their hair and "star boys" with tall cone-shaped hats, carrying shiny gold stars on sticks. At the depth of winter, Lucia and her party—local kids in costume—bring back light, hope, the sun.

The actual Saint Lucy was an Italian who tore her own eyes out when their beauty attracted unwanted masculine attention. No one is exactly sure how she came to be linked with the Swedish winter-solstice custom, which dates from at least the late eighteenth century. Certainly there are clues. Lucy's name means "light." And her blindness, the useless pair of eyes that she sent to one suitor on a platter, is symbolic of winter's darkness. In Italy her feast day used to be welcomed with bonfires, and in some parts of the country she was said to bring gifts on this day.

The cardamom-, butter- and raisin-flavored *lussekatter* are shaped like fanciful wheels, with spirals whirling out from a central point. Clearly they resemble the awakening sun. The saffron in the recipe gives them a rich golden hue.

# December 14

To a samurai, death always came before dishonor. Thus a samurai who had been captured, humiliated, or otherwise brought to the end of his rope had no choice but to commit *seppuku*, aka *hara-kiri* or "cutting the belly," in which the participant disembowels himself with a weapon while a helpful comrade stands by holding a sword with which to behead him.

Samurai lived and fought under the aegis of masters, to whom they were fiercely devoted. So when a courtier called Kira Kozukenosuke tricked a master named Asano into humiliating—and then killing—himself, Asano's forty-seven loyal warriors rose up in righteous anger. Upon the death of their lord they had been rendered no longer samurai but *ronin*, drifting ones, men of the waves: masterless fighters. For years they dreamed of vengeance; after much plotting, they killed Kira at his fortress-home in Tokyo. Then having done their duty, they all committed seppuku together. The tale of the forty-seven ronin, subject of many Japanese plays and movies, is called *Chushingura*. Their bodies were buried at Tokyo's Sengaku-ji Temple, where an annual memorial service every December 14 honors them. Highlighting the ceremony is a parade of stalwarts in historical warrior garb.

# December 15

This was Rome's second annual festival in honor of Consus, the god of seed sowing and of the stored-up harvest. (See August 21, the date of the first annual *Consualia*.) Although not nearly as famous as other Roman deities, Consus is undoubtedly much older than most. His roots are in the ancient agricultural communities that flourished in Italy before the advent of Rome.

Because Consus was an earth deity, his altar, like that of the goddess Ops, was buried underground. (It was, wrote the chronicler Tertullian, *sub terra*.) On the two Consualia festivals, priests disinterred the god's altar in the Circus Maximus to perform the rites and make their offerings. Because horses and mules were beasts of burden commonly used in agricultural work and thus were associated with Consus, these animals got a day off for the Consualia. Their manes were decorated with flower garlands, ancient sources tell us. And then—although this seems more of a holiday for the spectators than for the animals—the horses and mules were raced in the Circus Maximus.

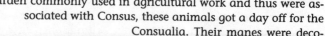

# December 16

*A* reenactment of the Holy Family's fruitless search for lodgings, Mexico's *Posadas*, literally "inns," evokes frustration, humiliation, desperation—and, finally, joy.

A posadas procession is a neighborhood affair. At dusk, a cluster of people traipses from house to house carrying a slender platform on which are arranged clay figurines of angels, stars, trees, the pregnant Virgin riding a burro, and Joseph on foot walking alongside. All sing litanies as they knock, by custom, on door after door. As each door is opened to them, the party begs, in song, for a night's lodging. And, by custom, at each door they are rudely turned away, often with threats. At last one householder is convinced of their need and welcomes them inside, where—by custom—a refreshment table awaits them, as does a *piñata*.

The rite is repeated nightly from December 16 until Christmas Eve, which is called *la noche buena*. Finally the journey is ended and the whole neighborhood shares a feast of tamales and three-colored noche buena salad. Afterwards they sing:

> *Oh beautiful Holy Mary,*
> *Full of glory and sweetness,*
> *The desired night has arrived*
> *Of your confinement, Virgin Pure.*

# December 17

The *Saturnalia* was Rome's favorite holiday. Masters gave their slaves a week's freedom and, in the topsy-turvy whimsy of the season, waited on *them* hand and foot, and dressed them in fine clothes, and even encouraged the slaves to mock those who owned them. Throughout the empire, all schools, law courts, shops, and offices were closed, and all battles and household chores ceased. People of every class gave themselves up to leisure—all in imitation of a legendary "Golden Age" that was embodied by Saturnus, the mythical proto-king for whom the holiday (and the word *Saturday*) was named.

On the 17th, a public pig sacrifice was held at the Forum. Then came the *convivium publicum,* a public feast, after which the senators exchanged their togas for the more casual garment called the *synthesis.* For the rest of the week, individuals performed private piglet sacrifices and ritual baths. Friends and family members visited one another. They feasted, played with dice, and exchanged gifts, a custom still surviving in the form of Christmas presents. These predecessors of Christmas gifts included *cerei,* wax candles, which signified the return of warmth and the sun. They also gave little terra-cotta dolls called *sigillaria.* In some parts of the empire, a "lord of misrule" was chosen to preside over events, to make hilarious declarations and ludicrous laws. The chronicler Seneca marveled, "All Rome seems to go mad on this holiday."

# December 18

## The Virgin of Solitude

### La Virgen de la Soledad

**O**axaca's favorite Virgin, patron of both the city and the state, is the Virgin of Solitude. (Sometimes her name is translated to mean "the Virgin of Loneliness.") To be with her on her feast day, pilgrims come into town from mountains and valleys, from up and down the coast. As the 18th draws nearer, more and more people bustle in and out of the church, whispering prayers, lighting candles before the statue with its pearl-studded crown. They pray that the Virgin will have the mercy to end their loneliness, as this is her specialty. Out in the street, pilgrims hover around sidewalk booths that offer lard-dipped, syrup-soaked fritters, *buñuelos*. These are a Oaxaca Christmastime specialty; custom rather recklessly demands that once the fritter is eaten, the diner must smash the plate on which it was served.

On the night of the 18th, locals organize into neighborhood groups that wind their way to church by lantern light, bearing flowers, branches, paper birds, and lacy colored-paper cutouts fluttering on sticks. As the evening ends, the winter sky explodes with a brilliant filigree of fireworks.

# December 19

The Romans celebrated two holidays in honor of their goddess Ops. The *Opiconsivia* was August 25. Observed during the *Saturnalia*, December 19's *Opalia* was one of the final festivals in the Roman year.

The December date does not correspond with any noteworthy part of the farming cycle, although it has been suggested that at this time, the year's very last olives were being gathered. In that case, the Romans did well to ask the abundance-bringing Ops for her blessing just now.

One chronicler reports that on the day of the Opalia, Romans gave their friends year-end good-luck gifts in the form of holly sprigs. Also, they decorated their temples with green boughs, including holly boughs. If this is so, then the pagan Romans were "decking the halls" centuries before the English started singing about it.

# December 20

## Commerce-God Festival

### Ebisu-ko

The ancestry of Japan's jolly Ebisu, god of business and fair dealing (not to mention tradesmen, merchants, luck, fishing, and food), is a bit of a mystery. Some say he is a Buddhist bodhisattva, and thus Japanese by way of India. But the Shinto faith claims Ebisu, too, calling him the third child of Izanagi and Izanami, the divine couple who stirred the Japanese islands out of oily chaos, then settled down and birthed everything else. Still others say he's not their child but their grandchild.

In any case, Ebisu smiles. He smiles on the making and the spending of money; beatifically he smiles on financial success. Depicted as a robust, bearded angler with a big pink fish—the *tai,* sea bream—tucked under one arm, he presides over many a cash register, many an adding machine. In the culturally rich Edo period, the 20th day of every month was declared sacred to Ebisu (see November 20), and guilds or businessmen's associations always used to hold their monthly meetings on that day. Fewer and fewer are doing so now. But the custom of holding special year-end sales on the year's final *Ebisu-ko,* December 20, still survives. Big-city department stores eagerly participate, and on this day many small towns stage year-end "bargain markets" in hopes of attracting shoppers from far and wide.

# December 21

**F**ew days—or nights—cry out for a celebration so stridently as December 21, the winter solstice. Now the daylight hours are the shortest in the year, a mere glimmer before night gobbles them up. Ancient solstice rites calmed the celebrants' natural fear of the dark, while offering the promise that after this, things could only get brighter. In *The Golden Bough,* Sir James Frazer explains that among many ancient cultures, "the winter solstice . . . was regarded as the Nativity of the Sun, because the day begins to lengthen and the power of the sun to increase from that turning point of the year. The ritual of the nativity, as it appears to have been celebrated in Syria and Egypt, was remarkable. The celebrants retired into certain inner shrines, from which at midnight they issued with a loud cry, 'The Virgin has brought forth! The light is waxing!' The Egyptians even represented the newborn sun by the image of an infant which on his birthday, the winter solstice, they brought forth and exhibited to his worshipers. No doubt the Virgin who thus conceived and bore a son . . . was the great Oriental goddess whom the Semites called the Heavenly Virgin or simply the Heavenly Goddess." The winter solstice, as Yule, is a major holiday among modern witches and pagans.

# December 22

## Saints Chaeremon and Ischyrion's Day

The year 250 was not a good time to be a Christian in Egypt. Saint Dionysius of Alexandria, in a now-famous letter to Fabian of Antioch, described how scores of people were fleeing the city and seeking refuge in the desert. There, he explained, the refugees were dying of exposure, hunger, and thirst. Some were killed by wild animals; some were captured by local tribespeople and sold into slavery. Dionysus's letter tells in detail about Chaeremon, who had been bishop of Nilopolis. Already a "very old man" when the persecutions heated up, Chaeremon had gone with one or several companions to hide "in the mountains of Arabia." They were never seen again; "search was made by the brethren but not even their bodies were found."

The letter also tells of Ischyrion, an officer who worked for a certain city magistrate. Ischyrion was disrespectful of his boss's gods, and so the irate magistrate impaled him on a stake. As the figureheads of a whole wave of martyrs, most of whom remain nameless, these two Egyptian saints share a feast day, which has special resonance in their native East.

# December 23

The name of the Roman goddess to whom this day was dedicated may have been—as the holiday's name suggests—Larentia. Then again, depending on which source you prefer, it might have been Lara. Or Laurentina, Larunda, Acca Larentia, Mater Larum; possibly Tacita, possibly Muta. Her dominion, however, is generally agreed upon: She is said to have been the mother of the ghosts—that is, the good ghosts, the mellow *lares*. (These are not to be confused with the other kind of Roman ghosts, the terrifying *lemures*, which had to be annually banished by the spewing of mouthfuls of beans; see May 9.) She wasn't exactly their biological mother but their guardian—the divine equivalent of a Cub Scout troop's den mother or Peter Pan's Wendy.

On the festival day, priests made offerings at her altar, taking care to mention in their prayers the beloved dead, including the departed spirits of slaves. Of the goddess and her rite, the poet Ovid mused: "Nor would I pass by thee in silence, Larentia, nurse of so great a nation. . . . Your honor will find its place when I come to tell of the *Larentalia;* that festival falls in December, the month so dear to the mirthful spirits."

# December 24

## Christmas Eve

**C**hristmas Eve celebrations often out-shine those of Christmas itself.

In Denmark, Christmas Eve (*Juleaften*) is the biggest occasion of the year. The partying goes on all night, with traditional prune-stuffed roast goose, red cabbage, fried pastries, and cinnamon-laced rice pudding, *grod.* The Christmas elves, *Julenisse,* are appeased with offerings of rice pudding, and dishes of seeds are placed outdoors for wild birds. Rumanians serve a myriad-layered cake called *turta,* said to represent Jesus' swaddling clothes. In France, children set out their shoes in hopes that *le petit Jesus* will fill them during the night with small gifts. Mexicans attend a midnight service called *la misa del gallo,* "the rooster's mass," and sing lullabies to — NOCHE BUENA Jesus. Norwegians eat lye-treated codfish and wash it down with boiled potatoes, rice porridge, gingerbread, and punch. Swedes eat lye-treated codfish, too, and welcome the Christmas elves and the *Julbok,* the Christmas goat generally held responsible for the distribution of presents. The Swiss wait breathlessly for the Christ child, *Christkindli,* to arrive with gifts for all in his reindeer-drawn sleigh. Meanwhile, Czechs eat a soup made of cod roe and tempt each other with tales of a mythical golden pig.

# December 25

## Christmas

**W**hole books have been written about this festival-of-good-cheer, which Christians hold to be the birthday of Jesus and which in the ancient world was just as fervently held to be the birthday of the fiery sun god, Mithras. Clinging to the coattails of the winter solstice, Christmas celebrations in all their myriad permutations hint at hope, at light in the darkness, warmth within the chill.

The Germans popularized the now-universal Christmas tree as well as certain prominent holiday carols. Their Christmas dinner often features roast goose and *Christstollen,* bread loaves stuffed with raisins, citron, and nuts. (Berliners, however, eat carp.) The Portuguese *cepo de Natal,* "Christmas log," is a hank of oak that burns on the hearth all through the day while people enjoy a lingering *consoada,* the Christmas feast. In Spain, where Christmas is *Navidad,* people go to church, exchange presents, and many play on swingsets set up specially for the occasion. Swinging at solstice time evokes an ancient desire to encourage the sun, urging it to "swing" ever higher in the sky. Bulgarians make Christmas wishes around the fire and eat blood sausage. Albanians, like Finns and Danes and a great many Europeans, attend early-morning mass. Afterwards they sit down to a rich egg-lemon soup with tripe. Rumanians tote big wooden stars through the streets and put on puppet shows based on the life of Jesus. Belgians, meanwhile, tell ghost stories.

Kwanzaa
12|26 – 1|1

# December 26

## Saint Stephen's Day

Stephen's feast day is the first day after Christmas because, it is said, Stephen was the first person ever to die for his faith in Jesus. It is possible that Stephen's allegiance to the Prince of Peace derives from a certain veterinary miracle, for Stephen is said to have been a devoted horseman, one of whose ailing beasts, according to a tenth-century poem, Jesus restored to health. Several equine customs surround Saint Stephen's Day. As of the mid-twentieth century, priests in various parts of rural Europe were still blessing horses, not to mention bins of oats and hay, on the morning of the 26th. Sanctified and festooned, the horses would be made to circle the church three times in a row. In Poland, the dessert of the day is *podkovy*, "Saint Stephen's horns," lemony yeast dough stuffed with jam, poppy seeds, nuts, or cheese, brushed gently with cream and baked in the shape of horseshoes.

Saint Stephen's Day has long been considered a time for giving alms to the poor. "Good King Wenceslaus looked out," goes the carol about the charitable Bohemian sovereign, "on the feast of Stephen." Thus evolved the now-mostly-defunct English tradition of Boxing Day, in which boxes of treats would be distributed to household servants—in later years, to postmen and such.

A far more ancient custom, once practiced throughout England and Ireland, involved the hunting and killing of wrens.

# December 27

## Boar's Head Supper

The roasted head of a wild boar used to be the indispensable entree at English Christmas dinners. The custom of eating such a thing at this time of year is said to derive from a Norse custom involving the goddess Freya. Like many other goddesses who rode the skies astride wild beasts, Freya's steed was said to have been a golden-bristled boar. Thus, perversely, her worshipers devoutly offered her a boar's head at solstice time.

The dish remained extremely popular throughout the Middle Ages and well beyond. In the sixteenth century it inspired numerous carols such as the one that proclaimed:

> *The boar's head that we bring here*
> *Betokeneth a Prince without peer . . . Noel! Noel!*
> *A boar is a sovereign beast*
> *Acceptable in every feast . . . Noel! Noel!*

Turkey, goose, and the roasted "joint" of beef have long since supplanted boar's head as the entree of choice in British households. But the custom is still remembered at Saint John's College, Cambridge University, whose students sit down to a fancy boar's-head supper every December 27. Queen's College at Oxford University serves its annual boar's head a bit earlier in December. The platter is carried in amidst the hoot of hunting horns, and the "Boar's Head Carol" is sung in Latin.

# December 28

## Holy Innocents' Day

Established so that Christians might never forget Herod's slaughter of innocent children, Holy Innocents' Day took on a reputation as the year's unluckiest day. It was a time when people warned each other against starting any new projects, trimming their hair or nails, and—most emphatically—marrying. King Edward IV's coronation was postponed for a day because as originally scheduled it fell on Holy Innocents' Day. To dramatically evoke the horror of Herod's deed, medieval parents would whip their own children on the morning of the 28th. These beatings had the beneficial effect—or so the parents rationalized—of ensuring a child's good health throughout the coming year.

In Mexico, *El Día de los Inocentes* is unlucky, too. But here it functions as a kind of April Fools' Day, on which newspapers print bogus editions and radio stations issue hilarious fake broadcasts. People play practical jokes on each other. Many send "surprise" packages, loathsome contents gaily wrapped, via messenger. Another trick is to offer food that turns out to be cleverly disguised cotton or sawdust. Those foolish enough to loan anything on this day will most likely be rewarded with snide laughter and a note reading:

> *Innocent little dove,*
> *You have let yourself be fooled,*
> *Knowing that on this day*
> *You should lend nothing.*

# December 29

**E**ngland's King Henry II and the clever young cleric, Thomas à Becket, were thick as thieves—at first. Together they dreamed and schemed, and Thomas was as courtly a churchman as ever lived. But when Henry made Thomas bishop of Canterbury, things soured between the two. Suddenly strict and austere in all respects save his care for the poor, Thomas became a self-described "shepherd of souls" instead of a "patron of play-actors and a follower of hounds." This disappointed the king, and they sparred. In 1164 a frightened Thomas took refuge in France. He returned six years later, only to find himself, three weeks after his arrival in England, held up at sword-point by a quartet of Henry's knights. In Thomas's own cathedral in Canterbury they killed him.

Thomas was canonized within three years of his murder, and Canterbury, where he was enshrined, was one of the top three European pilgrimage destinations for nearly four hundred years thereafter. It was here that the pilgrims in Chaucer's *Canterbury Tales* were bound, "the holy blissful martyr for to seek." While Henry VIII in his own time attempted to banish Thomas worship, calling the martyred bishop "a rebell and traytor to his prince," the English weren't having any of it.

# December 30

Kwanzaa

**P**rofessor Maulana (formerly Ron) Karenga of the black studies department at California State University, Long Beach, created this holiday in 1966. While its name comes from the Swahili for "first," as in "first fruits," *Kwanzaa* is not actually African and was deliberately designed for African *Americans*. It is a harvest feast only figuratively: Kwanzaa's ingathering is not of crops but of family, cultural heroes, achievements, and dreams.

A feast of lights that commences every December 26 and lasts for a week thereafter, *Kwanzaa* has distinctive symbols that include the straw mat, *mkeka;* the candleholder, *kinara;* and the seven candles, *mshumaa saba,* whose red, black, and green colors represent the ancestors' spilled blood, the celebrants' black skin, and the green of good land. Each night of the holiday is dedicated to one of seven sacred principles: *umoja,* unity; *kujichagulia,* self-determination; *ujima,* collective action; *ujamaa,* cooperative economics; *nia,* purpose; *kuumba,* creativity; and *imani,* faith. Accenting each night's discussion, families often read from relevant literature or commemorate historical figures who exemplify a particular principle. Kwanzaa meals (whole cookbooks have been written on the subject) plumb the traditions of South America, the Caribbean, the American South, Africa, and beyond.

Originally designed as an at-home affair, Kwanzaa has inspired many universities, libraries, community centers, and other institutions to stage celebrations at this time of year.

# December 31

*A* day—or, more precisely, a night—pregnant with omens, with countless symbolic good-byes and hellos, New Year's Eve can be downright terrifying. Bulgarians perform fortune-telling tricks with leaves and water glasses. Finns have been known to do the same with molten tin and buckets. In Germany, the day is known as *Sylvesterabend,* in honor of Saint Sylvester, whom the Germans toast with fish dinners and a sweetened, spiced wine named especially for him. In the lower Rhine, it was once customary to play cards frenziedly until the stroke of midnight. The Greeks, too, play cards and sing songs about Saint Basil; and the Belgians and Swiss remember Sylvester with the custom of calling the last person to awaken in a household on New Year's Eve morning, man or woman, a "Sylvester." An old custom in Madrid involved standing at the foot of the Puerta del Sol, in front of the Department of the Interior, where a huge clock strikes the hours, and to swallow, at the stroke of twelve, twelve grapes one after the other. The Viennese counterpart was the custom of releasing live pigs in restaurants at midnight, at which point the diners raced around chasing them. More sedate Austrians call New Year's Eve *Raauchnacht,* "smoke night," and content themselves with ritually purifying homes and storehouses with incense and holy water. Latvians hold masquerade parties, and Rumanians sing a carol concerning Emperor Trajan and a bull.

# Selected Bibliography

The following are among the hundreds of books consulted while assembling this volume.

Attwater, Donald. *The Penguin Dictionary of Saints.* Harmondsworth, Middlesex: Penguin Books, 1965.

Ausubel, Nathan. *The Book of Jewish Knowledge.* New York: Crown Publishers, 1964.

Burland, C. A. *Echoes of Magic.* Totowa, N.J.: Rowman & Littlefield, 1972.

Caxton, William. *The Golden Legend or Lives of the Saints.* London: J. M. Dent & Co., 1900.

Cohen, Hennig, and Tristram P. Coffin, eds. *The Folklore of American Holidays.* Detroit, Mi.: Gale Research Co., 1987.

Fergusson, Erna. *Dancing Gods.* Albuquerque: Univ. of New Mexico Press, 1931.

Field, Carol. *Celebrating Italy.* New York: William Morrow & Co., 1990.

Fowler, W. Warde. *The Roman Festivals of the Period of the Republic.* 1899. Reprint, Port Washington, N.Y.: Kennikat Press, 1969.

Frazer, Sir James George. *The Golden Bough.* New York: The Macmillan Co., 1927.

Gascoine, Margaret. *Discovering English Customs and Traditions.* Aylesbury, Buckinghamshire: Shire Publications, 1969.

Hammerton, John Alexander, ed. *Manners and Customs of Mankind,* vols. 1–4. London: The Amalgamated Press, 1938.

Kojima, Setsuko. *Dictionary of Japanese Culture.* Union City, Ca.: Heian, 1991.

Milne, Jean. *Fiesta Time in Latin America.* Los Angeles: Ward Ritchie Press, 1965.

Shuel, Brian. *The National Trust Guide to Traditional Customs of Britain.* Exeter, Devon: Webb & Bower, 1985.

Toor, Frances. *A Treasury of Mexican Folkways.* New York: Bonanza Books, 1947.